BANNERS TO THE BREEZE

GREAT CAMPAIGNS OF THE CIVIL WAR

SERIES EDITORS

Anne J. Bailey
*Georgia College &
State University*

Brooks D. Simpson
Arizona State University

EARL J. HESS

Banners to the Breeze

The Kentucky Campaign,
Corinth, and Stones River

University of Nebraska Press
Lincoln and London

© 2000 by
the University of
Nebraska Press
All rights reserved
Manufactured in the
United States of America
∞
Library of Congress
Cataloging-in-Publication Data
Hess, Earl J.
Banners to the breeze : the Kentucky Campaign,
Corinth, and Stones River / Earl J. Hess.
p.   cm.—(Great campaigns of the Civil War)
Includes bibliographical references and index.
ISBN 0-8032-2380-3 (cloth : alk. paper)
1. Kentucky—History—Civil War,
1861–1865—Campaigns.
2. Tennessee—History—Civil War,
1861–1865—Campaigns.
3. Corinth (Miss.), Battle of, 1862.
4. Murfreesboro (Tenn.), Battle of, 1862–1863.
5. United States—History—Civil War,
1861–1865—Campaigns.
I. Title.   II. Series.
E474.7.H47   2000
973.7'3—dc21
99-30826
CIP

For Pratibha,
my beloved wife
and soulmate

Contents

Illustrations

Maps

Series Editors' Introduction

Americans remain fascinated by the Civil War. Movies, television, and video—even computer software—have augmented the ever-expanding list of books on the war. Although it stands to reason that a large portion of recent work concentrates on military aspects of the conflict, historians have expanded our scope of inquiry to include civilians, especially women; the destruction of slavery and the evolving understanding of what freedom meant to millions of former slaves; and an even greater emphasis on the experiences of the common soldier on both sides. Other studies have demonstrated the interrelationships of war, politics, and policy and how civilians' concerns back home influenced both soldiers and politicians. Although one cannot fully comprehend this central event in American history without understanding that military operations were fundamental in determining the course and outcome of the war, it is time for students of battles and campaigns to incorporate nonmilitary themes in their accounts. The most pressing challenge facing Civil War scholarship today is the integration of various perspectives and emphases into a new narrative that explains not only what happened, why, and how, but also why it mattered.

The series Great Campaigns of the Civil War offers readers concise syntheses of the major campaigns of the war, reflecting the findings of recent scholarship. The series points to new ways of viewing military campaigns by looking beyond the battlefield and the headquarters tent to the wider political and social context within which these campaigns unfolded; it also shows how campaigns and battles left their imprint on many Americans, from presidents and generals down to privates and civilians. The ends and means of waging war reflect larger political objectives and priorities as well as social values. Historians may continue to debate among themselves as to which of these campaigns constituted true turning points, but each of the campaigns treated in this series contributed to shaping the course of the conflict, opening opportunities, and eliminating alternatives.

Late 1862 was a critical time for the armies fighting in the western theater. The Rebels had abandoned Kentucky and much of Tennessee earlier in the year and by the summer had even relinquished Corinth, a valuable railroad depot in northeastern Mississippi. To rebound from these losses, the Confederacy mounted three fall offensives: an invasion of Kentucky, a strike in Mississippi, and a raid into Maryland. These campaigns resulted in three significant battles, Perryville, Corinth, and Antietam. Although Robert E. Lee regrouped after Sharpsburg to win the battle of Fredericksburg in December, the Confederates in the West would see no such success. William S. Rosecrans, the Union victor at Corinth in early October, attacked the Rebels at Murfreesboro in December and forced Braxton Bragg to retreat south. As a result, Bragg's men did not receive the same psychological boost to end the year that Lee's men experienced in Virginia.

Earl J. Hess provides an insightful account of why the last half of 1862 was so important to the side able to gain the upper hand in the western theater. He sees the period from June 1862 until January 1863 as the Confederacy's best opportunity to seize the strategic intiative and astutely shows how the battles in Mississippi, Kentucky, and Tennessee affected morale both on and off the battlefield. Lincoln, who had received little encouraging news from Virginia, could savor his western victories. More important, the battles in 1862 established a pattern, for the Confederate armies in the West had suffered more defeats than offsetting victories. This trend would continue until the war's end.

Preface

The three campaigns discussed in this book represent desperate Confederate efforts to reverse the strategic course of the war in the West. They involved a mighty struggle for control of the Upper South—Tennessee and Kentucky—with its sizable population, rich agricultural resources, and strategic importance. Control of this region would put the Confederates on the North's doorstep; loss of it would place Federal troops on the verge of invading the Deep South. It was a critical phase of the western war, which was predominantly a contest of far-flung offensives spanning huge reaches of territory.

In the end, the Confederates lost more than they gained. Gen. Braxton Bragg's invasion of Kentucky failed to bring that state under Confederate control but saved Chattanooga and much of Middle Tennessee. That action set the stage for Maj. Gen. William S. Rosecrans's Stones River campaign, which placed a bit more of the Upper South under Federal control. Maj. Gen. Earl Van Dorn failed in his attempt to retake Corinth, Mississippi, but he also inadvertently prepared the way for a major Union offensive against Vicksburg. As was true of Gen. Robert E. Lee's contemporary raid into Maryland, the glittering possibility of Confederate strategic gains in the summer and fall of 1862 bore relatively little fruit. By the time these campaigns ended, Rebel armies were again on the defensive in all theaters of the war.

This book tells the story of these attempts by the Confederates in the West to recover territory lost to the Federals during the previous winter and spring. It covers the period from June 1862 through January 1863 and is part of a sixteen-volume series titled The Great Campaigns of the Civil War. While the Kentucky campaign, Corinth, and Stones River have been studied by previous historians, I hope not only to provide a full, well-rounded narrative explaining the origins, course, and conduct of the campaigns but also to illustrate some lesser-known aspects of them. Thus I have included insights on terrain, geography, and the use of fortifications whenever possible. Analysis is blended with storytelling; the view of commanders is mixed with the experiences of common soldiers; and the human drama of war is given its due. I hope the reader will better understand the significance of these campaigns and realize how tumultuous and traumatic they were. They represent a phase of military operations that might have redirected the course of the war, if not for certain failings and limitations and the sheer bad fortune that plagued Confederate arms.

I would like to thank Professor William L. Shea for sharing some primary sources with me that were helpful in writing this book and for reading and commenting on an early draft of it. William G. Jackson kindly gave permission for me to use two photographs of Battery Robinett in his possession. Stacy D. Allen and Shiloh National Military Park graciously allowed me to use postwar photographs of the covered way at Battery Robinett as well. I also wish to thank the editors of The Great Campaigns of the Civil War series for their assistance.

BANNERS TO THE BREEZE

CHAPTER ONE

Banners to the Breeze

The first half of 1862 was disastrous for the Confederate army in the West. Beginning with Forts Henry and Donelson in February, the South suffered one defeat after another. An entire field army of some fifteen thousand men surrendered at Fort Donelson, leading to the collapse of Confederate defenses in southern Kentucky and western and central Tennessee. That vast area, with its rich storehouse of goods and agricultural products, was laid open to the Yankee invaders. The Federal offensive temporarily came to a halt at Shiloh when the Army of the Mississippi under Gen. Albert Sidney Johnston surprised the Army of the Tennessee under Maj. Gen. Ulysses S. Grant in its camps on a peaceful spring morning. The fighting that day, April 6, 1862, was fierce and bloody, but Grant's troops blunted the Confederate attacks and held their forward base of supplies at Pittsburg Landing on the Tennessee River. Grant was joined that night by the Army of the Ohio under Maj. Gen. Don Carlos Buell. Together, the two Federal armies drove the outnumbered Rebels away. Johnston was killed, shot accidentally by his own men, on April 6. Now led by Gen. Pierre G. T. Beauregard, the Army of the Mississippi retreated safely back to Corinth. The Rebels failed to crush Grant or prevent his juncture with Buell and had suffered nearly twelve thousand casualties, but they put almost thirteen thousand Federal troops out of action in the two-day battle.

Reinforcements from the Trans-Mississippi and new regiments from the North enabled Grant and Buell to hold the strategic advantage. But they would not be given the opportunity to continue the advance toward Corinth on their own. Their superior, Maj. Gen. Henry Wager Halleck, hastened to take personal charge of their combined armies, which numbered over one hundred thousand men. Not until the Atlanta campaign of 1864 would the

Union gather such a powerful host. Halleck began an overly cautious advance from Pittsburg Landing toward Corinth, fortifying his camps each night to avoid being caught by a surprise Confederate attack. Beauregard, with only fifty-five thousand men, could not risk an assault unless Halleck became careless and gave him an opportunity. The Federal general, engaged in the only field campaign of his career, did not offer his opponent such a chance. As a result, the famed "siege" of Corinth resulted in several small fights but no significant battle. Halleck accomplished his goal through maneuver and relying on earthworks to protect his painfully slow progress. Beauregard was forced to evacuate the town on May 30, 1862, with his army intact.

The fall of Corinth was hailed by the press, as a great triumph of Federal arms, even though Halleck had failed to damage the Confederate army. His own soldiers did not believe this assessment. They were disappointed that, after all their marching, digging, and high expectations, Beauregard's troops were still a strong, potent force barring their way south. Yet the capture of Corinth was the culmination of an immense gain of territory. The Union offensive that accomplished this feat was unprecedented in size and in the geographic expanse it covered. No previous campaign in American history had involved the movement of so many troops over such a large area. All of Kentucky had been cleared of Confederate troops and all of western and central Tennessee was either in Union hands or open to Federal occupation forces. Nashville became the first Confederate state capital to fall to the North. The entire length of the Mississippi River through the Upper South was cleared of Rebel forces, and several heavily fortified strongholds, including Columbus, Kentucky, Island No. 10 on the border between Missouri and Tennessee, and Fort Pillow, sixty miles north of Memphis, had fallen with little loss of life. The important commercial port of Memphis was under Northern control after a brief but showy gunboat battle on the river. The rest of the Mississippi River south of Memphis lay open to further attacks by combined land and naval forces. Only two strongpoints were still held by Confederate forces on the long stretch of the river between Memphis and New Orleans, Vicksburg and Port Hudson. They would be under attack a few weeks after the fall of Corinth.

Farther west, other Federal forces duplicated the success of Grant and Buell east of the Mississippi. The small but tenacious Army of the Southwest, under Brig. Gen. Samuel Ryan Curtis, had driven into northwestern Arkansas and fought a pivotal battle at Pea Ridge, blunting an attempted invasion of Union-held Missouri by the Confederate Army of the West under

Maj. Gen. Earl Van Dorn. Still farther west, a Confederate attempt to invade New Mexico Territory was defeated by a combination of logistical problems and stiff resistance by the scattered Federal forces in that distant region.

Even in Virginia, where much larger armies lumbered over much shorter distances with huge mountains of supplies, Federal armies were on the move. The nation's attention was focused on the Army of the Potomac and its young commander, Maj. Gen. George B. McClellan. By the time Corinth fell to Halleck's men, McClellan landed his army on the Yorktown Peninsula and began a slow, careful advance toward Richmond. Displaying even more caution and digging just as many earthworks to protect his gains as Halleck had, McClellan spent the month of April 1862 dislodging a much smaller Confederate force from its heavily fortified position at Yorktown. He suffered another delay on May 30 and June 1, 1862, when the Confederate army of Gen. Joseph E. Johnston attacked him near Seven Pines and Fair Oaks, only a dozen miles from Richmond. Although the Rebel assaults were repulsed and Johnston was severely wounded, McClellan was plagued by false reports that the Confederate army outnumbered his own. He also was plagued by his own fear of failure and proceeded at an even slower and more cautious pace during the month of June. Still, despite Johnston's replacement by Gen. Robert E. Lee and the renaming of the army as the Army of Northern Virginia, a name that would later strike fear into many a Federal commander's heart, there was every reason to expect great things from McClellan and his men as spring gave way to summer.

Yet this impressive string of Northern successes was in danger of unraveling. There were many reasons for this possibility, chief among them the overwhelming need for the Federal armies in the West to consolidate the tremendous gains they had made thus far. Halleck felt he had to disperse troops to key towns along the logistical network that supplied his army, which already was several hundreds of miles from its major supply depots in the North. These logistical matters were vital. The system of rivers and railroads that Grant and Buell had used to bring their armies thus far had been a strategic boon to the western Unionists, making it possible for them to come so far and conquer so much territory in a comparatively short time. This transportation system greatly aided in the conquest of the Upper South, but it did not so conveniently extend into the Deep South. Below Corinth, only one rail line penetrated the vast stretches of territory in central Mississippi, a region less well endowed with prosperous farms, good wagon roads, and navigable rivers than Kentucky and Tennessee. New logistical arrangements had to be considered before a further push south of Corinth was feasible.

In short, the Union army in the West had reached the end of its rope. It had been easy enough to operate in the Upper South, for that area was adjacent to Northern territory and was well suited to the movement of large armies and their supplies. It had a long-settled population, dating back to the 1770s, and an excellent system of pikes and wagon roads. Railroads spanned the region, connecting the major cities with the rest of the country. The Tennessee, Cumberland, and Mississippi Rivers flowed north to south, giving Union commanders an opportunity to drive deeply into the region and easily supply their armies.

The Deep South posed far more difficult problems for Halleck and his subordinates than did the Upper South. Mississippi and Alabama extended some four hundred miles north to south. These states had been largely settled only during the three decades before the firing on Fort Sumter. Their drier climate and less fertile soil failed to yield a diversified agriculture like that in Kentucky and Tennessee. Cotton was the key crop of the Deep South. A traveler through Mississippi and Alabama would have found the region dotted with large plantations separated by huge tracts of endless pine forests, with many small hardscrabble farms scattered across the land. Important cities were few and far between and railroads failed to penetrate large areas of this region. The river system did not take up where the railroads left off. Traveling upstream, a visitor on the Tennessee and Cumberland would veer eastward before penetrating the Deep South and find the waterways increasingly unnavigable. The rivers that penetrate the heart of Mississippi and Alabama flow largely in the southern halves of those states and are small and shallow. The only exception is the expansive sweep of the Mississippi, which gave Federal forces the opportunity to penetrate the Deep South on a very narrow front. The landlocked interior of the region remained a very poor place for the maneuvering and feeding of large numbers of troops.

In short, the Deep South was an inhospital area for military operations. Federal forces could easily disperse in the Upper South to occupy important points that were connected by good roads and rail lines. There, the Civil War was truly a war to reclaim lost territory, show the flag in many towns large and small, and protect Unionists with permanent garrisons. Operations in the Deep South would have to be different. It would be impossible to spread out and occupy all regions there. The North simply did not have the manpower or the time to do that, and there were vast areas of the Deep

South that were not worth holding. Instead, the strategy of the war in the Deep South would be dictated by the region's geography. Federal commanders would have to decide which areas were important enough to take and then prepare extensively to send armies into them. Penetrations of the Deep South would be on a very narrow, limited front, such as expeditions down the Mississippi or along the rail line from Chattanooga to Atlanta. They would have limited objectives rather than the all-embracing goal of reclaiming huge chunks of territory from the Confederate government. And logistics would play an even more crucial role in the success of these expeditions than in the Upper South. The operational and administrative capacities of the Union army would be tested to the extreme, and supply officers would be forced to develop and improve their technique as the war shifted from the Upper South to the lower states. The western Federals faced this problem long before their counterparts in Virginia for the war in the eastern theater never moved from the Upper to the Deep South. The war in the West was primarily a conflict of distances, of varied geography, climate, and land forms, of movement, and of real progress or failure measured by the shifting of forces over the map. Westerners would have to learn to become hardy campaigners as well as tough fighters on the battlefield, for their part of the war was won as much by moving over vast distances as by slugging it out with their enemy on a small field of battle.

For all of these reasons Halleck was forced to stop after entering Corinth in late May. He refused to rush in pursuit of Beauregard's army, which retreated some sixty miles southward to Tupelo. His massive army would not have been able to feed itself adequately with the single line of railroad that led into central Mississippi. Two years later, Maj. Gen. William T. Sherman would succeed in moving a similar number of men down the single track of line that penetrated northwestern Georgia during the Atlanta campaign. But that happened only because the Federal Army of the Cumberland, Buell's old army, had spent the intervening two years building up the equipment, supplies, and techniques for moving huge amounts of goods on a single track. Sherman could feed, provide ammunition, send reinforcements, and evacuate wounded men quickly over the rail line from Louisville to Nashville to Chattanooga all the way up to his advancing army. Halleck's army did not have that capability in the summer of 1862. And the only objective in Mississippi worth campaigning for, control of the Mississippi River, might well be gained without an overland invasion. Even then, an expedition was beginning to take shape among the forces that had captured New Orleans in April and had moved northward up the river to occupy

Natchez and Baton Rouge. This combined force of oceangoing ships under Rear Adm. David G. Farragut and a small contingent of infantry under Brig. Gen. Thomas Williams might well clear the Mississippi without the aid of Halleck's army. Halleck had every reason to stop at Corinth and carefully consider his next move.

He decided to direct his attention toward the west and east rather than the south. The need to consolidate Union gains seemed more important than moving into an uncertain campaign in difficult territory. West of the Mississippi, Samuel Ryan Curtis's small army was in danger. After Pea Ridge, Curtis had begun to march across Arkansas as Van Dorn moved eastward to join Beauregard at Corinth. Curtis was at the end of a precarious supply line of wagon trains that trundled over the rugged Ozark Mountains from Rolla, Missouri, more than two hundred miles away. Despite that problem, Curtis dallied at Batesville, hoping to move on and capture Little Rock, but he eventually decided to cut his supply line and march to Helena on the Mississippi. Halleck tried to help him by sending a supply fleet up the White River (which barely missed meeting Curtis's army) and then reconnecting Curtis's supply line down the river to Helena when the Army of the Southwest reached that town in July. Curtis had come close to occupying what would have been the second Confederate state capital to fall into Union hands. As it was, he demonstrated one successful tactic an invading army could use to solve logistical problems, living off the land. And he opened up the most advanced base of operations on the Mississippi River, sixty miles south of Memphis, for those forces that were tentatively moving south down the waterway.

When Halleck turned his attention eastward, he found that consolidating Federal control over the rest of the Upper South would be far more difficult than supporting Curtis's little army. The Union concentration of manpower that had combined the Army of the Ohio with the Army of the Tennessee for the drive on Corinth had taken troops from huge areas of Kentucky and Tennessee. This concentration had allowed Grant and Buell to penetrate the Upper South on a very narrow front, essentially along the Tennessee and Cumberland Rivers. The Confederates had also concentrated their troops from the Upper South at Corinth to oppose this advance, adding men from as far away as Mobile, Pensacola, and the Trans-Mississippi. As a result, large areas of Tennessee were not controlled by either army and some parts of it were still held by comparatively small, isolated contingents. The Federals firmly held Nashville and most of Kentucky but little else. A small division of about eight thousand Federals under Brig. Gen. Ormsby McKnight

Mitchell, from Buell's army, had penetrated northern Alabama in March, when the Army of the Ohio left Nashville to join Grant at Pittsburg Landing. Mitchell made it to Huntsville, a town in the Appalachian Mountains on the Memphis and Charleston Railroad that connected Corinth with Chattanooga. His small force lived precariously, forced to rely on supplies shipped by wagon from Nashville and on whatever the men could forage from the countryside. Mitchell survived by aggressively prowling the area to prevent the buildup of Confederate guerrillas and because the Rebels were too preoccupied with trying to stop Grant and Buell in western Tennessee to pay much attention to his division.

Fortunately for him, the only sizable Confederate force in the area was nearly as vulnerable as he was. Maj. Gen. Edmund Kirby Smith commanded fewer than ten thousand men who were strung out across the width of eastern Tennessee from Cumberland Gap, on the borders of Kentucky, Tennessee, and Virginia, to Knoxville and to Chattanooga. Smith was barely able to maintain his position; his vulnerability was amply demonstrated in June, when a Federal division of some ten thousand men under Brig. Gen. George W. Morgan captured Cumberland Gap without a struggle. Morgan moved toward the gap down the Wilderness Road from the Bluegrass region of Kentucky. Although Cumberland Gap was an impressive topographic feature that amply deserved to be called the Gibraltar of the West, it could easily be turned by using any number of smaller passes that lay north and south. Morgan did this and was able to force the outnumbered garrison to give up the place. Cumberland Gap gave the Federals an avenue of advance into the heart of eastern Tennessee, including Knoxville, but it offered nothing else of strategic value. Yet its fall was a sign that the Federals were beginning the process of consolidating their positions all across the Upper South. Smith's men were in real danger of losing all of eastern Tennessee, including the vital railroad junction of Chattanooga. That city was the logistical gateway to Georgia and other areas of the Deep South, offering a rail line to any future Federal invasion of the southeastern portion of the Confederacy. In addition, rail lines running east and west also ran through Chattanooga, connecting Virginia with the western Confederacy. This small mountain town on the banks of the Tennessee, with its imposing geography, was one of the true strategic points of the war.

By mid-June 1862 Halleck was ready to begin the process of securing the rest of the Upper South and preparing to invade Georgia. He sent Buell's Army of the Ohio eastward from Corinth to seize Chattanooga. Halleck ordered him to move "with all possible dispatch" and confidently expected his subordinate to be ready to invade Georgia in a few weeks. This was good news to Andrew Johnson, who had been appointed as military governor of Tennessee by President Abraham Lincoln the previous March. Johnson won this appointment because he had been the only member of the United States Senate from a seceded state who remained loyal to the Union. Although born in North Carolina, he had grown up in eastern Tennessee knowing the hard hand of poverty and the value of a strong Union, developing a hatred of slave owners that was stronger than his prejudice against black people. The prospect of freeing the many other Unionists in the mountains of Tennessee was a passion of his. "They are being treated worse than beasts of the forest and are appealing to the Government for relief & protection," he wrote to Halleck. The time was right for such a move on purely military grounds. Halleck assured Johnson that "East Tennessee will very soon be attended to."

But Buell was not one to rush things. Born in Ohio forty-four years before, he had graduated in the lower ranks of the West Point class of 1841, a class that provided twenty generals to the Union and Confederate armies. Buell managed to compile an impressive military record before the war, serving in Florida, on the western frontier, and in Mexico. He was severely wounded at the battle of Churubusco during Winfield Scott's famous campaign to Mexico City but spent most of the postwar years on staff duty in the Adjutant General's Office. He received a brigadier general's commission immediately upon the outbreak of war and was instrumental in helping to organize the rapidly growing volunteer army of the North. A friend and colleague of McClellan, Buell was quickly given one of the most important field posts in the North, command of the Army of the Ohio. He was charged with defending Kentucky and advancing into the important central theater of operations that lay between the Mississippi Valley and the Appalachian Highlands.

Buell displayed his chief failing as a field commander in Kentucky, one which he shared with McClellan, which was a far too healthy respect for the possibility of failure. He initiated no offensives during the winter of 1861–62, preferring to wait for dry spring weather to put into operation his plan to advance to Nashville. But Grant's spectacular victory at Fort Donelson cleared Buell's path by forcing the Confederates to abandon their positions in southern Kentucky and concentrate at Corinth. Thus the Army of the Ohio occupied a Confederate state capital it did not have to fight for. Buell agreed to combine his army with Grant's at Pittsburg Landing, abandoning for the time the central theater of operations. It gave him the opportunity to lead the army in its first battle on April 7, 1862. The second day at Shiloh was not nearly as deadly or prolonged as the first day had been, but it introduced the men of Buell's army to combat.

After Halleck's capture of Corinth, Buell was once again given the opportunity to lead an independent offensive into Rebel territory. He moved his headquarters from Corinth in mid-June and by the end of the month was safely at Huntsville, having traveled along the Memphis and Charleston Railroad. Buell decided to make his headquarters there, where Mitchell's division already had established its base. He posted his six divisions, totaling about forty thousand men, as they arrived from Corinth. Maj. Gen. Alexander McDowell McCook's Second Division and Maj. Gen. Thomas Leonidas Crittenden's Fifth Division were sent to a point east of Stevenson where Battle Creek flowed into the Tennessee River. The railroad eastward from Huntsville passed through Stevenson and continued along the valley of the Tennessee to Chattanooga. This route was the most direct line of advance to the strategic mountain town. By positioning half of his army at the mouth of Battle Creek, Buell could protect Stevenson where the Memphis and Charleston line connected with the Nashville and Chattanooga Railroad. These were the two lines he was determined to use on his campaign to Chattanooga. They gave him flexibility—he could receive reinforcements and supplies from the Mississippi Valley or from Nashville, and if one line was cut by cavalry raiders or guerrillas the other might provide enough supplies to keep his army in the field. Battle Creek would also be the closest point any of Buell's men would be stationed to Chattanooga, which was about thirty miles away. McCook and Crittenden assumed their posts there by mid-July.

Brig. Gen. Thomas J. Wood's Sixth Division was sent to Decherd, just west of the Cumberland Plateau. To the east the Nashville and Chattanooga line climbed up the rugged western face of the Cumberland Plateau and quickly began to descend the valley of Crow Creek to Stevenson. Two tunnels that took the line under the worst part of the plateau were obvious targets for any Southerners with a mind to play havoc with Yankee trains. Wood also took up his position in mid-July. Maj. Gen. William Nelson's Fourth Division took the most roundabout way to its assigned position. The men traveled by way of Nashville to Murfreesboro and then marched across the countryside to McMinnville, which also was just west of the plateau. Maj. Gen. George Henry Thomas's First Division was the last to leave Corinth and arrived at Huntsville on August 8. From there Buell sent it to Decherd, where it reinforced Wood's division. Thomas sent one of his brigades to Pelham to give wider coverage to this area, which constituted the left wing of Buell's army. Finally, Brig. Gen. Lovell Harrison Rousseau arrived to take command of Mitchell's Third Division, which was already at Huntsville, Mitchell having gone on sick leave. George W. Morgan's Seventh Division was already firmly in control of Cumberland Gap. As the most extended of Buell's divisions, Morgan's men were busy digging fortifications to defend that pass.

Thus the Army of the Ohio was spread out on a line that was sixty miles long on a front that generally faced east. The left was at McMinnville, the center at Decherd, and the right rested near Stevenson. One division was one hundred miles from the left wing at Cumberland Gap and another division was in reserve fifty miles to the rear of the right wing at Huntsville. Buell had to stop his advance here to secure his communications. He had found that the difficulties of sustaining a large campaign in this area were more enormous than anyone had predicted. Rousseau found that Mitchell's small division of only ten thousand men could barely survive in the mountains of northern Alabama. As they were chronically short on rations since March because the wagon trains could not haul enough food and the local farms were cleaned out, the division's fighting ability had plummeted. Buell found the command "in disorder" with troops pillaging the inhabitants at will. Capt. Charles Champion Gilbert later put it well when he wrote, "No supplies had been accumulated, and when the divisions of the Army of the Ohio arrived they were compelled to live from hand to mouth until order could be established. This condition of affairs was fatal to all projects for an immediate advance." If ten thousand men could not subsist themselves in this region without a secure rail line, then Buell's army of forty thousand men certainly would starve. The two railroads had to be repaired before he could even think about beginning a push to Chattanooga. The troops that Edmund Kirby Smith already had in place there were strong enough to hold the town against anything less than a full advance of Buell's entire army. The only recourse open to the Federals was to pay close attention to their supply lines.

That would involve a great deal of heavy labor, for the rail lines were already in rough shape and were exposed to enemy attack. The Memphis and Charleston line was the least troublesome from a technical point of view. This route entered the Tennessee River valley in northeastern Mississippi and followed it all the way to Chattanooga. The most vulnerable spot was the crossing of the river at Bridgeport, Alabama, with its mile-long bridge. The Nashville and Chattanooga line traversed more difficult terrain. It had three big bridges over major rivers and went through a tunnel south of Dech-erd that was over twenty-two hundred feet long. In addition to these two main lines, Buell worked hard to open a third route, the Nashville and De-catur line. It linked the Tennessee capital with the Memphis and Charleston line at Decatur, Alabama, over seventy miles west of Stevenson. The use of this railroad would provide insurance for Buell. If the Nashville and Chatta-nooga line were cut, he might shift supply shipments to it. But the Nashville and Decatur line was a far more serious challenge to his construction crews than either of the others. It ran through very rough terrain and used twelve big bridges on the forty-five-mile stretch between Nashville and Columbia alone. The line also ran across a trestle at Culleoka, Alabama, that was over a thousand feet long and a curving tunnel a quarter mile long at another point. The last obstacle was a seven-hundred-foot-long bridge over the Elk River that was fifty-eight feet high. The river was twenty feet deep at this point. Buell may have been well advised to ignore the Nashville and Decatur Rail-road for its repair took valuable manpower from construction sites along the other lines. Still, he dispatched elements of the First Michigan Engineers and Mechanics, reinforced them with detachments of infantrymen to do the heavy lifting, and hoped for the best. The work was slow, although the men worked twenty-four hours a day on the Elk River bridge. In contrast, the Nashville and Chattanooga line was opened by July 12. Buell put two regi-ments of infantry, a battery, and some cavalry at Murfreesboro to serve as a mobile force to protect the line.

The need to detach troops to guard all of Buell's rail lines was imperative, for guerrilla forces had already begun to attack them. Blockhouses were built along the Nashville and Chattanooga route while stockades were con-structed on the Memphis and Charleston line. The blockhouses, much stronger than mere stockades, were needed for protection against the better firearms and possibly even artillery possessed by the mobile cavalry forces operating in Middle Tennessee. The more flimsy stockades were all that were needed against the isolated guerrilla bands in the Tennessee River val-ley. Those stockades were made of trees up to twenty inches in diameter and enclosed a small area with a wooden wall nine feet tall. Loopholes for mus-kets were cut into the wall, and a ditch was dug outside the stockade to pre-vent the enemy from standing on the ground and firing into the enclosure through the loopholes. All of this took time, energy, and manpower.

Buell soon found that he had much more serious opposition to worry about than a few poorly armed guerrillas. On July 13, his garrison at Mur-freesboro was hit by fourteen hundred cavalrymen under Col. Nathan Bed-

ford Forrest. In one of the early raids that would make him one of the most
famous mounted leaders of the war, Forrest took the Federal pickets by surprise, fought a swirling action with several detached Union forces, and managed to capture up to twelve hundred Yankees before the day was over. He
also destroyed a quarter of a million dollars worth of Federal property, the
railroad depot, and a nearby bridge before escaping eastward. His exploits
delayed the first shipment of supplies to Buell along the newly rebuilt Nashville and Chattanooga line, forcing him to keep his army on half rations. On
July 21, Forrest added more complications to Federal plans by wrecking
three bridges near Nashville which were not repaired for at least a week.
The line was finally reopened on July 29 and the first trainload of supplies
reached Stevenson, allowing Buell's men to return to full rations. But Stevenson was as far as the train could go for Buell still did not have the long
bridge over the Tennessee ready because of a delay in bringing forward the
necessary bridging material. The supply problem was slightly eased when
the very difficult Nashville and Decatur line was finally ready for use on
August 11.

Another famous Rebel horseman surpassed Forrest in frustrating Buell.
Col. John Hunt Morgan of Kentucky set out on a raid that resulted in far
more damage. Morgan hit the Louisville and Nashville line at Gallatin, Tennessee, twenty-five miles north of Nashville, on August 12. He easily captured the small garrison of 125 men without a struggle and then played
havoc with the railroad. His men loaded several flatcars with flammable material, set them afire, and pushed them into the Big South Tunnel. The fire
burned the wooden supports and caused a cave-in, filling the tunnel with
rocks and debris. Morgan also burned forty railroad cars and a quantity of
stores, destroyed a bridge south of the tunnel, another bridge south of Gallatin, a trestle, and six hundred feet of track. This was a very serious setback
for the Union. It would take nearly three months to repair the tunnel, and
wagons could not easily bypass it because of the rugged terrain in the area. A
short siding had to be constructed north of the tunnel and a loading dock
built to allow wagons to haul supplies all the way from there to Nashville before they could be reloaded onto cars.

Putting his men on half rations again as a result of Morgan's raid, Buell
found no comfort in assessing his other supply options. The Cumberland
and Tennessee Rivers had fallen so low by mid-July that heavily laden boats
could not move upriver from either Nashville or Pittsburg Landing. The
Memphis and Charleston line also proved to be inadequate. It could easily
support enough shipments from Memphis to feed Grant's garrison at Cor-

inth, but the area east of that point was wide open to attack. Guerrillas were hitting the railroad in the area between Tuscumbia and Decatur, avoiding the stockades built along the line, and cutting it by July 25. Foraging on the countryside was out of the question, as Mitchell's division had proven even before the army's Chattanooga campaign began. Buell did not even want to try living off the land, for he thought it would inevitably lead to a breakdown of discipline among his troops. Also, he shared McClellan's political views that the war should be fought in a limited, purely military way. Both generals wanted to respect private property and protect the constitutional rights of residents in the occupied territory as the best way to redeem the South and foster a renewed sense of loyalty among the people. Buell had many logistical and political obstacles to deal with as he tried to figure out a way to bring his men to the gates of Chattanooga.

Buell's campaign took place at a critical time in his career. The patience of his superiors in Washington was wearing thin because of the slowness of all his moves since he assumed command of the army the previous fall. His friend and mentor, McClellan, had a similar history of slowness which exasperated Lincoln even more. The example of Grant offered a stark contrast to Buell. He initiated the offensive that had rolled Union arms to victory at Fort Donelson and Shiloh, building for himself a reputation as a tough fighter who could get things done. Buell and McClellan were sliding out of favor for political reasons as well; neither general favored more radical means for carrying on the war. They were conservative generals, both militarily as well as politically, believing that war should be made only on armies and that the object of strategy was to outmaneuver the enemy rather than to kill him. Neither general had a sense for the jugular, an overriding desire to close with the Rebels, or a willingness to embrace the messy uncertainty of a life-or-death struggle.

Political factors put a great deal of pressure on Buell. Lincoln and many other Northerners had long wanted to help the Unionists living in eastern Tennessee. That part of the state had consistently voted against secession and even attempted to break away from the rest of Tennessee when the war opened. They were subdued by the shifting of Confederate troops from Nashville. Even though occupied by their own Southerners, the mountaineers rose in revolt. In November, many of them burned key bridges along the rail lines in preparation for what they thought would be a Federal invasion of the region, but Buell delayed and then postponed the advance. As a result, many loyalists were arrested and executed. The plight of these and other Unionists was given wide currency in the North by the speeches

and writings of Parson William G. Brownlow, an articulate and sincere pro-
pagandist for his Appalachian people.

Throughout the winter months of 1861–62, the cause of East Tennessee
loomed like a grail for many Northern politicians, and they were highly critical of any commander who did not share their enthusiasm. As president,
Lincoln saw only the political importance of helping the Unionists while
Buell saw only the military considerations. The army leader correctly
viewed East Tennessee as an inhospitable place for maneuvering a large
army. There was nothing of strategic importance there, except Chattanooga, to warrant an invasion, and he consistently refused to be drawn into
one. Now, in the late summer of 1862, his only interest in East Tennessee
was occupying Chattanooga and preparing for an advance into Georgia. He
did not envision spreading out his limited strength into garrisons for all the
small mountain towns where friends of the North lived. Lincoln did not see
this fine point; he was quite happy that a Federal army was on its way to the
region and assumed it would liberate all Unionists there.

But the president had also been acting as his own general in chief since
McClellan resigned from that post the previous winter. The bulk of his attention was devoted to operations in Virginia, and trying to coordinate
troops to trap Maj. Gen. Thomas J. "Stonewall" Jackson in the Shenandoah
Valley became almost an obsession for him. Then McClellan's Peninsula
campaign heated up, and the dramatic turnaround of the Seven Days absorbed his efforts. He also organized the Army of Virginia and put a westerner, Maj. Gen. John Pope, in command of it.

The president offered little advice to Buell except to endorse heartily his
move toward East Tennessee. In late June, as the Seven Days' fighting
raged, Lincoln took a comprehensive view of Union strategy in a memoran-
dum to Secretary of State William Henry Seward. He wrongly assumed that
the evacuation of Corinth would allow the Confederates to reinforce Lee so
he could attack McClellan outside Richmond. It would make little sense for
Halleck to send reinforcements to the Army of the Potomac, for that would
endanger Union gains in Tennessee and Mississippi. Instead, the president
outlined a strategy to call up additional, new regiments for McClellan, holding what had already been gained in the West, reopening the Mississippi
River, and taking Chattanooga and the rest of East Tennessee. "I expect to
maintain this contest until successful, or till I die, or am conquered, or my
term expires, or Congress or the country forsakes me," stated Lincoln. The
president meekly asked Halleck for the transfer of twenty-five thousand
troops to the East if they could be spared, but such a transfer would not be

warranted if it might threaten the move toward Chattanooga. Lincoln wrote to Halleck, "To take and hold the Rail-road at, or East of, Cleveland in East Tennessee, I think fully as important as the taking and holding of Richmond." Halleck was able to convince Lincoln that sending so many men would indeed endanger Buell's campaign, but the president was so pressured by events in Virginia that he repeated his request on July 4, receiving the same reply from Halleck.

Lincoln felt overwhelmed by his dual duties as general in chief and chief executive, and he began to search for someone to fill the top military post. There was no question that Buell was unsuitable, both for political reasons and for his lack of military success. Governor Johnson had no faith in the general's ability to "redeem east Tennessee." Halleck seemed the most likely choice. He was an effective administrator although a terrible field commander, and Grant's successes had been made possible, in part, by his management of the western department. On July 11, Lincoln issued an order making Halleck general in chief. Other westerners, including Pope and Maj. Gen. Franz Sigel, had already been transferred to the East.

Buell also was in trouble because a political revolution was brewing in the North during the summer of 1862 which would swamp his fortunes. The war had begun as a limited, conservative effort by the Union. Few people other than abolitionists wanted to fight for the freedom of the slaves in 1861; nearly everyone wanted a short and bloodless war. The only way to assure this was to guarantee the protection of slavery if the South would call off the conflict and rejoin the Union. The Lincoln administration had no constitutional powers to eliminate slavery in the states, and everyone wanted to avoid the thorniest problem associated with emancipation—what to do with four million newly freed blacks. During the first few months of the conflict there seemed to be every reason to fight a war for purely political goals and avoid social revolution.

Then the Federal defeat in the Seven Days' fighting changed the public mood. This shift happened because one of the other reasons behind the limited war effort was a vague assumption, harbored by many in the North, that the majority of nonslaveholding Southerners could not have their heart in the bid for independence, that they had been coerced into supporting secession by the wealthy slave owners for their own benefit. The fierce fighting of ordinary Confederate soldiers and McClellan's shocking defeat disabused Northern minds of this conceit. Now they realized that the South was in earnest, that even poor whites intended to fight to the last man for independence, and that their own war effort had to change to meet this new reality. All across the North, more and more people began to demand radical measures to prosecute the war, and Lincoln responded by calling for three hundred thousand three-year volunteers early in July, which would nearly double the size of the Union army. He signed into law a confiscation bill passed by Congress on July 17 that empowered the government to seize the private property of those who aided the rebellion, including their slaves, which could then be used to help the Northern cause. Later in the summer, Lincoln issued a presidential proclamation suspending the writ of habeas corpus, thereby enabling the government to arrest, imprison, and hold anyone accused of "discouraging volunteer enlistments, resisting militia drafts, or guilty of any disloyal practice," without charging them with a crime. The limited, conservative war effort was turning into a radical, total war.

The most radical, provocative, and important war policy Lincoln adopted in the summer of 1862 was a decision to place his government squarely behind the drive to free the slaves. The time was right as it had never been before in American history. Although he still had no constitutional authority to do so, Lincoln based his decision on national necessity; he framed the policy in high-minded moral tones but, more important, as a needed war measure to bring the South to its knees. The president had considered it for a long time, but there was no public consensus in favor of the move before the Seven Days. His efforts on July 12 to convince loyal border state congressmen to accept some form of compensated emancipation came to nothing. The next day, Lincoln first mentioned to Seward and Secretary of the Navy Gideon Welles the possibility of issuing a proclamation to free the slaves in the seceded states, and he informed the entire cabinet of his decision on July 22. Several members enthusiastically endorsed the idea; others hesitated. Seward suggested that Lincoln wait until a major battlefield victory was won before letting the world know of his policy, or it would appear to be the weak and desperate effort of a losing war. Lincoln agreed. The overriding thought he had on this thorny issue was that "we must free the slaves or be ourselves subdued."

Although they would have to wait a while to learn of this most revolutionary part of their war effort, most Northerners were catching the fever of a renewed sense of purpose as the summer wore on. "There is a wonderful and increasing enthusiasm and determination to put down this Rebellion and sustain the integrity of the Union," noted Welles. "It is confined to no class, or party or description: rich and poor, the educated and ignorant, the gentle and refined as well as the stout, coarse, and athletic, the Democrats generally as well as the Republicans, are offering themselves to the country." Although Welles would soon learn that a great many Democrats could not stomach the radical policies, he was accurate when speaking of the widespread support for them among other groups.

Buell, like his friend McClellan, was no supporter of these policies, and he was quickly judged by his politics as well as by his military record. Secretary of the Treasury Salmon P. Chase was a strong supporter of emancipation and other radical policies that summer. He also was a vocal critic of Buell, noting his slow progress toward Chattanooga in early August. "No movement could be slower than his had been. East Tennessee ought to-day to have been in the occupation of the troops of the Union. . . . Gen. Buell though I believe him to be an [able] & faithful officer ought in my judgment, to be replaced [by] a more active *fearless* and energetic leader in the [present] emergency."

The political pressures on Buell were indirectly affected by the North's relations with foreign powers as well. The summer of 1862 was a tumultuous time in cross-Atlantic diplomacy. The British were the key to the Confederacy's prospects for foreign intervention or recognition of its bid for independence. The government of Prime Minister Lord Palmerston wanted to wait until the Northern people had become convinced that they could not defeat the South and force reunion on them, and McClellan's defeat in the Seven Days seemed to be a step toward that result. Ignoring the renewed energy for the war among the common people and forgetting that Federal armies had already captured a huge chunk of Confederate territory in the West, many influential Englishmen pointed to the Seven Days as proof that the South could not be subjugated. Southern cotton also loomed large as a factor in the prospect for intervention that summer. English textile mills had long relied heavily on the American South for their raw material, and now that the supply was cut off by the war, the resulting economic troubles might force the government to do something to restore prosperity. The unemployment rates in some areas of industrialized England were as high as 50 percent, a third of the cotton mills were closed or on the verge of collapse, and inflation was driving prices sky high. But counterbalancing the move toward intervention was the Northern blockade of the Confederate coastline, which the British recognized as legal even though most ships successfully ran through it. The biggest ace up Seward's sleeve in this game was that the British would do nothing until the Confederacy had clearly turned the military tide of the war and the North was in a mood for ending the conflict. Only then would the British, probably in conjunction with France and Russia, consider offering to mediate a negotiated settlement between the belligerents. This form of intervention was possible for the English, for they did not necessarily intend to follow it up with a formal recognition of Southern independence. They also did not want to provoke a retaliatory war with the North by prematurely offering to become involved in the conflict in any way. While the Confederate government obviously welcomed any form of intervention, Lincoln's administration consistently and strongly declared its unwillingness even to consider such a move.

Thus military events in Virginia had an enormous effect on the minds of Europeans. It is not surprising that they ignored Union successes in the West. Europeans naturally looked to the eastern seaboard for their news and their commercial contacts in America, and even Americans living in the East often tended to ignore or underplay the significance of what was happening in the interior of their own country. The national capitals of both belligerents were on the East Coast, and the biggest armies were grappling in Virginia rather than in Tennessee or Mississippi. As a result, English diplomats would pay very little attention to Buell's movements. But his campaign was just as much a part of the ebb and flow of military fortunes as was McClellan's, and it held its own potential for demonstrating whether the Northern war effort could succeed.

Thus Buell had complicated problems to face as he continued to push his hardworking soldiers to their utmost in the hot and humid summer of 1862. He began to wonder if his campaign might be in trouble when he pondered the significance of reports, which he had begun to receive as early as July 8, that sizable numbers of Rebel troops were leaving Tupelo, their route unknown. They could be moving toward Chattanooga or toward Buell's rear. Of all the logistical and political troubles the Ohio general faced that August, this was the most deadly.

The author of Buell's coming woes was Gen. Braxton Bragg. He had taken over command of the Army of the Mississippi on June 20 when Beauregard left to spend time at a health spa near Mobile. At first, as Beauregard's second in command, Bragg only held army command temporarily. Then, when it became apparent that Beauregard was using his supposed health problems to avoid shouldering responsibility for the army, it became permanent. It was a change for the better. Although good at projecting a romantic, cavalier image of himself, Beauregard was an inept field commander given to grandiose and unrealistic plans. He displayed little stomach for the daily grind of commanding a large, unruly army on the defensive and was best shunted off to command of marginal areas.

Bragg, in contrast, displayed qualities that indicated success. Born forty-five years before in North Carolina, graduating fifth in his West Point class, he had a reputation for capable administration and battlefield bravery before the war. The many stories circulating about his pettiness and attention to detail were the natural reaction of less qualified men to his administrative ability. Bragg deserved censure for his inability to get along with colleagues, and he was outspoken in his criticism of superiors when he believed they deserved it. As a light artillery officer in Mexico, he saw combat in several hard-fought battles, and he later married into a sugar planting family in Louisiana. He and Secretary of War Jefferson Davis fought over the issue of stationing artillery in frontier posts during the 1850s but mended their fences before important assignments were made in the early months of the Civil War. Bragg rose quickly to command a corps at Shiloh and then was booted to army command first by Johnston's death and then by Beauregard's abdication.

Bragg would need all his administrative ability, self-discipline, and respect for regulations, for his army had none of these qualities. He had a workaholic's eagerness to plunge into detail and, given the poor state of staff work and paper keeping in the army, he needed it. On the retreat from Corinth, Bragg worked himself and his staff members around the clock trying to impose as much order on the army as possible. Large amounts of provisions and supplies were left behind as the men marched sixty miles to Tupelo with inadequate food and even less discipline. "I think with the army we have our Generals will have to work themselves to death to do anything with them," observed Samuel H. Lockett, one of Bragg's staff officers. Bragg kept Lockett busy tracking down supplies, keeping columns closed up during the march, and trying to prevent stragglers from wandering off into the countryside. The soldiers tended to stop at every farmhouse to get water, steal livestock, or rest. Bragg ordered a man executed for carelessly firing into a barnyard and killing a slave. He also ordered another man to be "drawn up" for killing a pig and, in a fit of frustration, wanted to execute him as well but was persuaded to postpone such action until his case could be investigated. "These strong measures are the only ones that will do our army any good," asserted Lockett, "and from this time on all cases of desertion, lawlessness disobedience and unmilitary conduct is going to meet with speedy and severe punishments. We are going to have no more playing soldier in Genl Bragg's army and I hope we will soon see a very beneficial change."

From the beginning, officers and men of the Army of the Mississippi talked about taking the offensive against the Yankees. Even while retreating to Tupelo, staff officers discussed the different options open to them. They thought of drawing Halleck's huge army south from Corinth, then outflanking it and hitting its rear. They also discussed the possibility of moving to Chattanooga, joining Smith's small army in East Tennessee, and driving on to Nashville. Then they could "carry the war into Yankeedom and thus force Halleck to take the back track," as Samuel Lockett put it.

Bragg was eager to satisfy his army's yearning for offensive action. The only questions in his mind were where he should lead it, what his line of approach should be, and when the army would be ready to move. As indicated by Lockett's testimony, one option was to move directly northward. Even though Halleck showed no intention of allowing himself to be drawn into Mississippi, his army could be attacked in its positions at and near Corinth. Even after Buell began to move his Army of the Ohio eastward, however, Grant still had many more troops available for defense than Bragg had for offense. Another option was to move farther eastward and then drive north somewhere between Grant and Buell, perhaps threatening Buell's rear. This idea was appealing, offering the possibility of separating the two Union armies. But it also was dangerous, for it gave the Federals the equally inviting opportunity of concentrating on Bragg and crushing him in the middle. The third option proved to be the most attractive. If Bragg could quickly move his army over the rail system to Chattanooga he could relieve Smith, who was sending increasingly nervous appeals for help to anyone who would listen. From Chattanooga, Bragg would be in a position to move into the central portion of the state and force Buell to act on the defensive. Bragg could dictate the strategic course of the war for a change, instead of simply responding to Federal moves.

No matter which of the three options he chose, Bragg would have to postpone his move for several weeks while he created his army's offensive capability almost from scratch. The Army of the Mississippi had been pulled together quickly from several disparate commands and then thrown immediately into battle at Shiloh. It never had the long, nurturing birth of most field armies, which were created during the winter of waiting that preceded Fort Donelson. Bragg had to do his best as quickly as possible. His most immediate concern was a shortage of wagons, one of the reasons he had been forced to leave behind so many supplies at Corinth. While working on that problem, he tried to help Smith by sending a small division of only three thousand men under Maj. Gen. John P. McCown to Chattanooga. The division left Tupelo on June 26 and traveled via the rail system to Mobile, then on to Atlanta and Chattanooga, arriving on July 3. Another stopgap measure to help Smith hold East Tennessee was the sending of Forrest and Morgan on their respective raids to middle and northern Tennessee. Their success in temporarily breaking Buell's supply lines and limiting his preparations for a push on Chattanooga did more to help Smith than McCown's little division.

The day after McCown left Tupelo, Bragg announced to his army that the days of retreating were over. "Soldiers, great events are impending," he told them. "A few more days of needful preparation and organization and I shall give your banners to the breeze. . . . But be prepared to undergo privation and labor with cheerfulness and alacrity." The men were more than ready in spirit if not in material. Capt. T. J. Koger of the Forty-first Mississippi spoke for many when he wrote to his wife, "Let the word come 'forward' and set our faces to the enemy and we will tell a different tale. . . . It does seem to me that a little less ditch digging and a little more daring, go-ahead fighting would do better, even tho it cost . . . more lives."

It took Bragg almost a month to accumulate enough wagons to nearly fill his army's needs and to weigh the different options for an advance, a month afforded him by the slow progress Buell was making in solving his own logistical nightmare. Bragg eventually decided that attacking Grant's heavily fortified towns in northern Mississippi and western Tennessee was too difficult and that marching between Grant and Buell was too risky. The transport of McCown's division had shown that troops could be moved rapidly over the rail system that connected Mobile with Chattanooga. Bragg felt the ambition natural to any man who had just received a new and important command. On July 21 he officially informed Davis of his decision—the Army of the Mississippi would move immediately to Chattanooga. Thirty thousand infantrymen would ride the cars over six different rail lines with different gauges. They would travel over eight hundred miles before reaching their destination. There was no room for the cavalry, artillery, or wagons, all of which would have to march cross-country to Rome, Georgia, and then on to Chattanooga. The first units left Tupelo on July 23 and reached Chattanooga six days later. It would take time for the entire army to assemble there.

Bragg was careful not to abandon Mississippi. He left sixteen thousand men under Maj. Gen. Sterling Price near Tupelo and another sixteen thousand men under Van Dorn near Vicksburg, believing these two forces could unite when necessary to protect the state from further penetration by Grant's troops and save Vicksburg from falling to the rather feeble Union attempt to take it from downriver. More important, Bragg counted on Van

Dorn and Price to unite and take the offensive northward in support of his planned move into Tennessee. While he was retaking Nashville, the transplanted Trans-Mississippians could strike Grant in northern Mississippi. Not only was Bragg planning a bold offensive movement for his own army, he was trying to coordinate all the major Confederate forces in the West to support it.

The exhilaration that Bragg felt at the beginning of his first campaign as an independent commander began to be hedged about as soon as he reached Chattanooga on July 30. There, he learned to his surprise that Edmund Kirby Smith was also an independent commander, answerable directly to Jefferson Davis. If the two forces were to join, Bragg, as senior commander, would take control of the whole. But until that time, Bragg had to treat Smith as an equal partner. It was imperative that the two meet and take each other's measure, so Smith left his headquarters in Knoxville and rode the cars to Chattanooga. There, the two authors of the coming campaign closeted themselves for a conference on July 31 that lasted until the early morning hours of August 1.

They had much to discuss. Smith went to great lengths to assure Bragg that he was willing to cooperate with him on whatever plan was hatching for the recovery of lost territory, but he knew he was walking a tightrope between effective service for the good of the Confederacy and the potential loss of his independent command. His pairing with the ambitious Bragg was a delicate partnership whose problems were smoothed over with assuring words and a cordial relationship. Bragg believed that he came to a mutual understanding with Smith before the conference ended, but there is every reason to doubt Smith's sincerity. Since most of Bragg's army would not be ready to move out of Chattanooga for several days, if not weeks, it was decided that Smith should unite his command and retake Cumberland Gap. Then he could take his entire force to Chattanooga to join Bragg in the coming thrust into Middle Tennessee. The two would move on Buell's lines of communication and force the Federals to retire, hopefully all the way to Kentucky. There even was hope that Grant might be forced to evacuate western Tennessee if Bragg and Smith could interdict his supply lines northward, although that was only marginally possible. Certainly, with combined forces of forty thousand men, Bragg and Smith would be a match for Buell, and they also would have the advantage of striking first at his vulnerable rail lines. The recovery of Middle Tennessee was a very real possibility, and even a successful invasion of Kentucky was feasible if conducted smartly. In short, the plan was not only to recover lost territory but to capture land the Confederacy had never controlled. Most of Kentucky had been under Union occupation ever since that state's rather naive policy of neutrality had broken down in September 1861. Bragg and Smith were looking to a campaign of conquest, not just recovery.

When Smith left Chattanooga on August 1 to return to Knoxville, Bragg was confident all would work well. He later wrote to Smith that "mutual support and effective co-operation" would be the keynote of their partnership, and Smith assured Bragg that he agreed. Jefferson Davis, who was kept well informed of developments, was jubilant over the prospects of an offensive in the West. He naively wrote Bragg that Smith was "one of our ablest and purest officers. He has taken every position without indicating the least tendency to question its advantage to himself." Davis was confident that the two commanders could defeat Buell, capture Nashville, and force Grant to retreat northward. The result would be "a complete conquest over the enemy, involving the liberation of Tennessee and Kentucky."

But as soon as he returned to Knoxville, Smith deftly began to alter the course of events to suit himself. He did so with the greatest of care, playing off Bragg's good-natured willingness to allow him latitude in his movements. Smith was well respected by his colleagues. Born in Florida thirty-eight years before and graduating in the middle of the West Point class of 1845, he had seen combat in Mexico and served in Albert Sidney Johnston's Second U.S. Cavalry before the war. He was a major when Florida seceded from the Union and was quickly booted to brigade command in the Confederate army. His brigade arrived from the Shenandoah Valley just in time to play an important role in reversing the Union advance at the battle of First Bull Run. Smith was severely wounded in the chest, but his timely arrival on the battlefield caught the public imagination and he was lionized while recovering from his wound. His reward was promotion to major general and an independent command that was quickly becoming a focal point in the first Confederate offensive in the West. He intended to make the most of his opportunities.

On August 9, Smith admitted to Bragg that taking Cumberland Gap would not be easy. George W. Morgan's Federal force there was as large as Smith's, and it had stockpiled an enormous horde of supplies. Even if Smith were to cut off his line of communication, which was easy enough to do, Morgan could hold out in the gap for many weeks. Rather than tie his men down in this boring task, Smith suggested that he bypass the gap and move directly into the Bluegrass. Bragg responded on August 10 with a confusing mixture of caution and enthusiasm. He reminded Smith that Buell's army was the biggest roadblock to a successful invasion of Kentucky and that together they had a good chance to deal with it; if they were separated, the campaign might be in peril. Yet Bragg did not feel he could force Smith to comply with their initial plan and even promised to meet his headstrong and increasingly errant partner on the Ohio River. Smith responded with a promise, which seems very hollow in hindsight, to wait a while after bypassing Cumberland Gap until Bragg thought it was safe for him to advance toward Lexington. Ambitious and impatient, Smith was already beginning to indicate that he had no intention of joining his force with Bragg's and losing his independence. He clearly looked to Kentucky, not Middle Tennessee, as his chosen theater of operations. Bragg would be dragged into Smith's scheme.

Perhaps another reason that Bragg was willing to enlarge the initial plan of the campaign was that he was becoming just as infected with a desire to strike boldly into Kentucky as was Smith. Numerous influences were operating on both commanders during this time. The great success of John Hunt Morgan was one. The Kentucky cavalier was familiar with the Bluegrass region, which was his home. He sent back glowing reports from a recent raid into the state. "The whole country can be secured, and 25,000 or 30,000 men will join you at once," he wrote to Smith.

The flow of affairs was ripe for offensive action in the summer of 1862. The Confederate failures in the West had created an almost desperate desire among westerners to retrieve their fortunes, and Lee's great victory in the Seven Days inspired an expansive optimism among easterners. All Confederate patriots sensed that the time had come to take the war to their enemy rather than allow Northern armies to resume their grinding attacks on the Southern homeland. Halleck's need to consolidate Federal gains in the Upper South gave Bragg the opportunity to act on these public impulses.

Davis received a great deal of pressure and encouragement to push Confederate armies northward that summer, and everyone expected great, spectacular gains. As early as July 27, Josiah Gorgas, chief of ordnance in the Rebel army, believed that Bragg would at least force Buell away from Chattanooga and perhaps retake all of Tennessee and Kentucky. Jabez Lamar Monroe Curry, an Alabama delegate in the Confederate Congress, visited Bragg's army and reported to Davis that the men were "tired of inactivity and retreats and winning victories without making them available." They wanted "the privilege of fighting." The congressional delegation from Kentucky consistently implored the president to free their home. These Bluegrass politicians urged Davis to send as many Kentucky officers as possible with Bragg to facilitate recruiting there. Enthusiastic supporters of the invasion predicted that forty thousand men could be signed up for the army in Kentucky, for the populace was tired of squirming under the "oppression and tyranny of the Lincoln authorities." For his part, Davis was eager to see the Confederate colors fly over his native state. Writing to John Forsyth, the editor of the *Mobile Register*, he clearly spelled out his desire to free the South of invading armies: "There could be no difference of opinion as to the advantage of invading over being invaded. . . . My early declared purpose and continued hope was to feed upon the enemy and teach them the blessings of peace by making them feel in its most tangible form the evils of war."

Kentucky's political status in the Confederacy was anything but simple. The state never formally seceded, at least not in a way that was acceptable to everyone. Sentiment was so divided when secession began that a consensus one way or the other was impossible to achieve. While Gov. Beriah Magoffin was pro-Southern, the state legislature was pro-Northern. As a result, Magoffin decided to declare Kentucky neutral in the conflict, a policy that broke down in September when the Confederates made the first military move into the state. But he continued to act as governor even when most of the state was occupied by Federal troops, although he and the legislature could agree on almost nothing.

Those Kentuckians who could not accept Yankee rule held a meeting in Russellville, west of Bowling Green and well within Confederate lines, for the purpose of taking the state out of the Union on November 18. This convention denied the legitimacy of Magoffin's government in Frankfort, declared the state to be free, and voted George W. Johnson, one of the convention's organizers, as the new governor. Johnson immediately applied for Kentucky's admission to the Confederacy, which was granted on December 10. Governing with a ten-member council, consisting of a delegate from each congressional district, Johnson established his headquarters at Bowling Green and retreated from the state with Albert Sidney Johnston after the fall of Fort Donelson. A pugnacious man, Johnson served as a volunteer aide for Maj. Gen. John C. Breckinridge and fought in the ranks of Company E, Fourth Kentucky Infantry, on the first day at Shiloh. That night, he insisted on being mustered into the company as a private. He was hit twice in the next day's fighting and left on the field when Beauregard retreated. Alexander McDowell McCook, who had been a delegate with Johnson at the Democratic presidential convention in Charleston two years before, found him and saw to his care. Johnson died a few days later.

The council now voted to replace the chief executive with Richard C. Hawes, who also was a refugee. Hawes was sixty-four years old and had served as a commissary officer with Brig. Gen. Humphrey Marshall in eastern Kentucky during the fall of 1861. He joined the exiled government in late May and prepared to accompany Bragg in his drive north. Hawes aggressively pushed Kentucky's political agenda with the Davis government, visiting Richmond in late August to ask the president for money. The Confederate Congress had appropriated $3 million for the state, and Hawes believed that Johnson had taken a quarter of a million already, but he did not know how it was spent. He suggested that the remaining appropriation would greatly help the enrolling of troops in Kentucky, but Davis remained uncommitted. Hawes had to leave with no promise of money. He hoped that, by following Bragg into the state, he could "combine as far as practicable, our moral, political, & civil influences, with the military power of the Confederate army."

The leadership of Unionist Kentucky was in transition as Bragg's invasion plans took shape. Magoffin was discredited in the eyes of the people because of his views during the secession crisis, and he could not work effectively with the legislature. He finally decided to resign in the summer of 1862, but only if he could be followed by his hand-picked successor, state senator James F. Robinson. This transfer was arranged, and Magoffin stepped down on August 18. Robinson, a moderate conservative, was not associated with the controversies of the early months of the war and thus was able to work with the legislature on matters within the state. But he was highly critical of Lincoln's handling of the war, condemning the suspension of the writ of habeas corpus and attacking the emancipation policy. He was sure that abolition would result in racial conflict. But the governor cooperated with the Federals in providing troops and supplies for the Union war effort. He and the state government needed to be sustained by Lincoln in the coming crisis.

The Confederate president received encouragement from his generals as well as from various political leaders. Humphrey Marshall had been driven out of eastern Kentucky the previous January just as the Federal offensive that conquered the Upper South was getting under way. Ever since, he had taken refuge in southwestern Virginia hoping for an opportunity to return. "I cannot refrain from expressing in the very strongest terms my conviction that this is the golden moment," he assured Davis. Marshall was assembling a small force and planning to move back into the state in conjunction with Smith and Bragg.

Davis tried to coordinate the movements of these three commanders with those of his forces in the East, but this desirable goal was difficult to accomplish. The strategic needs and the flow of events were quite different in Virginia than in Tennessee and Kentucky, and Lee was a powerhouse intent on setting his own pace. The Confederacy's premier general took time to dash off a letter to Davis approving of a movement into Kentucky by Marshall, Smith, or Bragg noting that "it would produce a good effect." But he could not wait until those western generals had conquered their logistical problems or moved their forces over the long distances and rugged terrain that confronted them. Lee was planning a strike north from the Richmond area against John Pope's Army of Virginia by early August. His large army of some fifty-five thousand men would have to march about sixty miles on this campaign. Lee had to strike soon to prevent McClellan's Army of the Potomac from moving to Pope's support from its base on the Peninsula. There was no way that Bragg or Smith could move as quickly, so there would be only a loose coordination of effort between West and East that summer. Davis, who was acting as his own general in chief, could only encourage the various commanders to do their best at their own pace.

Unlike the North, the Confederate people were not witnessing a political revolution that summer. Their war effort had started out with three primary goals, to achieve independence, to protect their homeland, and to preserve slavery. Despite the pressure of military defeat in the West, those goals remained the same. The Rebels had no need for a confiscation policy because they were not invading Northern territory (at least not yet). When Davis tried to suspend the writ of habeas corpus, it caused so much political disaffection that he was forced to reinstate it. And there was certainly no political will among any group of Southerners for the emancipation of the slaves. That would have undercut one of the three goals of the war and created a social revolution that no Southerner wanted to see.

The only measure left to them was to attempt to increase the size of their armies. But the Confederates were already working on this problem. The Rebel Congress had passed the Conscription Act in April 1862, when it became apparent that the expiration of the initial one-year enlistment period of the volunteer regiments would threaten the war effort. This act was the most controversial move the Davis administration took. It mandated that all one-year volunteers would remain in service for the duration of the war, and it called up all able-bodied men between the ages of eighteen and forty for military duty. There were relatively few loopholes in this draft; it was a draconian measure designed to put men in uniform, not primarily to encourage voluntary enlistments. There was widespread resistance to it among a large minority of Southern citizens.

As the prospects of an invasion of Kentucky grew to reality, Confederate authorities looked toward imposing the Conscription Act on that state. The enrolling or drafting of tens of thousands of new troops would be a godsend to the thinning field armies in the West. The Rebels had far too few soldiers to defend huge tracts of territory, and there seemed to be no better way to compensate for this deficiency than to apply conscription to virgin land. Although food and forage were important, men seemed to be the real prize to be had by invading Kentucky.

The Confederates liked to think of themselves not as revolutionaries but as defenders of the original political tradition in America. They looked upon their war as a conservative movement, designed to retain their original rights against a North gone mad with "isms" and new ideas. They feared the tyranny of the majority would swamp the rights of the minority and destroy its peculiar interests, such as the need to preserve the outdated institution of slavery. Southerners were appalled when they read in Northern newspapers about the new policies and attitudes gaining currency among the Yankees. Catherine Ann Devereux Edmondston, a North Carolina plantation mistress, compared Lincoln to the czar of Russia and accused the Northerners of failing to "show either the genius of Christianity or the spirit of Civilization." For others, the radical war in the North inspired further devotion to the Southern cause. John B. Jones, a clerk in the War Department in Richmond, thought it would eliminate any hesitancy among the Confederates about the need for independence: "By their emancipation and confiscation measures, the Yankees have made this a war of extermination, and added new zeal and resolution to our brave defenders. . . . It is well. If the enemy had pursued a different course we should never have had the same unanimity. If they had made war only on men in arms, and spared private property, according to the usages of civilized nations, there would, at least, have been a neutral party in the South, and never the same energy and determination to contest the last inch of soil with the cruel invader." If there was a renewal of war spirit in the South that summer, it was propelled by a deepened sense of the need for defense. No new political moves would be made to achieve independence. Instead, Southerners concentrated on fighting harder and raising more troops. Perhaps a successful invasion of Kentucky would coincide with more battlefield victories by Lee in Virginia to bring on foreign intervention and recognition. Upon these hopes rested the future of the Confederacy.

By the middle of August, the entire strategic picture in the West was on the verge of a dramatic turnaround. The long Federal offensive from Fort

Henry to Corinth was long since over, and Union troops had not yet completed their occupation of the Upper South. Tired of retreating, the Confederates were on the move. They were beginning the campaign in Kentucky with a divided command structure and strategic goals that seemed to change on a weekly basis, and supplies would be a constant problem for them. But the men were eager for action. After losing so much ground, it was an amazing feat of resiliency to see Bragg's men ready to strike at their enemies. They moved out with spirit, as if their reverses had not damaged their morale. As Bragg had boasted in June, he meant to unfurl his "banners to the breeze" and take his army as far as it could go.

CHAPTER TWO

Bold Strike into the Bluegrass

Edmund Kirby Smith was ready to strike. He had gathered his men, made his plans for outflanking Cumberland Gap, and set his sights on even greater achievements. A mere three weeks before, he had been frantically sending pleas to Braxton Bragg for help to defend East Tennessee. Now he was about to launch the first move in a major Confederate invasion of Kentucky.

The geography of this theater of war would be an important factor in the coming campaign. Eastern Tennessee and eastern Kentucky were dominated by the southern portion of the Appalachian Highlands, which separated the eastern seaboard from the western states. The highlands stretched for over a thousand miles from New England to northern Alabama and were about three hundred miles wide with a varied topography. The eastern half of the highlands consisted of long, high ridges and jumbled mountains, the most prominent among the latter being the Great Smokies. Just west of the center of the highlands rolled the wide and fertile Tennessee River valley. With Knoxville and Chattanooga nestled in its bucolic landscape, the valley had the heaviest concentration of population and the most important railroad and river routes in southern Appalachia.

Bragg and Smith would traverse the western third of the Appalachian Highlands. There were two dominating ridges that stretched northeast to southwest through Virginia and Tennessee. One of these ridges, Cumberland Mountain, formed the boundary between Virginia and Kentucky. At a point on its top, just south of Cumberland Gap, the state lines of Virginia, Kentucky, and Tennessee intersected. The mountain continued to the southwest for another forty miles to LaFollette, Tennessee. Here it connected with a much larger geographic feature, the Cumberland Plateau, which sliced diagonally across the state to separate eastern Tennessee from

Middle Tennessee. The plateau was about sixty miles wide with a steep eastern escarpment and a rugged, irregular edge on the west. The top of the plateau was rolling terrain with occasional ridges and hills. From his starting
point in the Tennessee River valley, Smith would not have to worry about
the Cumberland Plateau, but he would have to find a way to take his men
across Cumberland Mountain south of Cumberland Gap. Fortunately for
him, there were several accessible gaps in the mountain at and north of
LaFollette. Bragg, however, would have to contend with the Cumberland
Plateau immediately after leaving Chattanooga, which was located where
the Tennessee River begins to slice through the eastern edge of the plateau.

Even after crossing Cumberland Mountain, Smith would have to contend with an even bigger and higher ridge, Pine Mountain, which paralleled
it to the northwest. After crossing Pine Mountain, Smith would enter a
large area of jumbled terrain, extending some fifty miles west and north,
known to local inhabitants as the Log Mountains. There was no order to
these heights, no long ridges or spacious valleys, only narrow creeks that
wound their torturous way among the peaks. The only major road through
this area was the Wilderness Road, first carved out of the woods by Daniel
Boone in 1775 from modern-day Kingsport, Tennessee, to Cumberland
Gap, and then northwest to the Bluegrass region. It had been widened into a
wagon toll road by the state of Kentucky in the 1790s and now served as the
transportation artery of the region. It was George W. Morgan's supply line
between Cumberland Gap and Lexington; Barboursville and London were
the chief towns along the route. Once Smith made it through the Log
Mountains and onto the Wilderness Road, he would have won his battle
with the region's impressive geography.

From here, he could advance quickly northward into the expansive, fertile Bluegrass, the home of Kentucky's first settlers and wealthiest land-
owners. The Bluegrass, with its principal city, Lexington, was the heart and
soul of Kentucky. It was the home of Mary Todd Lincoln, the northern
president's wife, and the repository of wealth, breeding, and prestige that
produced the state's best families. It also was the area of greatest Confederate sympathy. Its excellent pikes and prosperous farms made it an ideal theater of operations.

Stretching southwestward from the Bluegrass and bordering the western
edge of the Cumberland Plateau all the way to Nashville was the Plateau of
the Barrens. Named by early settlers because of its expansive forests of
cedar and pines, which they believed denoted infertile soil, it was characterized by rolling terrain dotted with small hills and ridges. This region

would be Bragg's main area of operations after he crossed the Cumberland Plateau. It had good roads and at least a few good farms. Limestone lay just under the surface of the land and often cropped up above the surface, making the region ill suited for cultivation but excellent for grazing. It also was well suited for rapid movement of troops but not necessarily for feeding a large army. If, on the other hand, Bragg decided to attack Nashville, he would find a different geographic region surrounding the city. Known as the Nashville Basin and extending seventy miles in each direction from the city, it was a region of flat, rolling land and fertile farms. Like the Bluegrass in Kentucky, the Nashville Basin was the location of Tennessee's most important city. It was the home of Andrew Jackson and James K. Polk, a transportation center for the Upper South, and the breeding ground for Tennessee's wealthiest and most influential people. In short, both wings of the coming Confederate offensive could look forward to glittering prizes at the end of a long, hard march through barren and mountainous country.

Smith planned his campaign with a keen awareness of geography. He targeted two gaps in Cumberland Mountain that were big enough to accommodate his men and trains and also far enough south of Cumberland Gap to prevent Morgan from interfering. The extra troops that Bragg loaned Smith made his campaign possible. He organized his available manpower into four divisions. One, under Brig. Gen. Carter L. Stevenson, would remain behind in East Tennessee to hold Morgan in place. Stevenson's nine thousand men began to move up to the gap and take positions immediately south of the pass. He had nearly as many men as Morgan, but the defenses of the gap were too strong to risk an attack.

Smith would take two other divisions under Brig. Gen. Patrick R. Cleburne and Brig. Gen. Thomas J. Churchill, a total of six thousand men, through Roger's Gap. It was a wide but shallow cut in the top of the mountain about twenty miles south of Cumberland Gap, passable by troops but unsuitable for artillery and wagons. Another division of three thousand men under Brig. Gen. Henry Heth would escort the supply wagons and artillery through a much easier passage, Big Creek Gap, just north of LaFollette. This gap, which had been cut through the mountain over eons of erosion by Big Creek, extended all the way to the base of the height and offered easy passage for wheeled vehicles. A small cavalry brigade of nine hundred men under Col. John S. Scott rode far ahead of Smith's infantry to clear the roads, secure key points, and provide much needed information.

The separate columns started out at different times. Those who had the longest distance to travel began early, leaving Knoxville on August 12. The

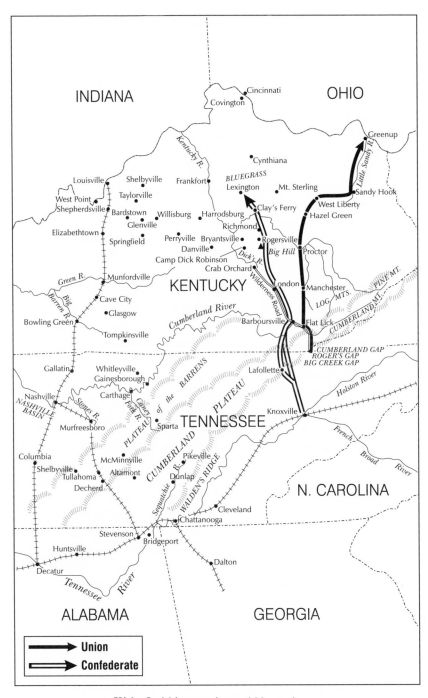

INDIANA

OHIO

Cincinnati
Covington

Greenup

Little Sandy R.

Cynthia
BLUEGRASS
Lexington
Mt. Sterling
Sandy Hook
West Liberty
Hazel Green

Kentucky R.

Louisville
Shelbyville
Frankfort
Taylorville
West Point
Shepherdsville
Bardstown
Willisburg
Harrodsburg
Clay's Ferry
Glenville
Elizabethtown
Springfield
Perryville
Bryantsville
Rogersville
Danville
Big Hill
Proctor
Camp Dick Robinson
Crab Orchard
Richmond
Dick's R.
Wilderness Road

KENTUCKY

Green R.
Munfordville
London
Manchester
Cave City
Barbourville
Flat Lick
Glasgow
Bowling Green
Tompkinsville
Cumberland River

Big Barren R.

PINE MT.
LOG MTS.
CUMBERLAND MT.

CUMBERLAND GAP
ROGER'S GAP
BIG CREEK GAP

Gallatin
Whitleyville
Gainesborough
Lafollette
Holston River
Nashville
Carthage
Knoxville
NASHVILLE BASIN
Stones R.
PLATEAU OF THE BARRENS
Murfreesboro
Sparta
French Broad River

TENNESSEE

Columbia
McMinnville
Shelbyville
Altamont
Tullahoma
Decherd
Dunlap
Pikeville

CUMBERLAND PLATEAU
WALDEN'S RIDGE
Sequatchie R.

N. CAROLINA

Broad River

Cleveland
Stevenson
Chattanooga
Huntsville
Bridgeport
Dalton
Decatur

Tennessee River

ALABAMA

GEORGIA

→ Union
→ Confederate

1. Kirby Smith's campaign and Morgan's retreat

march to Cumberland Mountain was relatively easy with plenty of ripening fruit hanging on the trees for the hungry soldiers to pick. But as the divisions made their way through Big Creek Gap and Roger's Gap, they entered a region that was much more desolate and forbidding than the Tennessee River valley. It was the driest season of the year and the small mountain streams provided little water. Farms were less numerous and productive. The soldiers in Cleburne's and Churchill's divisions had to rely on what they could carry, for the supply wagons were miles away and having a difficult time of it. The passage of Pine Mountain was torturous for both columns, and the jumbled nature of the Log Mountains presented a trying ordeal. In places, the artillery had to be manhandled over the peaks with up to thirty men tugging at long ropes attached to guns and caissons. Lean on provisions and marching in hot, dry weather, the infantrymen trudged on through an inhospitable country. They found the inhabitants to be suspicious and unwilling to share their meager supplies. J. G. Law of the 154th Tennessee described the Log Mountains as a "wild and desolate region." The citizens appeared to be "wrapped in profound ignorance. Some of them do not know in what year they live and are under the impression that Andrew Jackson is President of the United States." Some units had a long haul through this region. The Forty-eighth Tennessee marched a total of ninety-eight miles in seven days from Knoxville to Barboursville.

The lead elements of Smith's command reached Barboursville on the morning of August 18 and completely surprised the few Federal soldiers who were stationed there. The town was located on the upper side of a graceful northward curve of the Cumberland River. A small, unimpressive town, Barboursville was at the mouth of a creek that occupied a wide valley running several miles from north to south, draining into the river. Thus it was one of the few open places in the region. Smith easily captured fifty prisoners and learned from them that Morgan had stockpiles of supplies at Cumberland Gap that could feed his men for up to thirty days. He concluded that Morgan's position was impregnable and that only a lengthy siege would oust him. He had no intention of tying up his eighteen thousand men in that task, especially now that he had cut off Morgan's line of communication and had an avenue of advance to the Bluegrass.

Smith quickly began to prepare for a continued drive northward. It would take several days for the rest of his two columns, especially the wagons and artillery, to make it to Barboursville, so he ordered the regiments to camp and rest. They found little to eat and had to be content with green corn, apples, and a little beef. While he prepared for the push northward, Smith indulged in a spate of letter writing. To his wife, he bragged about his accomplishments in taking nine thousand men over rugged terrain, even comparing the march to that of Hernando Cortez into the heartland of the Aztec nation in 1519. He complained of the fierce Unionist sentiment in the mountains of Kentucky, the increasing incidents of sniping and guerrilla attacks, the shortages of food and water, and the "almost impassable roads and mountain passes." His men were "ragged, famished, barefooted," but that only seemed to make their accomplishment thus far in the campaign even more impressive. Smith also informed Bragg and Davis that he could not afford to wait for them to approve of his advance into the heartland of Kentucky. Now, far ahead of his would-be partner, Smith was in his element. There was no longer any danger of consolidating his army with Bragg's and losing his independent command. He was in a position to dictate strategy to his superior and win the glory he had craved since First Manassas.

Smith wanted more men, so he ordered Carter L. Stevenson to send him a brigade of three thousand troops under Col. Alexander W. Reynolds by way of Big Creek Gap. But he later decided that he could not afford to wait for Reynolds. Heth's division reached Barboursville on August 22 with the artillery, and Smith decided it should remain in town and wait for the supply wagons that were still struggling up the road from Big Creek Gap. Reynolds's brigade could join Heth at Barboursville. Meanwhile, Smith would lead Cleburne's and Churchill's divisions northward and strike for Lexington as quickly as possible. He believed that time was of the essence if he were to reach the Kentucky River, which ran east to west between Richmond and Lexington. If he could cross that major stream without interference, he was confident of his ability to control the Bluegrass. "We should make no retrograde movements now in this State," wrote Smith's chief of staff, Col. John Pegram, to cavalry commander Scott. Smith wanted "the most perfect decorum of conduct toward the citizens and their property," a tall order for an army that was only one or two meals away from starvation. "It must be our policy to conciliate the inhabitants of a State whose every interest lies with our own country, and who have only been thus far kept from joining us by the infamous misrepresentations of the Yankee leaders and newspapers. It is for your command, as being the advance of this army, to show them that you come not to destroy but to protect their property."

John S. Scott did not need these instructions, for his men were too busy ranging across the countryside securing key points along Smith's line of advance to engage in plunder. Scott's little force performed excellent service and was a key element in the campaign. He had ridden his Louisiana, Georgia, and Kentucky horsemen well ahead of the infantry, attacking a small group of Federals stationed atop Big Hill on August 23 and easily capturing them. Big Hill was a commanding eminence at the edge of the mountains sixty miles north of Barboursville. From its seven-hundred-foot height, one could gaze northward for many miles across the rolling terrain of the Bluegrass. Because it would serve as Smith's entrepôt to the land he desired, its easy capture was encouraging. Smith moved out of Barboursville with Cleburne's division in the lead on August 27, leaving the Wilderness Road north of London to take a direct route to Big Hill. The Confederates crossed Rockcastle River the next day and continued northward. The countryside was even more barren of settlers, food, and water than the route from Cumberland Mountain to Barboursville, but the dry weather hardened the unimproved mountain roads, which speeded the march.

Smith reached Big Hill at dawn on August 29 and was delighted that his cavalry had stolen a march on the Federals and seized this important point. His infantry rested that day after carefully making their way along the road that snaked down the side of this steep mountain. Federal cavalrymen attacked his pickets that night, but they were easily repulsed. Smith did not know exactly what lay out there in the darkness, but two divisions and a few batteries of his army were out of the wilderness and poised at the edge of the Bluegrass. He even took heart in the cavalry clash, believing that it meant whatever Federal force lay before him intended to fight in the open landscape rather than block his passage over the Kentucky River. He was sure his veterans of Shiloh and Pea Ridge could handle anything that might lie in their path as long as it was an open fight on a battlefield with no particular terrain advantage or fortifications to aid the enemy. Smith and his men rested that night knowing that a battle was likely the next day and also knowing that the fighting would decide whether his invasion was a foolish disaster or a brilliant feat of arms. As one of his staff members, Paul F. Hammond, put it after the war, "doubt was ruin; to hesitate was to be destroyed. Behind us was a barren mountain country, and a ferocious and bitterly hostile population; beyond the enemy in our front the 'blue-grass region,' the garden of Kentucky, teeming with inexhaustible supplies."

Smith could have rested more easily that night if he had known that he had taken his opponents by surprise. The Federal forces in the Bluegrass were ill prepared to meet him. All they could do was to throw together a force of newly raised regiments, all of them unbloodied and most of them barely proficient in drill or target firing. They were even more ignorant of the strength and composition of Smith's force than Smith was of theirs. The Confederates would have all the advantages in the first battle of the campaign for Kentucky.

Buell had barely begun the task of preparing the state for defense. In mid-August, when it became apparent that Bragg was massing large numbers of troops at Chattanooga, the Federal general became alarmed. He began to shift commanders and troops around to protect his rear. First, he sent George Henry Thomas from his division at Decherd to take charge of McMinnville, the left end of his attenuated line. William Nelson was then detached from his division at McMinnville and sent all the way to Kentucky. His job was to take charge of the defense of Louisville and the railroad line that supplied Buell's army.

Nelson reached Louisville on August 22. There he discovered, much to his surprise, that the authorities in Washington had been meddling with the boundaries of Buell's authority. An entirely new command had been created, termed the Department of the Ohio, under Major General Horatio G. Wright. Its area included all of Kentucky, which had been taken away from Buell's command. Nelson found that he was Wright's senior in rank, but for the sake of the cause, he declared himself willing to serve under him.

There was no time to waste in squabbling over rank or complaining about departmental boundaries. The troops in Wright's command were mainly located at Richmond to protect the line of communication with Morgan, a line that already was being cut by Smith's hard-marching army. Wright agreed that the rail line to Buell's army also needed protection, so he assigned Nelson the job. He was to gather the regiments that were being raised in the Midwest under President Lincoln's July call for an additional three hundred thousand men and that were being shipped across the Ohio River as soon as they became available. He was to accumulate the scattered railroad guards and any other troops he could find and deploy the lot along Buell's line of communication.

Nelson's first step was to go to Richmond and begin repositioning the troops already there. He reached this small town, some twenty-five miles south of Lexington, on August 26. Nelson had several capable officers to aid him. He divided the infantry into two brigades under Brig. Gen. Mahlon Manson and Brig. Gen. Charles Cruft. Then Nelson sent Brig. Gen. James S. Jackson to Nicholasville, some fifteen miles southwest of Lexington, to collect the cavalry. Manson and Cruft had a total of six thousand men who were better positioned at Danville, Nelson thought, where they would be connected to Buell's line of communication by a branch of the Louisville and Nashville Railroad that ran to Bardstown and Lebanon.

Nelson left instructions with Manson to prepare the infantry for this move to Danville and then he rode to Lexington. On August 29, the day Smith's infantry reached Big Hill, Nelson sent Capt. Charles C. Gilbert to Cincinnati with information for Wright. The captain served as an effective liaison, convincing Wright that Nelson's plan would support both Buell and Morgan. Gilbert also relayed Nelson's suggestion that the railroad garrisons be protected by stockades similar to those currently in use on the line from Nashville to Huntsville. Wright approved all of Nelson's arrangements. He encouraged the midwestern governors to renewed efforts, telling them to send the newly raised regiments from Ohio to Lexington so they could be used to protect Morgan's supply line, while the regiments from Indiana and Illinois were to go to Louisville to protect Buell's line. In effect, both Wright and Nelson ignored Buell's insistence that he be given priority and Halleck's insistence that Morgan be given priority.

Unknown to either Wright or Nelson, their carefully laid plans had already been broken by forces beyond their control. On August 29, Manson learned from his cavalry patrols that Rebel horsemen, Scott's cavalry, were pushing northward up the road from Big Hill. He quickly decided to prepare for battle and wanted to secure a bit of high ground, just a mile and a half south of his camp, before any Confederate troops planted artillery there. If the Rebels reached that point before he did, the Federals would have to retreat north of Richmond. Manson quickly marched his infantry brigade there and halted Scott's advance. Instead of stopping there, he impulsively pushed Scott south to the small village of Rogersville, nearly two miles away. Here he encamped his infantry while sending his small cavalry force to continue the pursuit. The Federal horsemen rashly attacked Cleburne's division at the base of Big Hill that night, unaware of what they were hitting in the darkness. After their blunt repulse, the Union cavalrymen rode all the way back to Rogersville.

The next morning, Saturday, August 30, both sides got an early start. Cleburne's division moved out before dawn while Manson's men left their encampment at Rogersville at 6 A.M. The Federal commander sent a message to Cruft to hurry his brigade from Richmond while Cleburne was counting on Churchill's division to follow him northward. Manson and Cleburne met about a half mile south of Rogersville, near a stout brick church called Mt. Zion, five and a half miles south of Richmond. Manson put most of his men to the left, or east, side of the road, the Fifty-fifth Indiana and the Sixteenth Indiana forming his battle line, with the Seventy-first Indiana in reserve. The Sixty-ninth Indiana took position to the west of the road. None of these Federal regiments had much combat experience. The Seventy-first Indiana had received its first issue of ammunition less than two weeks before and had tried its first battalion drill on the morning of August 29.

Manson deployed at the point where the road began to descend a long slope down into the headwaters of Hayes Fork Creek. It was fairly good defensive ground except that a series of cornfields to his left could give cover to an advancing enemy, and he did not have enough men to cover the area west of the road, where a ravine offered an avenue of advance to outflank his right. Cleburne would give Manson no time to scout the countryside properly. He immediately deployed his division five hundred yards from the Federal line, placing Col. Benjamin Hill's brigade to the east of the road and leaving Col. Preston Smith's brigade in reserve. For two hours the two forces exchanged artillery fire and skirmished. Cleburne was under orders from Smith to wait for Churchill's division before bringing on a general engagement, but that did not prevent the Irishman from scouting to the east to locate Manson's left flank. Indeed, both commanders nervously began to send more troops to the east to prevent their opponent from outflanking them. Manson moved the Seventy-first Indiana and all but three companies of the Sixty-ninth Indiana in that direction, while Cleburne sent all of Smith's brigade and the Thirteenth and Fifteenth Arkansas from Hill's brigade. While riding back and forth to see that these movements were properly carried out, Cleburne stopped to talk with Col. Lucius Polk, who had been wounded. A spent Federal bullet cut through his left cheek and fell into his mouth as he spoke, resulting in a lot of bleeding but no serious damage. Still, Cleburne found it impossible to talk for a while, so he gave command of his division to Preston Smith while he went to the rear for medical treatment.

Cleburne left the battlefield just when the action reached a turning point. Churchill's division had come up, and Smith, who had been on the field since 8 A.M. but had not interfered with Cleburne's work, ordered one of his brigades under Col. T. H. McCray to undertake a flanking march to the west. McCray moved through a field of tall, green corn and up the ravine, unseen by the Federals, to hit Manson's exposed right flank. By this time, Cleburne's regiments had worked their way through the cornfields to the east and were putting pressure on Manson's left flank. Even the arrival of

Cruft's leading regiments on the field, after a hard seven-mile march, could not save Manson. Only two of Cruft's regiments arrived in time to take part in the battle, and both were immediately caught in the escalating retreat that Manson's brigade had already begun to make. The Eighteenth Kentucky of Cruft's brigade stood defiantly to slow the advance of the Confederates, which now included Hill's brigade coming up the road, but it had to join the retreating mass. Manson and Cruft were in rapid retreat by 10:30, with much confusion and heavy losses in some regiments. Nevertheless, Manson managed to stop most of the men and reform his battle line about a mile and three-quarters farther north, near the high ground that he had been so keen on securing the previous day, on land owned by a farmer named White.

The combined strength of the two Union brigades, about sixty-five hundred men, equaled that of Cleburne's and Churchill's divisions, but many Federal soldiers did not stop at Manson's second battle line on White's farm. Here Manson deployed Cruft's brigade to the west of the road, stretching on to some high ground. The two right regiments took position in a patch of woods while the left two regiments, next to the road, positioned themselves behind a fence that bordered a long cornfield. Manson's brigade deployed to the east of the road with two batteries of artillery as support. The Confederates were eager to continue the fight and immediately attacked after coming up to this position. McCray's brigade continued to advance west of the road while Cleburne's division continued to try to outflank the Federal left. Just as the Confederates began their advance, Manson glanced at his watch. It was 12:30, and he felt confident that his line would hold. Ironically, he just then received a message from Nelson, advising him not to fight a battle but to retreat by way of the road to Lancaster. It was far too late for such advice; five minutes after this note arrived, the firing began.

Manson's hopes for a stand on White's farm were doomed. McCray's brigade pushed forward through the cornfield and came under a terrific hail of artillery and musket fire. These veterans quickened their pace and moved forward until they came to a fence that was two hundred yards from Cruft's battle line. Here McCray ordered them to halt and lie down for protection. They hugged the earth for twenty minutes while shells and minié balls flew over their heads. This long rest encouraged the men of the Ninety-fifth Ohio and the Sixty-sixth Indiana, who thought it meant that McCray's troops were demoralized. They impulsively moved out from their strong position to attack the Confederates. It was a horrible mistake. When McCray saw what was happening, he told his men to prepare a volley but to remain hidden. The Rebels waited until the cheering Yankees were within a few yards of the mid-field fence, then they rose up and fired at nearly point-blank range. The Federals were staggered. When they regained their senses, most of them turned and beat a hasty retreat just as McCray's men reloaded and clambered over the fence in hot pursuit. The Ohio and Indiana troops did not stop when they reached the end of the cornfield but continued to retreat northward up the road toward Richmond, pulling the rest of Cruft's brigade with them. Manson had no choice but to order everyone to follow. The Confederates had won the engagement at White's farm by about 1:45 and inspired an even worse hemorrhage of strength from the Federal army as it raced toward Richmond.

William Nelson joined the retreating mass along the way. He had been in the saddle all day, riding a total of fifty miles from Lexington to Lancaster, and then, when he received word of the battle, toward Richmond. Nelson had not wanted a fight between his untried soldiers and an unknown force of Rebel troops, but now he had no choice but to help Manson and Cruft make the best of it. As he raged back and forth, berating the soldiers to stand and fight, even using his fists and the flat of his sword to reinforce the point, the weather reached its hottest point of the day. The temperature rose to ninety-five degrees and the sun turned the road into a hard-baked surface. The only water available seemed to be the green, stagnant liquid settling into wagon ruts, but the dry soldiers scooped it up and drank it.

Nelson and his subordinates managed to establish a battle line at the eastern edge of Richmond along a low ridge. About twenty-five hundred men took position here, many of them taking cover behind a low stone wall that bordered the city cemetery. Some Federals even used the tombstones as cover. The Confederates could taste victory even more clearly now than at any other time during the day, but they too were exhausted and overheated. Smith sent Scott's cavalry to swing around Richmond and interdict the Yankee retreat out of town. To give Scott time to position himself and to allow his infantry some rest, Smith ordered the men to halt in Manson's old camp. This delay gave Nelson much needed time to organize his battle line at the cemetery, but it did Smith little harm. The Federals were badly outnumbered as well as badly shaken by this late stage of the battle.

The Confederate army approached the cemetery at 5 P.M., Churchill's division on the left and Cleburne's on the right. The Federals put up a stiff fight for at least thirty minutes. Many Confederates believed this last engagement was the most fiercely fought of the day, but the Yankees were outflanked and forced to withdraw. Nelson was hit while boldly exposing himself to inspire his men. "Boys, if they can't hit something as big as I am, they can't hit anything!" he shouted just before being shot in the abdomen. For a third time, the two Union brigades turned and ran for dear life. As Cruft put it, "the whole line broke in wild confusion and reckless of all restraint or command, and rushed pell-mell to the rear, amidst a mingled mass of horses, wagons, artillery etc., in an utter rout."

The harried Yankees streamed through the streets of Richmond, passed the Madison County Court House in the center of town, and ran into the countryside on their way toward Lexington. They hit an imposing road-block a few miles north. Scott had positioned his nine hundred horsemen in a line that stretched from the Lexington Road westward to the Lancaster Road. He managed to capture hundreds of Federals, so many that he could not hold all of them, and many managed to escape. The Union army was a long stream of disorganized men when it left Richmond; now it fragmented into clusters of fugitives desperately trying to evade Rebel horsemen. Manson rode into a body of cavalry but refused to surrender. His horse was shot under him, and as he tried to escape it fell, pinning him to the ground, and the Rebels took him prisoner. Cruft managed to evade the Rebels, however, but Nelson was caught. His wound was not serious enough to prevent him from taking advantage of the first chance to escape. After hiding for a while in a cornfield, he made his way northward.

Most of the Federals who eluded Scott's cavalrymen crossed the Kentucky River at Clay's Ferry and trudged on to Lexington. That night a sorry straggle of beaten men came into town. Smith's Confederates were tired, and the day was fast slipping away; they made no effective pursuit. Not even the hard-riding Scott, who had trouble handling his prisoners, tried to chase the remaining Yankees northward.

As the sun came up on the morning of Sunday, August 31, the Confederates awoke to a deeper realization of the extent of their victory. Few other battles in the Civil War saw such a collapse of Union strength. Not even the debacle at First Bull Run was as complete as the thrashing Manson's and Cruft's brigades received south of Richmond. Of the 6,500 Unionists engaged, 5,353 were lost. There were 206 killed, 844 wounded, and an astounding 4,303 either captured or missing. The Federals lost their wagon trains, artillery, and one of their commanders. The Confederates bought all this at a surprisingly light cost in blood. Of the 6,850 Confederate troops engaged, only 451 were lost. It had been a Union battlefield disaster of epic proportions.

The most telling result of this sorry defeat was that it opened the way for Smith to sieze the Bluegrass. The Union high command could do nothing to stop him. Nelson rested on the night of August 30 at the home of Cassius M. Clay, near Richmond, and sent a message to Wright asking permission to go to Cincinnati to have his abdominal wound treated. It was considered a dangerous injury, particularly because Nelson "had of late been growing corpulent," according to his staff member Gilbert. As Nelson made his way northward on August 31, Wright made his way south, reaching Lexington at noon. He found the city in panic. Fragments of broken units were straggling in from Richmond all day long, and Indiana and Ohio soldiers were deserting to their homes. Wright's first problem was that he had no field commander to replace Nelson. Only Cruft and Jackson remained, but neither felt confident of their ability to deal with the chaos. They recommended that Gilbert be given a field promotion to major general and assume command of the scattered army. Capt. William R. Terrill, another member of Nelson's entourage, was promoted to brigadier general to replace Manson. These impromptu promotions were later sanctioned by higher authorities. Thus was a staff captain booted up to command the Army of Kentucky and another staff captain made a brigade commander on the spot.

Wright also decided that the troops gathering at Lexington should be sent to Louisville. Cincinnati, on the north bank of the Ohio River, was less vulnerable. Louisville was the key to Buell's supply line and to continued Federal control of Kentucky. A column of weary and dispirited men began the long march west by way of Frankfort on the evening of August 31, with 150 wagons loaded with supplies from the Lexington depot. They had five artillery pieces but no trained gunners to operate them. They reached Louisville on September 5, abandoning the Bluegrass to its fate.

Most residents of the Bluegrass were happy with their fate, for Southern sympathies ran high in the region. Smith moved cautiously to secure his prize. His men spent all of August 31 cleaning up the battlefields south of Richmond, gathering the wounded, rounding up prisoners, and collecting abandoned equipment. They found lots of supplies left behind by the Federals, including canned fruit, condensed milk, and cheese, a profusion of food compared to their meager fare while crossing the mountains. Any building big enough to hold a few wounded men became a hospital. Churches, private homes, even the courthouse were filled with the cries of the wounded and the smell of medicine. Dozens of civilians from the local area carted food and other supplies into town to help the unfortunate soldiers, often staying to volunteer as nurses. It was the first taste of fighting the region had known, and it greatly impressed everyone.

After paroling all the prisoners his men could gather, Smith began a laborious march to Lexington on the morning of September 1. He found a lone cavalry regiment guarding the crossing of the Kentucky River at Clay's Ferry, but the troopers immediately retreated when the head of the Confederate column appeared. Smith ordered his men to halt at noon, only four miles north of the river and ten miles south of Lexington. They were exhausted from weeks of hard marching over mountainous terrain, the shortage of food, and the fighting at Richmond. So many of them were straggling that Paul Hammond estimated that only twenty-five hundred could have been gathered to form a battle line if the column was attacked. Smith did not know that his enemy had abandoned Lexington, and he feared that unknown quantities of blue-clad soldiers might be around the next bend. He decided to wait.

Meanwhile, Heth had marched his division from Barboursville to Richmond and dispatched two thousand men on a forced march to reach Smith by dawn on September 2. Such exertion was unnecessary. Deciding to play a bluff, Smith had sent John Pegram with a flag of truce into Lexington on the night of September 1, demanding the city's surrender. Pegram was astonished to find that no pickets barred his way. Indeed, he arrived after everyone had gone to sleep and had difficulty finding anyone in authority. He finally roused the mayor from his bed, and the city was promptly surrendered. A much relieved Smith immediately sent a regiment into town to keep order.

When they entered Lexington on September 2, the tired soldiers were overwhelmed with gratitude, cheering, and congratulations. The happiness more than made up for the tiring campaign and the hot battle. The residents "seemed mad with joy," thought Jemison Mims of the Forty-third Alabama. The men had been received in a similar fashion by some residents of Richmond, but the enthusiasm was far more intense and widespread here. People brought food into the streets, waved their hats, and shouted hurrahs for the Confederacy. Several women laid flowers at the feet of Smith's horse as he rode into town at the head of his column.

Not surprisingly, when he settled into his quarters, Smith began to write gushingly enthusiastic letters to his superiors. His reception proved that the people of the Bluegrass "regard us as their deliverers from oppression" and "that the heart of Kentucky is with the South in this struggle." He was immensely proud of what his army had done and bragged to his wife that "all of Kentucky to the Ohio is at our feet." Smith naturally predicted that his ranks would swell with recruits. Pegram estimated that twenty thousand men would soon join the colors if only Smith had the means to arm them.

After cooling down from the excitement of his reception, Smith was forced to acknowledge that, by its very success, his campaign had suddenly grown much more complicated. He had achieved his immediate objective, control of the Bluegrass, and now had to decide what else he could accomplish. For the time being, no viable military force barred his way to either Louisville or Cincinnati, but he was not certain if he had strength enough to hold either place for very long. Even with the addition of Heth's division and Reynolds's brigade he had only eleven thousand men. It was thought that Humphrey Marshall had entered eastern Kentucky from Virginia through Pound Gap and might add his small force to Smith's. John Hunt Morgan had joined Smith in Lexington soon after the fall of the city, fresh from his tunnel-bashing raid on the Louisville and Nashville Railroad.

Still, Smith was closer to Northern territory than any Confederate force had been so far in the war, and he did not know the location of his supporting troops. Smith had not heard from Bragg since he left Barboursville. He had no information on the location of either Bragg's or Buell's armies. Morgan had a division at Cumberland Gap that was nearly as large as his own force, and he was likely to retreat toward Smith. Discussions about the next Confederate move flowed freely among his staff members. Some suggested taking the artillery to Covington, on the south bank of the Ohio River, and threatening to shell nearby Cincinnati. Because there was no permanent bridge over the river there, Smith had little chance of occupying the city, but some of his officers hoped to force the citizens to pay ransom to prevent the destruction of the town. Those who advocated the capture of Louisville were reminded that Buell might be moving quickly from Tennessee, faster than Bragg, and bring an overwhelming force to bear on Smith. Morgan might even move up from Cumberland Gap and capture the supplies that Smith was beginning to gather at Lexington, destroying them on his retreat to Cincinnati.

In the end, Smith decided on the most cautious policy, in direct contrast to the bold nature of his campaign up to this point. He would stay in Lexington to secure his hold on the Bluegrass and wait for Bragg to fulfill his role in the campaign. He sent small forces to Frankfort and Cynthiana and ordered cavalry raids to Shelbyville and even to the outskirts of Louisville but made no real effort to enter that important city. The only large movement outside of Lexington was the march of nearly eight thousand men under Henry Heth toward Covington. What Smith hoped to gain from this, beyond scaring the Federals out of their wits, was unclear.

Paul Hammond described Smith's decision to stay in Lexington as "undoubtedly the most prudent" course of action. He had decided to play it safe after some very bold maneuvers through forbidding country. Smith would not overextend himself or risk losing the Bluegrass. Instead, he would accumulate supplies, make up for the scarcities his men had suffered, and reap the material benefits of his campaign while Bragg consolidated the larger strategic gains.

Heth's little excursion toward Cincinnati caused panic among many people in Ohio but prompted an overwhelming response from others. Wright called on Maj. Gen. Lew Wallace to take charge of the defense of this city of nearly two hundred thousand people. A veteran of Fort Donelson and Shiloh, Wallace began to work quickly and decisively. He found hardly any organized troops available but began to assemble newly raised regiments in the city. The local and state authorities helped him by authorizing the calling out of militia and volunteer emergency men. Only five days after taking charge, Wallace had 12,000 volunteer troops, newly raised under Lincoln's call for 300,000 men. He also had 60,000 irregulars, so-called Minute Men called up by the governor of Ohio. They had streamed into Cincinnati from all over the state armed with the shotguns and hunting rifles they already owned. Called the Squirrel Hunters, they would have been completely unreliable against Heth's veterans, but their response symbolized the fierce determination of Ohio to resist Confederate invasion. A few days later, Wallace was reinforced by an additional 10,500 state volunteers and 2,300 militia, making a total of nearly 85,000 men. Hardly an individual in that host had experience under fire, but their numbers alone would make the Confederates think twice about attacking the city.

Wallace did not hesitate to take charge of Cincinnati itself. He declared martial law, banned the sale of alcohol, closed businesses, and required all able men to join the militia or work on the defenses being constructed at Covington. The people willingly cooperated, and soon fifteen thousand men were gathered in the streets with muskets or entrenching tools, obeying either drill master or engineer. The Covington defenses were still in rough shape when Heth appeared before the town. Only eight unfinished battery positions and some connecting lines of infantry trenches were up, but they were enough to make the Confederates pause.

Heth was uncertain about his mission. With Reynolds's brigade, Churchill's division of two brigades, Hill's brigade of Cleburne's division, and Col. Benjamin J. Allston's cavalry brigade, he had a comparatively large force. Most of it was placed at Florence, eight miles southwest of Covington. On September 10, a very small reconnoitering force advanced to the defenses and skirmished outside Fort Mitchell. Few if any men were lost on either side. After that tiny show of force, Heth pulled out of Florence on the night of September 11 and returned to Lexington. The great excitement in Cincinnati was over; the city was secure. The Squirrel Hunters went home full of stories about their bloodless exploits. Work on the Covington fortifications continued for the next two years to make sure Cincinnati would never again be caught unprepared. They became one of the most formidable earthworks of the war, consisting of four large forts, twenty-three batteries, and twelve miles of connecting infantry trenches.

Smith gathered the resources of the area while Heth made a show of force to the north. He began to purchase corn, wheat, bacon, and woolen goods from local merchants. Without gold, he had to convince sellers to accept Confederate treasury notes. Horses and mules owned by the Federal government were seized whenever found. Smith also began to recruit volunteers from among the young men who were still in the area but found this much more difficult than doing business with the Bluegrass merchants. It was a source of wonder to the Confederates that, following their ecstatic reception, so few Kentuckians wanted to join the army. Paul Hammond believed this was because they had suffered under Federal rule for a year. "They were, in reality, subjugated. The adventurous spirits were already in the Southern ranks; there were no leaders; they had not studied the great questions at issue so thoroughly as we had; their sympathies were certainly with us, but they could not see very clearly that their interests were also." He believed that their attitude would change with the passage of time, but Smith could not afford to wait. Meanwhile, Confederate ranks did not swell with fresh blood, and those few who joined wanted to serve in cavalry regiments rather than the infantry. No more than four thousand men enlisted, adding a regiment of horsemen to Morgan's command and some volunteers to Marshall's tiny force. Parts of five other cavalry regiments were organized before the campaign ended.

Smith worried about Morgan's division at Cumberland Gap because it was the only remaining loose end to be tied up from his campaign. Morgan also found himself at loose ends. He was isolated deep behind the Confederate theater of operations, over two hundred miles from friendly territory in Ohio. He could not count on help from the Bluegrass, from Louisville, or from Buell's army. Morgan and his men were on their own.

They had been confronted by Stevenson's division ever since August 16. The Confederates had advanced to Cumberland Gap and positioned themselves behind Poor Valley Ridge, which paralleled Cumberland Mountain at a distance of a mile along the Tennessee and Virginia side. Although Stevenson did not dig in, he had a strong position. The natural strength of Morgan's post was greatly enhanced by the heavy fortifications his men had been digging ever since they occupied the gap in June. They had found seven lightly built Confederate forts on the Kentucky side and strengthened them with thicker, heavier parapets. They constructed four new forts and, when Stevenson made his appearance in August, hastily built seven battery emplacements partway down the steep eastern slope of the mountain. Nearly two miles of connecting infantry trenches snaked up and down the rocky slopes on both sides of this imposing eminence. From the Pinnacle, the peak that flanked the north side of the gap, Morgan was a thousand feet above the valley floor that separated him from Stevenson's position on Poor Valley Ridge, which was only about one-third as high as Cumberland Mountain.

The two sides stared at each other for a full month, neither commander willing to risk an attack on the other. Stevenson could look from his observation post directly into the gap and see much of his enemy's activity, while Morgan could look through his telescope and see the same in the Confederate camps. With his men on half rations and the countryside around the gap utterly devoid of crops or food, Morgan could do little but wait. His line of communication was cut when Smith reached Barboursville. Morgan knew that there was no possibility of relief when rumors of the debacle at Richmond arrived, but he decided to wait as long as possible.

The only contact between the two forces occurred along the mountain south of Cumberland Gap. Both sides sent out patrols to scout the passes that were scattered along the length of the height to prevent raids or flanking movements. There were several skirmishes, one of which resulted in a unique feature of the war, the scalping of Union soldiers. On September 13, a detachment of the Forty-ninth Indiana patrolling Baptist Gap, three miles south of Cumberland Gap, skirmished with two companies of the Thomas Legion. Raised from among the eastern band of Cherokees in the mountains of North Carolina, the legion contributed these companies to the growing force that Stevenson had assembled to bottle Morgan in the gap. One of their beloved officers, Lieutenant Astoogatogeh, was killed, and his men became enraged. Before white officers could restrain them, they had driven off the Federals and scalped several dead and wounded men. It was one of at least four documented incidents of scalping by Indian troops wearing the gray.

Small skirmishes like the one at Baptist Gap did not alter the stalemate that had settled over the gap. With no hope of relief and facing imminent

starvation, Morgan called a council of officers on September 14. They unan-
imously urged an evacuation, and Morgan agreed. Engineers planted mines
to destroy powder magazines and storehouses; they rigged explosives in the
saddle of the gap and the mountain side to cause landslides and block the
pass. Morgan had thirty-two guns and planned to take most of them with
him, plus all the wagons and food he could handle. Four thirty-pounder
guns were spiked and shoved off the top of the mountain, where their broken tubes and carriages littered the valley floor. The trains set out on the
night of September 16 with an infantry and artillery escort. The rest of the
men followed at 8 P.M., September 17, muffling their noise so as not to alert
the Confederate pickets. Near dawn, the engineers ignited the mines and
the whole area lit up with blinding flashes of light and thunderous noise.
Morgan remembered that the gap seemed to have been turned into "a volcano on fire, and from time to time till after dawn we heard the explosion of
mines, shells, or grenades."

Morgan had stolen a march on his opponents. Stevenson could not pursue him because the gap was blocked and the closest pass capable of admitting large numbers of troops was Roger's Gap, twenty miles away. But Morgan's ordeal had only begun. It was too risky to retreat northward along the
Wilderness Road for Smith could easily move to block him. That left only a
hazardous route along crude mountain roads through the heart of Appalachian Kentucky. Morgan had already marked out this route by drawing a
red line across his map, and he had interviewed residents of the region who
were serving in the Kentucky regiments of his division. Everyone told him
that taking ten thousand men with wagons and artillery over these roads in
the driest season of the year was difficult in the extreme, but Morgan refused
to abandon his trains or guns. He would not be frightened; indeed, he had
no choice but to sneak through the back roads if he hoped to escape to Ohio.

The result was one of the truly memorable marches of the war. The Federals moved northward along the Wilderness Road to Flat Lick, eight miles
southeast of Barboursville. Then Morgan set out on a series of backwoods
roads. He ascended Stinking Creek to its headwaters at a saddle between two
mountains and began to descend Goose Creek to Manchester. The steep-
sided mountains towered into the sky along both streams, and branches
drained into the creeks at regular intervals. Both creeks had wide valleys at
their mouths but very narrow gorges at their headwaters. The roads snaked
along the creek bottoms between the heavily forested slopes, verdant and
green in the late summer, with only a few hardscrabble farms in the bottomland.

Morgan reached Manchester on the night of September 19 and rested for two days. He decided to split his force north of town. Two brigades would go via Booneville and two others on a more direct road to Proctor, on the Kentucky River. The Federals had been harassed by a small cavalry force to the rear before reaching Manchester and even by a few scattered guerrilla attacks, but no sizable force seemed to be anywhere near Morgan. That situation began to change when the two columns reached Proctor. Elements of John Hunt Morgan's cavalry brigade had occupied the town and burned a mill there the night before the Federals arrived. The town was located nearly halfway from Cumberland Gap to the Ohio, near the junction of the North Fork, the Middle Fork, and the South Fork of the Kentucky River. The stream was wide with steep banks, and its narrow valley was surrounded by high mountains. Fortunately, no Confederates tried to dispute Morgan's passage. To help divert trouble, Morgan sent his commissary officer, Capt. George M. Adams, with two men toward Mount Sterling, in the Bluegrass. Adams was a sacrificial lamb. Morgan knew he would be caught and questioned by the Confederates, who would find orders in his pocket to buy supplies at Mount Sterling for his division. Thus Morgan was able to fool some Confederates into thinking that he intended to march farther west than the red line he had drawn on his map. The ploy at least created some confusion in Confederate planning.

After crossing the Kentucky River, Morgan again divided his force into two columns. Two brigades escorted the wagons and the heavier artillery along the North Fork Road. It had been damaged by previous rains but mostly ran in the creek and river bottoms, making it easier for the teams to haul their loads and providing water for the animals. The other two brigades marched along the aptly named Ridge Road. It snaked along the top of a series of ridges with a magnificent view in all directions but absolutely no water. The men would have a dry surface to walk along but little refreshment.

The difficulties encountered by Morgan's men increased with each mile. Water was so scarce along the Ridge Road that the Forty-second Ohio did not have a drop to drink for fifty hours at a stretch. When they did find some liquid, it was hardly worth drinking. "Our tongues were parched with thirst," remembered Owen Johnston Hopkins, "and when at length water was obtained in the horse tracks on a low, flat piece of ground, it was fought for by us like so many wolves." But he suffered far more from hunger than thirst. Hopkins and his comrades marched for forty-eight hours without a bit of food.

By noon of September 25, the two columns reunited at Hazel Green, a tiny settlement in the middle of a wide, spacious valley. It was the most inviting spot along the line of march, and Morgan's men rested one day. They even rounded up a few cattle. Two Confederate officers, here on recruiting duty, were taken as well. Then the march resumed and Confederate activity began to pick up. A company of cavalry attacked the rear guard on the first day out of Hazel Green and scattered the small herd of cattle, so there would be no fresh beef for Morgan's hard-marching men. Instead, they ate corn gathered along the way. The soft ears were roasted over campfires and then eaten; the hard ears were grated, then the kernels were roasted. Each mess assigned a man to rub the kernels off the cob all day long while marching or riding in a wagon. The inadequate food, lack of good water, and nearly incessant marching began to wear on the men the farther they moved into the mountains. Frank H. Mason wrote, "For days and days together horses were not unharnessed nor cartridge boxes unslung. The men slept in their clothing by the roadside, in the woods, wherever the command halt! met them; they rose and fell into their places mechanically when the bugle sounded the advance."

The column entered West Liberty after crossing the Licking River. Morgan had expected to meet Marshall's Confederates here but was relieved to find they had retired upon learning of his approach. He rested his men for two days and ordered them to lighten their load as much as possible, for the worst terrain still lay ahead. Bonfires were built, and hundreds of blankets, greatcoats, and other articles were thrown on them. John Hunt Morgan's command had by this time moved in front of the Federal column. His gray cavalrymen were the only mobile force Smith could call on to intercept the Yankees. Marshall was in a position to do so, but that political general was utterly incompetent and had no heart for an engagement. Morgan's brigade of horsemen was, at best, only one-fourth as numerous as the blue-clad infantrymen, and he could not hope to stop them in open battle. Instead, he tried to block or at least delay the march by obstructing the most difficult portion of the route. The road north of West Liberty followed a wide valley and crossed a narrow defile into another valley that drained into the Little Sandy River fifteen miles north of town. This also was a wide, spacious valley for at least four miles, to the village of Sandy Hook. North of this town, however, the river flowed through a narrow gorge for at least ten miles. Here was the bottleneck Morgan hoped to create for his opponents. His men worked like beavers to fell trees and roll rocks onto the narrow road in the bottom of the gorge. They did their job very well.

The Federals broke out the entrenching tools they had used to dig the fortifications at Cumberland Gap and went to work. Because they were well supplied with equipment, whole brigades were deployed along the road to quicken the pace. If the blockade was too good, the Federals cut a crude road atop the gorge for a mile or two. The progress could be maddeningly slow. At one point in the march, it took Morgan twenty-two hours to make eight miles. The historian of the Forty-second Ohio counted seven block- ades cleared up or bypassed in one day. Morgan recalled that his men built a bypass of four miles to circumvent a blockade that stretched for only one mile. Whenever possible, the Federals pushed ahead to interrupt the Con- federates as they felled trees, fighting several skirmishes with them. The Federal commander recalled with a touch of irony that "while the one Mor- gan was clearing out the obstructions at the entrance to a defile, the other Morgan was blocking the exit from the same defile with enormous rocks and felled trees." The men did all this while subsisting on little water and very little food. They were so hungry that they gathered up the ripened acorns lying on the ground and roasted them.

The Federals refused to be trapped. By the time they worked their way through the gorge, Smith had sent a message to Morgan to call off the pur- suit. If the cavalryman could not stop the column in the narrow defiles, he could not hope to do so in the more open country north of Grayson. That town was in the wide valley of the Little Sandy River. The way to the Ohio was clear, and Morgan's men pushed on to Greenup, at the junction of the Little Sandy and the Ohio, by October 3. When the first units saw the wide expanse of the river the cry "The Ohio! The Ohio!" rippled along the col- umn. The soldiers were embarrassed to march into town for their clothes were in rags. Owen Johnston Hopkins had lost one of his boots and the bet- ter part of his pants below the knees. "A whole pair of boots or shoes was not to be found amongst the rank and file. Some marched in their drawers; others, without blouses; *all* looked like beggars." The starved men had to wait until transported across the river to Ohio before they could get ade- quate food and shelter from the loyal citizens of that state, who marveled at their epic journey.

In sixteen days Morgan's men had marched 219 miles over some of the worst roads imaginable, with little food or water and no outside help. They had avoided major contact with a sizable force and brought out all their wagons and artillery. Morgan lost about eighty men along the way. Every- one in the North praised his plucky move, but the evacuation of Cumber- land Gap infuriated Halleck, who insisted on holding an inquiry into the matter. Morgan was exonerated. Although his regiments had taken themselves out of the campaign for Kentucky, they would go on to perform good service in the Vicksburg campaign of December 1862.

Because the evacuation of Cumberland Gap eliminated a potential thorn in Smith's plans to control Kentucky, the Confederate commander could easily afford to let the Federal division escape. As September drew to a close, Smith continued to gather supplies in the Bluegrass and watch the progress of his colleague in dealing with Buell's army. His work had been an unqualified success. As Paul Hammond put it, "When we entered Lexington, General Smith's campaign, as originally conceived, was accomplished. All that was at first intended had been achieved, more easily, more fully, and with more complete success than could have been anticipated." Now, everyone in Smith's army knew, the rest was up to Bragg.

Northern reaction to the Confederate success was predictably glum. The editors of the *Indianapolis Daily Journal* spoke for all when they moaned that the "recent disaster in Kentucky has filled all hearts with sorrow." But the news of Smith's victory exploded on the Southern consciousness and lifted spirits. "Great hopes are entertained of the campaign in Kentucky," wrote Josiah Gorgas. By mid-September he assumed that Smith was knocking on the door of Cincinnati; "now is the time for audacity," he thought. It was not only the fact of the victory but the utter collapse of Union strength in the Bluegrass that encouraged Confederate civilians. Catherine Ann Devereux Edmondston rejoiced that "we are having it all our own way in Kentucky." Everyone across the South received grossly inflated reports about the enlistment of thousands of Kentuckians, the almost certain fall of Cincinnati, and the spread of resistance to Federal rule in Missouri and Arkansas. "Everything seems to indicate the 'breaking up' of the armies of our enemies, as if our prayers had been answered, and the hosts of Lincoln were really to be 'brought to confusion,'" crowed J. B. Jones in Richmond. The public was accurately informed of Smith's occupation of Frankfort, which sent the Unionist governor Robinson fleeing for his safety, and of the jubilant reception given his soldiers by the citizens of Lexington. But the expectations for a quick end to the war through invasion of the border states were inflated. No one wanted to take an objective view; they simply hoped with a desperation born of adversity for a miracle to come from the confusing swirl of activity in both East and West. As Mrs. Edmondston admitted in her journal, the "war has assumed such giant proportions that I cannot take it all in."

The Confederates were even more encouraged by the movements of Lee's army. Following the Seven Days' campaign, Lee took his men on a bold strike northward from Richmond. He left enough troops to guard the capital against the remote possibility that McClellan might strike at it from his base on the James River and set the rest on a campaign against John Pope's Army of Virginia some sixty miles to the north. Stonewall Jackson led the way. He maneuvered his men around Pope, won a victory at Cedar Mountain on August 9, and then captured Manassas Junction in Pope's rear. The Confederates ransacked the military stores and then took up a strong defensive position behind an unfinished railroad grade. Here, on August 29, Pope flung his army in piecemeal attacks that littered the landscape with his dead and wounded but failed to break Jackson. Pope paid no attention to signs that the rest of Lee's army, under Maj. Gen. James Longstreet, had followed Jackson and had quietly taken position to support him. On August 30, the same day that Smith whipped Nelson's men at Richmond, Longstreet attacked and crushed Pope in one of the most dismal and costly defeats the Union army suffered in the war. More than thirteen thousand Federals were killed, wounded, or missing, while Lee lost over eight thousand men.

McClellan was reluctant to reinforce Pope from the Peninsula, correctly viewing the westerner as his rival, and thus only a part of the Army of the Potomac participated in the battle of Second Bull Run. But Lee did not wait before making his next move. He immediately launched an invasion of Maryland. A border slave state, like Kentucky, Maryland had been occupied by Federal troops during the first few weeks of the war. Lee had been expanding the theater of operations in the East ever since he took command at the gates of Richmond. Now, flushed with success, he impulsively took his army out of Confederate territory to achieve much the same goals as the Rebels in Kentucky. Lincoln had to act quickly to meet this threat. He disbanded the Army of Virginia, sent Pope off to a frontier command, and consolidated his units into the Army of the Potomac. McClellan now had the dual task of protecting Washington and pushing Lee out of Maryland.

The southern victory at Second Bull Run brought the possibility of a joint offer of mediation from England and France to a boil. The English government, in particular, was concerned that the American war was reaching a threatening level of intensity. Lincoln's radical policies seemed to portend a very bitter, bloody conflict that could last indefinitely and create political instability in North America. The cotton shortage was not yet a major factor in British diplomacy; not until the spring of 1863 would English mills be so starved for raw material as to cause true economic hardship. There was fear that Northern radical moves might spark a race war in the South if Lincoln decided to emancipate the slaves in the middle of this terrible conflict. The desire to find a way to stop the fighting greatly increased when the news of Pope's defeat reached London, but Lee's quick move into Maryland caused the diplomats to hesitate. They wanted to wait and see what would result from this invasion before playing their cards.

Thus, as the summer began to give way to fall, the fate of the country hung in the balance. Much more attention continued to be directed toward Lee's movements than to Smith's or Bragg's, but the hard-marching Confederates in the West could not let that bother them. They were on the cutting edge of great success and needed only to take advantage of all that was offered to achieve it.

CHAPTER THREE

Bragg, Buell, and Kentucky

Braxton Bragg was eager to play his part in the grand campaign that was unfolding, but he was forced to spend several weeks preparing his army with no hope of accumulating all the supplies and equipment he needed. While Edmund Kirby Smith was winding his way through the mountains of eastern Kentucky, Bragg was slowly shuttling his divisions across the Tennessee River near Chattanooga. Most of the Confederate troops were forced to cross on ferries at different locations upriver and downstream from the town. Some divisions needed several days to transport all their men, horses, and artillery over the river, giving the infantry a welcome opportunity to bathe in the river. Some soldiers later realized that this would be their last chance to wash themselves before entering Kentucky. An artillery officer recently transferred to Bragg's army from duty in Alabama marveled at how smoothly the river crossing took place. "It is a great sight to see a big army in motion," commented Henry C. Semple. "I saw 5000 men cross the Tenn a few days since in perfect order & silence—Not half as much confusion as in the breaking up of the congregation at our Church."

Bragg oversaw all this with an attentive and hopeful spirit. Captain Semple had known Bragg from earlier service in the war and found his old commander to be "in fine spirits, his plans are all working well and he anticipates a great triumph." The army commander told Semple that Cumberland Gap would be in Confederate hands any day, while the men in his army expected to fight a battle somewhere near Nashville or Louisville. Semple was very impressed with the quality of the army, except its means of transport. The mules and horses belonging to the wagon trains and artillery batteries were "in very low condition." Bragg realized there was nothing he could do to improve that weakness short of postponing the advance. He would have to make do with these and other deficiencies.

While the troops shuffled over the wide river and prepared for a difficult march, Bragg did what he could to smooth the way. A pioneer company of forty-five mechanics were set to work improving the road over Walden's Ridge, the first major obstacle Bragg would have to tackle. The ridge was the eastern escarpment of the Cumberland Plateau, only ten miles north and west of Chattanooga.

Bragg assembled an army of more than twenty-seven thousand men on the north bank of the Tennessee by August 27. He divided them into two corps. Maj. Gen. Leonidas Polk commanded the right wing, consisting of Maj. Gen. Jones Mitchell Withers's division, Maj. Gen. Benjamin Franklin Cheatham's division, and a brigade of cavalry under Col. John A. Wharton. Maj. Gen. William Joseph Hardee led the left wing, with Brig. Gen. Simon Bolivar Buckner's division, Brig. Gen. James Patton Anderson's division, and a cavalry brigade under Col. Joseph Wheeler. The Army of the Mississippi moved out on its momentous campaign, the first strategic strike of its career, on August 28.

The country that Bragg would traverse was formidable. The route took his army across the Cumberland Plateau, forcing it to climb and descend four steep slopes along the way. The plateau was split nearly in half by the Sequatchie Valley, a wide and deep gorge cut by the river of the same name which drained into the Tennessee several miles downstream from Chattanooga. Thus the army would have to travel up the eastern escarpment of the plateau, down the eastern side of the valley, up the western side of the valley, and down the western escarpment of the plateau. In a way, the shortage of wagons was a blessing in disguise, for it lessened the problems of moving a large field army over difficult terrain. The Army of the Mississippi, which later would adopt its more famous name, the Army of Tennessee, would carry the burden of the Confederate war effort in the far-flung West for the remainder of the war, but it would have no marches more difficult in its long history than the one it was about to undertake.

The lead units of Bragg's army moved out on the Anderson Pike over Walden's Ridge, making a hairpin turn partway up the escarpment that was so sharp it nearly formed a circle. The landscape was level but undulating atop the plateau, and the pike offered a good road surface for the men. They descended the western slope of Walden's Ridge through a wide ravine. The pike was literally dug into the steep slopes of this gorge before it leveled out on the wide and flat bottom of the Sequatchie River valley. Here Bragg's men had good marching northward along the banks of the river, a relatively modest stream that meandered back and forth across this beautiful mountain vale.

By August 30, the day that Smith was drubbing the Federals at Richmond, Bragg had moved his headquarters to Dunlap. The leading elements of Polk's wing were a few miles farther north, up the valley, and Hardee's wing was still climbing Walden's Ridge. The Army of the Mississippi could no longer afford to allow itself the luxury of continuing northward up the Sequatchie. Polk had to turn west and climb the western slope of the valley and head for the open country of the Barrens plateau before Buell blocked Bragg in the mountains. Heading west from Pikeville, Polk met the steepest slope the army had to face on the whole march, a nearly vertical wall of rock with a narrow road cut into one of the ravines that partially broke the imposing facade. This was the critical phase of Bragg's march thus far, for only twenty-five miles due west of Dunlap was a division of Federal troops under McCook, sent to Altamont by a nervous Buell to stop or at least delay the Confederate march. Wheeler's cavalry brigade was sent out to screen Polk's movement from McCook and give warning of any further Union advance.

Buell had been scrambling to deal with this surprising Confederate offensive, which quickly put an end to his long-delayed hope of capturing Chattanooga. It had become clear to him by August 22 that the Confederates were massing troops at the mountain town, so he moved his headquarters from Huntsville to Decherd, shifting his army's supplies from Stevenson, Bridgeport, and Huntsville as well. The biggest question he had to answer was where to concentrate his army to meet Bragg, a problem made more difficult by the lack of certainty about his objective. Buell assumed that Nashville was probably Bragg's target so, at first, he decided to assume a position blocking the approaches to the capital. Altamont, located atop the western half of the Cumberland Plateau, was on the most direct line from Bragg's position north of the Tennessee River toward Nashville. Four roads stretched westward from Altamont toward the low ground. In addition, Bragg could place his army between the two halves of Buell's force if he occupied the town. Two divisions under Thomas were north at McMinnville, and the other three divisions were still south of Altamont, maneuvering so as to concentrate the army at whatever point was chosen.

Thomas disagreed with Buell. He believed that McMinnville was the proper point of concentration. There was little water or forage near Altamont, and the army would have to climb the western edge of the Cumber-

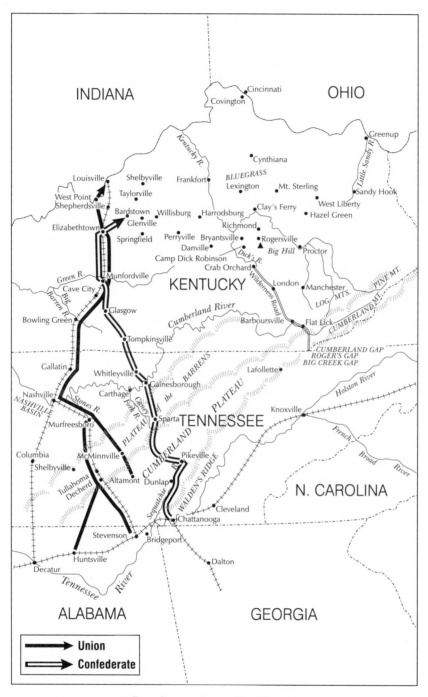

2. Bragg's campaign and Buell's retreat

land Plateau to reach the town. It would be relatively easy for Bragg to by-pass Altamont to the north and escape from the plateau before Buell could climb back down the highland and give chase. In contrast, McMinnville lay on the Plateau of the Barrens, allowing the Federals ample opportunity to detect Bragg's point of departure from the highland and to move rapidly to meet him. The supply problem would be alleviated by the existence of a spur railroad that linked McMinnville with the Nashville and Chattanooga line at Tullahoma. Later, when testifying before a court of inquiry investi-gating Buell's handling of the campaign, Thomas even suggested that Sparta, which was farther north up the Plateau of the Barrens, could have served as an effective concentration point. But Thomas was then speaking from hindsight, knowing Bragg's true line of advance.

Employing the same hindsight, it was easy for observers to see that McMinnville was probably the best place to assemble to meet Bragg. But that did not alter the ironic fact that, despite his widespread reputation for caution, Buell had overridden his subordinate and adopted a much more aggressive stance in dealing with this vexing problem. He ordered a concen-tration of all his available troops at Altamont. Five divisions set out to exe-cute that order. A sixth division under Rousseau moved directly from Huntsville to Nashville. Thomas's two divisions reached Altamont on Au-gust 25 and found no Confederates in the vicinity so he decided to take mat-ters into his own hands. Without asking permission, Thomas retired from Altamont back to McMinnville, informing Buell of his decision. The army commander had no choice but to concede, and orders were issued quickly enough to stop two of the three remaining divisions before they began the hard march up the edge of the Cumberland Plateau. Only McCook was not stopped in time. He reached Altamont on August 29 and waited, uncertain what to do.

The next day, Joseph Wheeler made up his mind for him. Wheeler's cav-alry rode out to screen this Federal force from interfering with Polk's and Hardee's climb over the mountains, and Wheeler demonstrated the aggres-sive qualities that would make him one of the best cavalry commanders of the war. He attacked McCook's outposts near Altamont, a small skirmish to be sure, but more than enough to convince McCook to retreat westward. This news must have convinced Buell that Bragg was indeed marching via Altamont. He decided to fall back and concentrate the entire army at Mur-freesboro. By September 5 all five of his divisions were there, only thirty miles southeast of Nashville.

The way was now open for Bragg not only to cross the mountains in peace but to move in almost any direction he chose after reaching the low ground. Buell would later come under severe criticism for opening the gate. After initially adopting an aggressive but impractical plan, he caved in and opted for the most conservative policy. By withdrawing to Murfreesboro, he was closing in on the most valuable prize in his theater of operations, Nashville, and he meant to save it at all costs. Most likely Bragg would have decided to bypass the state capital and go north at any rate, but Buell's withdrawal made a Confederate attack on Nashville highly unlikely. Buell pushed his divisions on to the capital shortly after they arrived at Murfreesboro. He had given up the strategic initiative to his opponent, who had every intention of making the most of this opportunity.

From this point on, the two armies were in a high-stakes race for the north. Buell outnumbered the Confederates with about forty-five thousand men, having received substantial reinforcements. He also had the railroad to Louisville, although there were still a couple of breaks in the line. But Bragg had the initiative and a shorter line of march. The prize would be Kentucky.

Buell left three divisions under Thomas in Nashville to defend the city and set out with six divisions. He realized that Nashville was in no danger by September 12 and ordered Thomas to bring one of his divisions northward. After some very hard marching, his leading elements crossed the state line and reached Bowling Green on September 14. This town had been one of the strongpoints in the Confederate defenses that stretched across southern Kentucky. Now, one year after the collapse of the state's neutrality, the Federals were faced with the necessity of securing it anew.

Bragg's army continued its progress over the mountain without interference. The Confederates ascended the western side of the Sequatchie Valley west of Pikeville and marched across the rolling terrain of the Cumberland Plateau until they came to a long and deep gorge that stretched for several miles into the highland. Formed by the Caney Fork River, with several tributaries feeding into it, the gorge offered Bragg his earliest opportunity to descend from the top of the plateau and march along creek and river bottoms onto the rolling countryside of the Barrens plateau. The slope into Cane Creek valley, one of the river's tributaries, was very steep and treacherous. Once in the bottomland, however, the going was much easier, and Bragg's men made great headway. They emerged from the shadow of the mountains, turned northward, and crossed the Caney Fork River. Bragg was now in the open. He rapidly marched to Sparta, crossing the Calfkiller River, and decided to split his army. By sending Hardee's wing westward to

Carthage, he hoped to fool Buell into thinking that Nashville was still his objective. Polk would continue due north via Cookeville, and Hardee was instructed to move from Carthage and rejoin him at Tompkinsville, Kentucky. The maneuver probably delayed Buell's movement of some troops from Nashville for a few days, but it did not play a significant role in the outcome of the campaign.

While Hardee moved off to the west, Polk continued the march for Kentucky. The last serious obstacle was the Cumberland River, but Bragg had selected an excellent place to cross it. Moving on to Gainesboro, Polk descended into the Doe Creek valley a few miles south of town and followed it to the river. He found the Cumberland to be a wide, deep stream flowing out of the mountains. Once across, the Confederates marched for many miles along the wide, fertile bottomland that bordered the north side of the river. This was the most pastoral spot they had seen since the beginning of the campaign. While turning north into the valley of Jennings Creek and passing through the village of Whitleyville, Polk's infantry was screened by Wheeler's cavalry. From Whitleyville, the column marched farther up several creek valleys that narrowed and grew more barren. These streams, with names like Pine Lick Creek and Keeling Branch, gradually led the footsore Confederates out of the Cumberland River valley. Bragg had marched his men for about fifteen miles through bottomlands to cross the great river, negotiating slopes that were barely half as high but nearly as steep as those that braced the Cumberland Plateau.

It was easy for Bragg's veterans to march the remaining miles over the rolling terrain of the Barrens. They crossed the Kentucky state line on September 5 and found a large sign nailed to a tree by the pioneer company, "You now cross from Tennessee to Kentucky." The men cheered lustily at this visible sign of their hard-won progress. Hardee rendezvoused with Polk at Tompkinsville as planned, and the Army of the Mississippi was once again united. When it reached Glasgow on September 12, Bragg rested the men and scribbled a proclamation to the citizens of the state. He assured them of his friendship and help "to free yourselves from the tyranny of a despotic ruler." Promising to safeguard their property, the Confederate commander challenged the citizenry to take sides. If they wanted "Federal rule, show it by your frowns, and we shall return whence we came. If you choose rather to come within the folds of our brotherhood, then cheer us with the smiles of your women and lend your willing hands to secure you in your heritage of liberty." Just as they had done for Smith's men in Lexington, many citizens responded enthusiastically to the Rebels. Bragg's men were cheered, offered food, cider, even wine by the people of Glasgow. Many regiments entered town amid a sea of waving, homemade Confederate flags and white handkerchiefs.

It was an encouraging sign for the weary soldiers, but they had little opportunity to savor it. The campaign, which was veering closer to success, now took a dramatic and pivotal turn, to be enacted outside the small town of Munfordville and the important crossing of the Louisville and Nashville Railroad over the Green River. The Green flowed through a deep gorge cut into the layers of limestone that rested just below the surface of the plateau. Munfordville was forty-five miles north of Bowling Green, and the iron railroad bridge that spanned the river there was a marvel of civil engineering. This was the southernmost point on the Louisville and Nashville line that Buell had occupied before the fall of Fort Donelson. Thus Bragg's presence in the area signified the success of his campaign of maneuver. His men began to tread on soil that had never been occupied by the Confederacy.

On the night of September 12, the day of his arrival at Glasgow, Bragg sent a brigade of Mississippi infantry under Brig. Gen. James Chalmers to Cave City, a station on the railroad fifteen miles south of Munfordville. His job was to cut the line and secure any supplies that might be found. Chalmers captured some men but found few supplies. He received a message from Col. John Scott while at Cave City. Scott's cavalry brigade had been sent to the region by Edmund Kirby Smith to harass the Federals. Scott told Chalmers that only a small force of Unionists held Munfordville, a much more strategic spot than Cave City, and that it should be easy to take the place. Chalmers was captivated by the idea and the consequences of success. Capt. E. T. Sykes of the Tenth Mississippi later wrote that his brigade leader "considered it a fine opportunity to win a Major-General's star." He set out on the night of September 13 without authority from Bragg. As the sun began to rise on the morning of September 14, Chalmers drove in the Federal pickets near Munfordville and quickly devised a plan of attack.

Munfordville was held by a force that was hastily assembled from a variety of sources by Col. John Thomas Wilder, a pugnacious businessman from Indiana. He was there by accident. Wilder had left Louisville on September 1 with 214 fresh recruits for his regiment, the Seventeenth Indiana, then stationed at Nashville. The train was stopped a few miles north, near Clarksville, when the engineer discovered that the bridge over the Red River had been burned. Returning to Bowling Green, Wilder received orders to go to Munfordville and hold that place. C. C. Gilbert, with his newly issued field promotion to general, was taking charge of the defense of Kentucky and readily recognized the importance of the Green River crossing. He even began to forward some reinforcements along the railroad to help him hold the iron bridge.

Wilder took command at Munfordville on September 8 and found that, in addition to his raw recruits, two hundred more enlistees bound for different Kentucky units and two Indiana regiments were available to defend the place. He quickly put them to work strengthening the fortifications that had been started the previous February when McCook's division occupied the town. A stockade big enough to hold fifty men already stood near the south bank of the river, about one hundred yards to the west of the railroad on a bit of high ground. A trench extended from the stockade southward for a few yards and then turned east to the railroad. It ran along the highest ground for at least a mile south of the river and thus had a good view of the southern approaches to the bridge. A half mile to the east, at the edge of a village called Woodsonville, Wilder ordered the construction of a redoubt named Fort Craig. It was on the top of a slope that commanded the stockade and its attendant fortification. Both defenses were excellently planned to take advantage of the terrain. They were strengthened by the addition of a few head logs on the infantry parapet at the bridge and the cutting of timber for several hundred yards to the south. The fallen trees were left lying to trip up an attacker. From both defensive positions, the outnumbered and largely untried Federals had an excellent chance of holding out even against Chalmers's veterans.

Wilder further prepared his post by sending into the countryside unarmed home guard recruits, who had gathered at Munfordville to join their units, to give him timely warning of a Confederate approach. Wilder also busily saw to the collection of ten days' worth of forage for his animals and food for his men from the surrounding farms. Gilbert sent dispatches encouraging him to hold out as long as possible. Buell was surely on his way, Gilbert said, and a few more men were coming from Louisville as well.

The Federals received their first challenge from Scott's cavalry. On the evening of September 12, when Bragg was dispatching Chalmers to Cave City, Scott appeared near Munfordville. He had been sent by Smith on September 4 to go as far as possible toward Louisville and disrupt the railroad. His mission had not been terribly successful, but Scott hoped to make up for it by quickly taking the crossing of the Green River. He sent a demand for surrender to Wilder, who rejected it. Early on the morning of September 13, Scott fired a few shots at the Federals but retired when Wilder fired back. That evening, Scott found Chalmers and urged him to come on and help. The eager Mississippian did not need a second invitation. Wilder's home guard scouts kept him well informed of Chalmers's approach.

As the sky began to lighten on the morning of September 14, Chalmers deployed his sixteen hundred men for an attack on Munfordville. The Tenth and Forty-fourth Mississippi faced the fortifications at the south end of the railroad bridge while the Seventh, Ninth, and Twenty-ninth Mississippi, plus Capt. William H. Ketchum's Alabama Battery, deployed opposite Fort Craig. The attack began simultaneously at 5:30, and in both areas it was a Confederate disaster. The Tenth Mississippi moved out on the west side of the railroad, advancing over ground that rose toward the Union fortifications above the level of the railroad. Shallow ravines drained eastward toward the railroad bed, some of them deep enough to hide a man. As the regiment came within musket range of the Union earthworks, a raging volley was fired. Col. Robert A. Smith was mortally wounded, but his men continued on. They reached a ravine only fifty yards short of the Federals and found it filled with cut timber. The Mississippians stopped and took cover, opening up a ragged skirmish fire at the Unionists that lasted for the next two hours. Seeing their comrades in trouble, the Forty-fourth Mississippi moved up east of the railroad but did not press its attack. Nevertheless, its commander, Col. James Moore, also was mortally wounded.

Chalmers's attack fared no better at Fort Craig. The earthwork was defended by only two hundred men and two twelve-pounder howitzers under Maj. Augustus H. Abbott of the Sixty-seventh Indiana. The nine hundred Confederates who attacked the fort were shielded from Abbott's fire by the rolling terrain until they were 250 yards away. The houses of Woodsonville and the charred remains of a Baptist church, which Wilder had burned earlier that morning because it was located only fifty yards from the fort, also helped to shield the attack. The Rebels managed to make it to the church ruins, where at least a part of their line took cover behind the shoulder of the hill. Chalmers ordered them to continue with a bayonet attack, which brought the Confederates to the ditch that surrounded the earthwork. It was eight feet deep and ten feet wide, and as Chalmers's men were trying to cross it they were hit by artillery fire from the rear. This unexpected blast ruined the attack, and became the source of much bitterness among the Mississippians for, ironically, it came from friendly guns. Scott's cavalry brigade desperately wanted to help the attack, and its light artillery opened up on the fort from a distance of five hundred yards without knowing that Chalmers's infantrymen were so near it. Chalmers naturally assumed the fire came from a Union battery that had sneaked up on his rear.

He recalled his regiments and sent them off to find and take the artillery. Only a timely message from Scott prevented an escalation of this sad affair into a wider tragedy.

Whether Chalmers could have taken Fort Craig without these difficulties was problematical. The green Federals inside fought tenaciously. Major Abbott was killed while trying to raise the flag on the parapet after it had been riddled with 146 bullets and fallen to the ground. The same spirit infused the Unionists at the bridge. Wilder later claimed that only five men in his force of roughly two thousand soldiers (only a portion of whom had guns) had seen combat before the attack. "In all the war I never saw a more brilliant charge or more complete or resolute defense than these undrilled and half-armed men made at this point," Wilder later wrote. The Federals lost 37 killed and wounded, while Chalmers suffered 288 casualties.

Not long after the firing stopped, at about 9:30 A.M., Chalmers sent a demand for surrender into the fortifications. Wilder thought it rather impudent, considering the sharp repulse his enemy had suffered. Chalmers complimented the Federals on their "gallant defense" and urged them "to avoid further bloodshed" by giving up. Wilder sarcastically replied, "If you wish to avoid further bloodshed, keep out of the range of my guns." Later that day, Wilder received reinforcements in the form of three hundred men under Col. Cyrus L. Dunham, compliments of Gilbert in Louisville. They had sidestepped Scott's cavalry north of the river to enter the defenses. Because Dunham's commission predated Wilder's by several days, he took charge of the defense.

Chalmers requested a truce to remove his wounded and bury his dead. As a sign of the improvised nature of his attack and the supply problem in Bragg's army, the Confederates had to borrow tools from their opponents to dig the graves. The truce lasted until 6 P.M., then the stalemate continued with the Rebels safely out of artillery range.

Bragg became angry when he received word of Chalmers's action. Terming it an "unauthorized and injudicious" attack, he nevertheless decided to move the entire army to Munfordville and seize the place. He had never planned to place himself on the railroad but to continue to move northward, and join Smith's force. He could have ordered Chalmers to rejoin him and continued northward, but, perhaps to maintain the army's morale by wiping out its humiliating defeat, he started for Munfordville on the evening of September 15.

The Army of the Mississippi took position before the Federal defenses the next day. There were no earthworks north of the river, where the ground was higher than the fortifications south of the stream. Bragg had an ace in the hole that enabled him to compel the Federals to surrender with little bloodshed. One of his division commanders, Simon Bolivar Buckner, was a native of Munfordville and knew the country well. He advised Bragg on the location of several fords upstream, which enabled him to send troops from Polk's wing to place artillery on the commanding ground to the north. Dunham was effectively surrounded.

Dunham was devastated when a member of Bragg's staff brought in a demand for surrender. He called a council of officers at 5 P.M. on September 16 and suggested they all give up. The telegraph line was still operating, so he sent a message to Louisville explaining the situation and advising Gilbert that he could not hold out. Gilbert immediately replied with instructions to resist and later sent another message for Dunham to give the command to Wilder. Then the telegraph line went dead. Wilder was willing to take charge and even put Dunham in arrest when the frustrated colonel refused to comply.

After taking care of Dunham, Wilder turned his attention to Bragg. He had had his fill of surrender demands. This was the third one he had received in three days, and Wilder, like a pragmatic businessman, had no intention of giving up until his enemy could prove that an overwhelming force opposed him. Thus began one of the most curious episodes of the Civil War. In a surprisingly frank, even innocent way, Wilder went into the no-man's land that separated the two forces to enter into negotiations with Simon Buckner. He knew the Confederate division commander by reputation and felt he could trust him. They met at an outpost between the lines and began to talk. Buckner assured him that Bragg's entire army was there and that Polk's position north of the river doomed the Federals. Wilder insisted on seeing this with his own eyes, so Buckner escorted him around the lines south of the river while another Confederate officer escorted one of Wilder's aides along Polk's lines. What they saw greatly impressed them. There were forty-six guns with Hardee south of the Green and twenty-six with Polk north of the river, plus nearly twenty-eight thousand infantrymen. With no sign of Buell's approach, it was obvious that the Federals had no hope of holding out.

Yet Buckner was so touched by what was happening between him and Wilder that he felt compelled to be completely honest, even supportive, in his tutelage. He and Wilder had quickly developed the relationship of a teacher and a student engaged in a military lesson with life-and-death consequences. Buckner advised Wilder that if he felt holding out against such great odds might bring some strategic benefit, then he should do so even if the cost was great. No, replied Wilder, he had made up his mind to surrender. Buckner then took him to Bragg's tent, even though it was already past dusk on September 17. They found the army commander busy writing dispatches. He kept Wilder waiting for several minutes before acknowledging his presence. Then, according to Wilder, Bragg "raised his head and surlily demanded: 'What do you want?'" When told of Wilder's demands, that his men be paroled and allowed to go to the Ohio River, Bragg was astonished. "Such terms are unheard of, and can not be considered. We have men and guns enough in position to crush you out of existence without losing a man." Such a contrast in personal styles between the two Rebel generals stunned Wilder, and he angrily told Bragg that he assumed the Confederate army had better save its ammunition to deal with Buell rather than to "crush out of existence" a pitifully small group of brave men.

Buckner now intervened to save the negotiations, leading Wilder out of the tent to separate the antagonists. "This is willful murder," Buckner told Wilder, and the still angry Hoosier replied, "That if it was, he [Bragg] had to commit it." While Wilder cooled his heels, Buckner returned to Bragg's tent and talked with him for a half hour, emerging with an agreement that essentially allowed Wilder his terms. Yet, even now, the Federal colonel sought to delay the process by arguing with Buckner over every detail. They talked for two hours in the early morning of September 18 over such things as whether the Confederates should march into the Union fortifications or allow the Federals to march out of them first. Wilder treated this as if it were a business negotiation while Buckner, who was a West Point graduate, maintained his patience as well as his respect for his opponent.

At 6 A.M. on September 18, a little surrender ceremony took place at Rowlett's Station, a couple of miles south of Munfordville. Wilder formally offered his sword to Buckner, who immediately returned it. He surrendered 3,546 men, 600 of whom still had no weapons, but they were not allowed to march to the Ohio River as agreed. Instead, the Confederates sent them on their way south to join Buell at Bowling Green.

Bragg now had his little victory, but what was he to do with it? He had not wanted to be here and later referred to the Munfordville incident as a "mere detour." But he decided to make the best of it by establishing a defensive position covering the Green River crossing and waiting for Smith to come to him with some of the supplies he had been gathering in the Bluegrass. This appears to have been Bragg's objective all along the route from Chattanooga, to join with Smith's force in the heart of Kentucky and establish firm Confederate control of the state. His defensive position incorporated Fort Craig and the earthworks at the south end of the bridge. Bragg and his subordinate commanders all were in the best of spirits on the morning of September 18, elated that they had beaten Buell to Kentucky and confident that they had the Army of the Ohio over a barrel. Buell would have to fight to regain his line of communication, and on ground of Bragg's choosing.

Buell had been receiving delayed information on the happenings at Munfordville. With relatively little cavalry and a cautious nature, he dallied for some time at Bowling Green before moving out on September 17. Soon after, word arrived of Bragg's defensive stance at Munfordville. This news led Buell to halt and call a council of war on the evening of September 17. His officers knew the ground at Munfordville, and all agreed that the Confederate position there was too strong to attack. Wilder confirmed this decision when he reached Buell's army on the evening of September 18, yet Buell felt he had to act. His enemy was firmly astride his lifeline to the north and could not be ignored. He cautiously moved on and placed his army just north of Cave City, nearly fifteen miles south of Bragg, by September 19. Buell took a careful course, challenging the Confederates but refusing to be bullied into an unwise frontal assault.

It was now up to Bragg to decide the outcome of the Munfordville incident. Suddenly his confidence evaporated. He knew Buell's army outnumbered his force, and, more important, he was dangerously short of supplies. Observers at Munfordville recalled that Bragg's wagons were nearly empty and that his men were eating green corn and fruit they had scavenged from nearby farms. Capt. Henry Semple later recalled that the draft animals of the army were in poor shape as well. His Alabama battery began the campaign with no spare horses, and he received no replacements until it came to an end in October, which reduced his available draft animals to below the minimum he considered necessary to pull his guns efficiently. He also received forage from the quartermaster on only three days during the entire campaign and was forced to use his own funds to buy food for the animals.

With these deficiencies weighing on his mind, Bragg decided not to contest the crossing of the Green River but to pull out of Munfordville and move on to join Smith at Bardstown to the northeast. It turned out to be one of the most controversial decisions of the Confederate war effort and the beginning of a long series of bitterly resented decisions Bragg was to make as commander of the army. His critics contended that an important opportunity to make the Kentucky campaign a success had been lost, that Bragg should have either stood and fought Buell or at least have moved on to capture Louisville regardless of Smith's movements.

Neither option was as easy as Bragg's critics saw them. Staying put would have been tedious and uncertain. Buell had no intention of rushing into an attack; instead, he intended to coerce Bragg into evacuating his strong position on the south side of the Green River. Buell had taken most of the supplies he had in north Alabama with him, which was one of the reasons his movement northward had been comparatively slower than Bragg's. He could afford to wait in his Cave City line, but Bragg could not afford to wait at Munfordville. His supply situation was critical. In addition, a junction with Smith would indeed have evened the odds with Buell. A more bold and opportunistic commander would have ignored these drawbacks, sensing a chance to seize the strategic moment and possibly win the Kentucky campaign in one bold stroke. But Bragg, like his opponent, opted for the less risky course, saying later that this campaign was to be won by marching, not fighting.

Marching on Louisville was a dream that captivated Bragg's officers, his critics, and indeed even his soldiers. Certainly, if he could have taken the city, he would have denied Buell his base of supplies. But Louisville was not an open city in late September. The battle of Richmond on August 30 had alerted everyone to the dangers of a Confederate invasion, and already there were as many as seventeen thousand infantrymen and two thousand cavalrymen in the city. Many of them were the defeated remnants of the Richmond battle, others were members of some of the newly raised regiments and thus were untrained and unbloodied, but several brigades were troops recently shifted to the city from Grant's army in southwestern Tennessee. These included veterans of Pea Ridge and Shiloh, men who had hard campaigning experience and knew the sound of a minié ball. Also, Gilbert had begun digging a line of earthworks around the city. Louisville was much better prepared for the Rebels than Cincinnati had been. Additionally, even if Bragg had taken the city, there was no way he could have remained there. It would have been very easy for Buell to trap him in Louisville with his back to Indiana and his line of retreat to the south blocked. He would have had to meet Buell outside the city in the countryside, and if he could do that with Smith's army by his side and his men's haversacks filled with Bluegrass food, he would have a fighting chance of winning Kentucky.

The Army of the Mississippi left its strong position at Munfordville on September 20 and headed northward once again. It left the rail line at Nolin and marched northeastward via Hodgenville, passing within a few miles of Abraham Lincoln's birthplace. The tired infantrymen reached Bardstown, thirty miles southeast of Louisville and fifteen miles east of the railroad. It offered a good place to communicate with Smith to the east and to watch the Federals. As at Glasgow, the Confederates were greeted with enthusiasm. Henry C. McNeill of the Thirty-third Tennessee remarked that women and children were "shouting enthusiastically for the rebels" as his regiment moved into town.

The public reception hardly made up for the sense of loss felt by Bragg's men. "The army was not a little disappointed when instead of 'On to Louisville' the head of the column was faced Eastward," lamented Maj. George Winchester. It seemed to nearly everyone that the campaign had ended too soon and in the wrong place. The disappointment was heightened by the great optimism the army had felt just a few days before. On September 14, while at Glasgow, Col. Henry D. Clayton of the Thirty-ninth Alabama jubilantly wrote his wife, "I think now it is pretty well settled that our destination is Louisville, Ky—do not think it is the intention of our government to invade the North, but will be satisfied to drive them from our own territory." The Confederates, according to Clayton, believed they outnumbered Buell and had the Federals cut off. Bragg's men were stunned and confused by the apparent throwing away of this advantage, allowing Buell to enter Louisville while they marched to Bardstown.

When word of Bragg's withdrawal from Munfordville reached Buell, he cautiously moved out of his Cave City line. Wheeler's cavalry harassed his advance and held briefly at the Green River crossing, but Buell had no difficulty outflanking him and moving over the river on September 22. The Federals began to march faster than they had moved during any part of the campaign, pushing the men rapidly northward in case Bragg decided to take a stab at Louisville. Wheeler kept Bragg informed of the Yankees' movements, hoping he might attack their exposed right flank. Even if Bragg had a desire to do this, it would not have been possible, for Buell took measures to avoid it. He left the Louisville Pike and the railroad at Elizabethtown and veered northwest to West Point, twenty-five miles downriver from Louisville, so his army would not offer an exposed flank to the Confederates. The Federals crossed the Salt River at West Point and marched northeast to Louisville. Buell traveled to the city by steamboat from West Point.

The Army of the Ohio suffered severe food shortages during this march from Munfordville to Louisville, and some Unionists wore out their shoes and clothes in the rapid marching. Like the Rebels, Buell's men began to curse their commander for the way the campaign had turned out. They had been forced to give up their forward positions so near Chattanooga and go all the way back to protect territory that had never been threatened before. There was a general feeling among the Federals that Buell was incompetent, a "traitor, tyrant, fool and coward." This was an overly harsh judgment, but it represented another stage in Buell's downfall as commander of the Army of the Ohio. His men had begun to lose faith in him, and if he did not do something quickly to throw the Confederates out of Kentucky, the whole country would lose faith in him as well.

Buell's army found Louisville alive with feverish activity. The place was rapidly being put into order despite the anxiety that pervaded the seventy thousand civilians who lived there. Louisville was one of the principal logistical centers of the Union army, and Gilbert was doing all he could to prepare its defense.

The pace of activity quickened when Nelson arrived from his medical leave on September 18. He assumed command of the Army of Kentucky from Gilbert and took up his residence at the Galt House, near the river. Soon a flurry of new measures were put into place. Nelson ordered the building of a second pontoon bridge across the Ohio, allowing hundreds of civilians to flee the city into Indiana without interfering with military traffic. He also closed hotels, bars, liquor stores, and schools. Even the Unionist governor of Kentucky, James F. Robinson, relied on Nelson's energy to create a safe haven for himself and his staff in the city. Robinson had been forced to leave Frankfort when Smith occupied the undefended capital. In the middle of all this activity, Nelson also reorganized the Army of Kentucky into six divisions under Cruft, Jackson, Brig. Gen. Philip Sheridan, Gilbert, Brig. Gen. Ebenezer Dumont, and Brig. Gen. Robert S. Granger.

The fortifications that were begun by Gilbert were finished by September 28. They ringed Louisville nearly all the way along its eastern, southern, and western edges. Except for a gap of three-quarters of a mile in the southeastern quarter, the fortifications were a continuous infantry trench with occasional gun emplacements and two large redoubts. Through the labor of numerous soldiers, civilian workers, African Americans, and even inmates from the county jail, the line was turned into an impressive defense work in a relatively short time.

If there had ever been a chance that Bragg could have taken Louisville, that opportunity was now gone. Yet it would take several days for news of the end of Bragg's march to reach all interested ears. On September 27, the chief of the Confederate engineer bureau, Col. Jeremy Francis Gilmer, felt encouraged by the sketchy information he received in Richmond. Gilmer had earlier served in the western army and had kept in close touch with its officers. "All hope Bragg will be in Louisville soon if he is not already in possession of the place," he wrote to his wife. He hoped that, at the very least, Bragg could pin the western Yankees in their place and prevent them from reinforcing McClellan in Maryland. "I have a little hope that the vigorous operations of our army may induce the yankees to think about stopping the war; it is getting to be a serious matter for them as well as for us."

Public reaction in the North was understandably shrill. Buell's long retreat back to Louisville deepened the gloom already produced by Smith's brilliant advance and by Lee's raid into Maryland. George Templeton Strong of New York worried that "Rebellion is on its legs again, East and West, rampant and aggressive at every point. Our lines are either receding or turned, from the Atlantic to the Mississippi." He thought the nation was "rapidly sinking just now" and refused to let his mind "dwell on the tremendous contingencies of the present hour." Anxiety was felt in Washington, D.C., by many people, including Elizabeth Blair Lee. The sister of Montgomery Blair, Lincoln's postmaster general, and the wife of a Northern naval officer, she had no faith in the Federal generals defending Kentucky. Elizabeth Lee feared that Louisville was doomed.

Midwestern reaction to the campaign was far more intense, for the Confederates were swooping toward the southern border of Indiana. The state capital's major newspaper, the *Indianapolis Daily Journal*, blamed it all on Buell. Referring to the "cold shade of his long uselessness," the paper editorialized that Buell "never has done anything yet that did not almost 'do itself,' and we hope for nothing from him." The editor assured his readers that he had no "feeling against General Buell except that created by his utter failure to do anything under any circumstances, with the finest army ever entrusted to any General in the West or East." Senator John Sherman of Ohio refused to defend the man. He fumed at the slowness of his movements, which were unaccountable to civilians who had no idea of his logistical difficulties. Sherman also reported to his brother, William T. Sherman, that the "sudden over running of Kentucky" had produced "a gloomy feeling" in the North. Everyone was eager to see some move by Buell to reverse the flow of events.

No one was a more bitter critic of Buell than Andrew Johnson. The military governor of Tennessee had begun to worry in July when Forrest attacked Murfreesboro. He whipped up the loyal citizens of Nashville to rally to the city's defense and felt that his capital had been saved only by the thinnest of margins. He then became convinced that Buell had no intention of securing eastern Tennessee, and the Federal retreat to Murfreesboro seemed to prove it. Johnson did not fear for the safety of Nashville when Buell retired to the city, for his whole army was available to defend it. But Bragg's bold movements killed any chance that the mountain loyalists might be saved for some time to come. Johnson bitterly accused Buell of favoring the "establishment of the Southern Confederacy" and fearing for "his own personal safety" by massing the Army of the Ohio at Nashville "as a kind of body guard to protect and defend him." Johnson worried about the Unionists who were now left to their own defense. "East Tennessee seems doomed," he informed Lincoln. "There is scarcely a hope left of her redemption, if ever, no one now can tell. May God save my country from some of the Generals that have been conducting this War."

While Northerners worried that their accomplishments in the West were coming undone, Lee's invasion of Maryland reached a bloody climax. McClellan moved against the Confederate army in the western part of the state while it was divided and separated. Lee assigned Stonewall Jackson and a large part of his force the task of capturing Harpers Ferry and retained the rest in the neighborhood of Sharpsburg. McClellan managed to move enough troops westward to force a passage through the gaps of South Mountain on September 14, the day that Chalmers made his unwise assault on Wilder's fortifications at Munfordville, before Lee could react with sufficient force to block him. Then, on September 17, the two armies met in the bloodiest single day of fighting in American history. While Buckner and Wilder negotiated over the surrender of Munfordville, the battle of Antietam became one of the defining moments of the Civil War. Lee's army fought magnificently on the defensive and barely saved itself from crushing assaults. Yet McClellan refused to employ about a third of his army, holding it back in reserve, and thus failed to win a decisive tactical victory. Lee was forced to retreat, although the remainder of his army returned from Harpers Ferry in time to participate in the battle. When his tired men recrossed the Potomac, the first Confederate invasion of Northern-held territory in the East came to an end.

The only thing that Jefferson Davis could do while the events in Maryland and Kentucky were unfolding was to urge his commanders to issue proclamations. Davis suggested that they assure everyone that the Confederacy was fighting for its preservation and wanted only peace with independence. Its forces were compelled to invade the border states to defend its own citizenry. The people of the North should take matters into their own hands and pressure Lincoln to come to the peace table or even start negotiations separately between Northern state governments and the Confederacy. If Davis could not coordinate the military movements of his invading forces, he could at least try to shape their political impact on civilians.

The Rebel president reaped none of the benefit of his efforts. Lee's defeat at Antietam relieved enormous pressure on the minds of the Northern people and led Lincoln to issue his preliminary Emancipation Proclamation. It would go into effect on January 1, 1863, and applied only to those slaves living in territory still controlled by Confederate armies as of that date. Although it excluded the border states and large chunks of Rebel territory already occupied by Federal troops, the proclamation was a watershed in American history. It was the first time the Federal government made a decisive move to eliminate slavery, and it added an immensely potent element of morality to the Northern war effort.

Antietam also forced the European powers to pause in their efforts to offer mediation in the war. England and France had been tending strongly to such a move after Second Bull Run. Antietam did not end the mediation effort, but it made the cautious diplomats stop to think about the result of this Union victory. The battle also seemed to prove to the people in London that the war would be deadlocked for some time to come, and thus there was even more need of mediation than ever. The emancipation policy that capped Lincoln's radical war effort seemed to be the Northern president's desperate ploy to incite a race war in the Confederacy. The events of September both eased and solidified foreign interpretations of the war, postponing indefinitely the prospects of mediation but making the European leaders even more convinced that the American conflict was a serious threat to their interests.

Bragg's campaign was not influenced by events in the East, and it had no discernible effect on foreign relations. His guiding light in this invasion was the action of Edmund Kirby Smith, who continued to stay in the Bluegrass rather than move to join his comrade at Bardstown. In the coming stage of the campaign, the failure to join the two forces into one army under a single commander would pay its worst dividends. The campaign was not yet lost, but a key turning point had been reached. Bragg suffered from another problem, one he shared with Lee in Maryland, that the Confederacy simply did not have the transportation and resources to support a deep penetration of Northern-held territory. Those operations turned into raids, temporary incursions for the purpose of collecting supplies, recruits, and forage. They could have led to permanent occupation of territory only if thousands of

Kentuckians and Marylanders rallied to the cause. In hindsight, it was difficult to see that Bragg had any reasonable hope of holding central Kentucky,
but the divided command arrangement with Smith and the fact that he allowed Buell to regain his logistical base further doomed this hope. Perhaps
Bragg's only real chance had been to make Buell pay dearly for reestablish-
ing control of his supply line at Munfordville, regardless of the risks to his
own army in fighting a larger force with inadequate supplies. Now the Federal army was secure in its base and once again had the strategic initiative.
For a few heady weeks, Bragg and Smith had called the shots, but now they
were on the defensive and had to pay the piper. The battle for Kentucky was
about to begin with all the advantages on the Federal side.

CHAPTER FOUR

Give Him Battle

The Kentucky campaign was already three months old and no decisive battle between Bragg and Buell had yet taken place. The Confederates had achieved many of their goals. They had positioned large, powerful forces in the heartland of the state, gathered enormous amounts of supplies, and taken the strategic initiative away from their opponents. But they had not been able to consolidate their hold on the state, and their position had become precarious. Buell now had an excellent opportunity to kick the Confederates out of Kentucky.

The Army of the Ohio began to enter Louisville on September 24 and continued to march into the city for five days. As soon as his headquarters reached Louisville, Buell began to prepare for an offensive against Bragg and Smith. He had no time to waste. The country was excited about the Confederate invasion, and Buell was under great pressure to take action immediately. To his credit, he accomplished a great deal in a short time. He thoroughly reorganized his army while at the same time incorporating many new units into it. Buell had received three divisions from Grant's army in northern Mississippi and western Tennessee and took in all the units of Nelson's Army of Kentucky. He divided the enlarged force into three new corps. McCook commanded the I Corps of thirteen thousand men, Crittenden led the II Corps with twenty-two thousand men, and Nelson commanded the III Corps of twenty-two thousand troops. Each corps had three divisions. Thomas, Buell's best subordinate, was named second in command of the army. With fifty-seven thousand men, Buell greatly outnumbered Bragg's and Smith's armies. Only by combining in a timely manner and acting under a single commander could the Confederates hope to have a chance of staying in Kentucky.

Buell's preparations reached a crisis on September 29, when several troubling events took place. Buell had planned a meeting of his corps commanders that day, but Nelson would be killed before he could attend. He ran afoul of Brig. Gen. Jefferson C. Davis, who had only recently come to Louisville in command of some of Grant's reinforcements. Nelson had assigned him to lead the citizen militia of Louisville, a humble position chosen because Davis was a protégé of Indiana governor Oliver P. Morton. Nelson was in the middle of a bitter grudge with Morton, who blamed the general for the terrible defeat at Richmond. Nelson in turn blamed the Indiana regiments for the debacle. He assumed Davis was a man to keep in the background and did his best to humble him. Nelson confronted Davis a few days after the subordinate assumed his new command and demanded detailed information on his work. Davis was unable to answer satisfactorily, and Nelson insulted him.

The Indiana general brooded for several days before confronting his superior early on the morning of September 29 in the lobby of the Galt House. He demanded satisfaction for the slur on his honor. Nelson made the situation worse by laughing, calling him a "damned puppy," and telling him to go away. Davis threw a crumpled hotel desk card in his commander's face and tempers flared. Nelson impulsively slapped his subordinate's face with the back of his hand and then turned and walked up the stairs to prepare for his meeting with Buell. The humiliated Davis went somewhere in the hotel to get a pistol and hunted Nelson down, found him in a hallway, and shot him without a word of explanation. The burly general stumbled down the hall into a room where he died thirty minutes later.

This unfortunate incident caused a wave of excitement all over Louisville. Nelson had been universally criticized, even hated, for his brutish manner with subordinates, and many people in the city hardly mourned his loss. But he did not deserve to die this way. Davis immediately regretted his hotheaded deed that early fall morning, refusing to comment on it or to cease brooding over it for the rest of his life. Governor Morton, who had witnessed the slapping incident in the lobby, apparently helped to convince the authorities not to bring Davis to trial. The general resumed his command soon afterward and served as a trusted division and corps leader for the remainder of the war.

The most serious consequence of Nelson's death was the need for a new commander for the III Corps. Buell unwisely chose Gilbert, who had been a captain only a month before and had relatively little combat experience. Gilbert had done well in picking up the pieces from the Richmond battle and in dealing with administrative matters in Louisville, yet he was unprepared to command a corps in an important campaign. His battlefield promotion to major general had not yet been recognized by the Senate, a fact that apparently escaped Buell's notice. Most important, he did not have the confidence of the III Corps. Gilbert became infamous for bullying soldiers on the march when they took fence rails to build fires or fresh fruit to eat. Rumors circulated throughout the corps that a silly martinet had been given command because of his personal connections with influential people. Neither McCook nor Crittenden would prove to be extraordinary corps commanders, but Gilbert was certainly in a situation that was far above his abilities.

The other crisis that hit Buell on September 29 was an order from Washington to give up his command to Thomas. Lincoln and his advisers had long been dissatisfied with Buell's performance, beginning with his delay in approaching Chattanooga and culminating with his failure to stop Bragg from invading Kentucky. He immediately prepared to transfer command, but Thomas put a stop to it. Taking command of the army on the eve of a major campaign that had been planned by Buell was hardly Thomas's idea of a promotion. "My position is very embarassing," he telegraphed Washington, "not being as well informed as I should be as the commander of the army on the assumption of such a responsibility." It was an effective argument. That evening, Halleck suspended the order replacing Buell. The long-suffering commander would have one more opportunity to live up to the expectations of his Washington superiors. In ordering Thomas to take charge of the army, Halleck had written, "The government expects energetic operations by the troops placed under your command. . . . Operate against the enemy; find him and give him battle."

Not only the Washington bureaucrats but all of the North wanted action now. Senator John Sherman feared that any delay in driving the Rebels out of Kentucky would give them ample opportunity to convince the citizens of that tortured state to side with the South. "If you leave [them] sixty days in Kentucky [they] will by conciliation—by threats—by bribery—by robbery—by [an] interest in confederate money—and by a common sympathy about negroes so consolidate confederate authority in Kentucky that the war will for a long time be along the Ohio River. Thousands of men who were for the Union will acquiesce in a successful revolution. I know that is the feeling with some of the strongest Union men in Ky. Nothing will save us but prompt offensive action that will prevent People from Committing themselves."

Buell planned the campaign well. His objective was to disguise his true line of advance, to confuse the enemy, and to force Bragg and Smith to spread their forces out to cover as much territory as possible. Buell was aided greatly by a lack of preparation on Bragg's part. The Confederate commander assumed the Federal force would take several weeks to prepare before leaving Louisville. It was an unreasonable assumption, considering the great public pressure in the North for action. Bragg had not yet combined his army with Smith's or planned any strategy.

Thus the Confederates were taken by surprise when Buell's army left Louisville on October 1. Most of the troops set out on a more or less direct line toward the Bardstown area. McCook's corps marched on the Taylorsville Road, Gilbert's men were on the Shepherdsville Road, and Crittenden's corps set out on the Bardstown Road. The movement was screened by the dispatch of two divisions, both under the command of Brig. Gen. Joshua W. Sill, directly eastward toward Frankfort. The short-term purpose of this column was to cover Louisville from a possible raid by Smith's cavalry or infantry, but Sill's more important task was to convince the Confederates that Buell intended to attack Frankfort. He succeeded beyond expectations. Bragg would agonize over his enemy's true line of advance throughout the campaign. The resulting hesitancy greatly contributed to the many difficulties he faced while trying to hold Kentucky.

The weather continued to be unusually hot and dry as the Federals advanced. "Our army suffers terribly for water," wrote John H. Tilford of the Seventy-ninth Indiana, "it is almost impossible to get any." The men had to resort to muddy holes in many cases, "hog puddles" as one Illinois soldier called them, holding their noses while drinking. Jesse B. Connelly of the Thirty-first Indiana remembered drinking water from "stagnant pools in the beds of creeks . . . very brackish and strong. A very little of it was all a man could drink at a time, and soon his thirst was more intense than ever." Food was in short supply as well. Despite the efforts of many officers to stop the men from foraging, they raided farms along the line of march as often as possible.

Bragg's situation could hardly have been worse. Few recruits had joined the Confederate cause to compensate for the disparity of strength between his own and Buell's army. He had the guns, nearly fifteen thousand small arms that had been brought for the new Kentucky troops everyone expected, but not the bodies. Bragg pleaded desperately to Richmond for an additional fifty thousand men. There was no possibility of getting reinforcements from further south. Bragg had hoped to receive aid from the Confederate forces operating under Sterling Price and Earl Van Dorn in northern Mississippi, but those troops were on the verge of fighting a major battle at Corinth. The officers of Bragg's army were mightily disappointed about the lack of support from Kentucky's population. "There are many who express southern principles who do not exemplify it," commented Maj. George Winchester. Bragg complained to Davis, "Enthusiasm runs high, but exhausts itself in words."

Even worse, Bragg could not fully count on the cooperation of Smith's army. That general, whose ambition for an independent command bordered on mutiny, continued to maintain his forces in the Lexington area, separate from Bragg's concentration at Bardstown. Bragg was willing to go along with this arrangement because the Bluegrass was a valuable area and because a widely dispersed occupation of northern Kentucky had strategic merit. Bragg wisely decided to establish his line of communication with the South by way of the Wilderness Road and Cumberland Gap, now firmly in Confederate hands. It was the only feasible line to establish, far away from Union forces and centrally located between his and Smith's armies. He assumed that, when the Union advance took place, Smith would join him in the area of Danville to protect access to this line.

But Bragg assumed that would be some time in the future. On September 28 he gave Polk temporary command of the Army of the Mississippi and left for Lexington to talk with Smith. He met Richard C. Hawes, the Confederate governor of Kentucky, at Danville that night. Hawes was eager to replace the Unionist governor Robinson as soon as possible and had traveled back to his home state by way of Chattanooga. He and Bragg reached Lexington on October 1, the same day that Buell's army set out from Louisville. It was decided that Smith would escort the party to Frankfort so Hawes could be installed. This was pushed through in part so that the Confederate conscription law could be enforced in Kentucky and some use could be found for all those small arms that were rusting in their boxes.

By this time Smith's force was much bigger and more powerful than ever before. Stevenson's division of eight thousand men had arrived from Cumberland Gap to replace Cleburne's men, who now began to make their way back to Hardee's corps. Col. Benjamin Allston's cavalry brigade also came with Stevenson. Smith now had about twenty-eight thousand men, five thousand of whom remained in the Lexington area while the rest moved on to Frankfort.

There was still a great deal of optimism among Southern civilians before the Federals began their movement, fed in part by false rumors that Bragg had already taken Louisville. Everyone, particularly the Confederate delegations from Tennessee and Kentucky, urged the authorities to recapture Nashville as well. "We hope to hear soon of active operations in Kentucky," wrote J. B. Jones toward the end of September. He also was encouraged by the passage of an act extending conscription to include men between thirty-five and forty-five years of age. All in all, the Confederates had every reason to hope for the best throughout the month of September. The editors of the *Augusta Daily Constitutionalist* celebrated the disappearance of those "dark days of despondency" that followed the fall of Fort Donelson. Since the double invasions of Maryland and Kentucky, "the sunlight of victory has burst over our land, and dispelled the gloom of despondency which has settled upon the minds of our people. In the East, and in the West, its bright rays have illumined the political horizon, restored courage and confidence to the weak and the doubting, and added strength and vigor to the brave and the hopeful."

As the columns of Buell's army made their way across the countryside, Confederate horsemen did their best to harass them. Wharton's and Wheeler's brigades of Bragg's army tried to bother the heads of McCook's, Crittenden's, and Gilbert's corps, while Scott's brigade hovered around the front of Sill's column. Bragg had received enough information by October 2 to believe that Sill was the vanguard of Buell's main advance. He was delighted. Sensing an opportunity to hit him in the flank, he lay plans to move Polk's and Hardee's corps from Bardstown to the north to attack the Federal right while Smith blocked him west of Frankfort. Orders were sent, but Polk had doubts. He had received enough information from Wharton to believe that a very large Federal force was moving directly from Louisville toward Bardstown. A council of officers advised Polk to ignore Bragg's order and instead to retire toward Danville. Gray columns began leaving Bardstown at five on the morning of October 4. Hardee moved out toward Harrodsburg by way of Glenville and Willisburg, while Polk marched toward Danville by a more southerly route via Springfield and Perryville. Wharton's and Wheeler's cavalry covered their retreat.

October 4 also was the day of Hawes's installation as governor of Kentucky. The party, including Bragg, Smith, Stevenson, Heth, and Buckner, had reached Frankfort the day before. The citizens of the capital flocked to the festivities by the thousands and cheered Hawes and his attendant generals. Smith personally commanded the military escort that accompanied Hawes through the streets, while artillery fired salutes and the Confederate flag was raised over the capitol dome. The installation ceremonies were held in the hall of the House of Representatives. It really was not an inaugural but an installation. Hawes did not retake his oath, but he gave a speech in which he promised to restore Confederate control over the state, "cost what it might."

Invited guests made their way to the Capital Hotel after the ceremony for a celebration dinner. Bragg acted on an important decision he had made the night before, that Sill was not, after all, the vanguard of Buell's main advance. He now wanted to concentrate both of his corps and Smith's force in the Harrodsburg area, something that Polk already was trying to do. Here he hoped to cover his line of communication to Cumberland Gap and Lexington as well. For now, at least, Smith appeared willing to cooperate and agreed to this concentration so Bragg wrote a note to Polk about it during dinner. Ominously, the faint thunder of artillery could be heard soon after the meal ended. Scott's cavalry was fighting a skirmish with Col. Edward Kirk's brigade of Sill's division about ten miles west of town. Bragg left Frankfort for Harrodsburg at 4 P.M. that day, followed quickly by Smith's army and Hawes himself. The good citizens must have been stunned. Their new governor was an executive in exile once again, and all they had was the memory of a Confederate flag flying over their capitol for one day.

For the next forty-eight hours it seemed that Bragg and Smith had settled on a workable plan that would finally bring their two armies together. But Smith's ambition soon got the better of him. When he met Bragg at Harrodsburg on October 6, Smith suggested he keep his force north of the Kentucky River so as to protect the Bluegrass and the supplies he had accumulated there. Smith argued that he could shift troops quickly enough south of the river, if it became necessary, to cooperate with Bragg before Buell concentrated in the Harrodsburg area. By now, Bragg was convinced that the Federals were conforming to his perception of the campaign; he incorrectly believed Buell was aiming at Harrodsburg. Smith's plan would work, he thought, and thus the idea of joining forces was scrapped. Bragg's main object from the beginning of the march from Chattanooga no longer seemed so important. Neither commander had enough accurate information on Buell's movements or his objectives, and both underestimated the amount of time needed to concentrate the scattered Confederate forces.

Buell had already taken a decisive advantage. He had managed to confuse his enemy about his true line of advance and therefore set the stage for Bragg's failure to coordinate his movements. Also, Buell was closer to the retreating columns of Hardee and Polk than Smith was, and neither Hardee nor Polk had very clear information on who was chasing them. It would be in this area, the line of retreat from Bardstown toward Danville, where the climactic battle for Kentucky would be fought, not in the Harrodsburg area where Bragg expected it. And this clash would come about more by accident than design, when neither army was fully prepared for it.

Hardee and Polk started from Bardstown by moving on different routes. By the evening of the first day, October 4, Hardee was falling behind schedule because of the poor condition of the roads leading to and from Glenville. Polk ordered him to change his direction south, march directly to Springfield, and follow his own corps to Danville. It was a fortunate move, for now the two corps would be in supporting distance of each other with Buell's army only hours behind Hardee. The Federals entered Bardstown on October 5. The Confederate cavalry reported such heavy fighting with the Federal vanguard the next day that Hardee began to believe it would be unwise to ignore the threat. Polk authorized Hardee to halt that evening at Perryville and force the pursuing Federals to deploy and develop their strength.

Although he had only Buckner's division and Wheeler's cavalry at Perryville, Hardee was determined to make Buell pay for his pursuit. "If he wishes to fight, let him come on," he told Wheeler that evening. Polk began sending units back to Perryville to help Hardee and informed Bragg that he had done so. But Polk unknowingly misled the army commander when he told him the Federal force following Hardee probably was not large.

This bit of faulty information was one of many inaccurate reports that filtered into Bragg's headquarters on October 7. This lack of good intelligence was decisive in Bragg's handling of the campaign, and it stemmed from his sorry lack of cavalry. The Army of the Mississippi had only two brigades of horsemen, and Smith's equally large army also had only two. These four brigades were far too few to accomplish the twin tasks of screening the Federal advance and gathering information.

Smith confused Bragg even more when, on October 7, he told him he was convinced that Sill's column was the vanguard of Buell's army. Bragg hastily agreed and revised his plan once again by concentrating his army and Smith's force at Frankfort instead of Harrodsburg and Lexington. The orders became irrelevant almost as quickly as they were issued. Smith changed his mind later that day and no longer felt Frankfort was the real target, forcing Bragg to cancel his new orders. This episode further contributed to Buell's advantage and to the atmosphere of confusion and indecision that had come to permeate Bragg's headquarters. Smith's staff officers described Bragg's "conversation and actions" as "unaccountable; they were like those of a wild man." It was an ungenerous view of a commander who was nearing his wits' end, not necessarily through any fault of his own.

Events were moving much faster than Bragg could manage them. On October 7, the day that Smith and Bragg considered moving their two armies to Frankfort, the first clash occurred between Hardee and Buell near Perryville. Hardee positioned Buckner's division west of town on a high hill owned by farmer Sam Bottom, between the Springfield and Mackville Roads, so as to cover these two routes from the west. McCook's corps was moving toward town on the Mackville Road, Gilbert's corps, with Buell, was marching by way of the Springfield Road, and Crittenden's command marched along the Lebanon Road from the southwest. As Wheeler engaged the Federal cavalry six miles from Perryville, the sounds of the firing could be heard by Hardee's infantrymen at Sam Bottom's house. Fearing this position was not strong enough, the infantry moved forward three-quarters of a mile to another hill, owned by Jacob Peter, and established a line parallel to the previous one. Not only was this a more forward position but it would deny the Federals access to the precious water in Bull Run, which ran between Bottom's Hill and Peter's Hill, and to Doctor's Creek in front of the Peter's Hill position. Patton Anderson's division arrived on October 7 and was posted to the rear of Buckner.

The Federals pushed Wheeler back to Buckner's position on Peter's Hill by the evening of the seventh, but Buell suffered an injury that limited his mobility. His horse, startled by artillery fire, threw him, injuring his thigh. He could not remount, so he crawled into an ambulance and established his headquarters at the Dorsey house, four miles from Perryville on the Springfield Road. He believed that all of Bragg's army was concentrated at Perryville, perhaps even Smith's force, so he determined to plan his next move carefully. Gilbert would deploy the next day and try to link up with McCook. Staff members scouted the rolling, hilly terrain, interspersed with open fields and woods, and reported that a line could be formed about two to three miles from Perryville in a great arc covering the western perimeter of the town. There would be a gap of half a mile between Gilbert's and McCook's commands where the line crossed Doctor's Creek. The army's position would be continued by Crittenden's men south of the Springfield Road on similar terrain. Thomas was traveling with Crittenden and could oversee the deployment of that wing. Buell hoped his three corps could establish their lines by 10 A.M. on October 8. He ordered his subordinates to take position, reconnoiter, and report before he gave the command to commence a general attack. It was to be a methodical, inflexible approach that would not serve the army well in the confusing swirl of events on the next day.

For his part, Bragg was still in a fog as to Buell's intentions and his dispositions. The Federal commander had given his opponent far too much credit as he contemplated the morrow. Although more divisions were coming to Perryville throughout the night of October 7, Bragg intended this to be only a temporary concentration for the purpose of stopping the close pursuit of one Federal column of undetermined strength. Bragg now made it clear that he believed Buell aimed at hitting him near Versailles. This prompted a worried Hardee to send a long letter to his commander pleading with him not to disperse the army, but it had no effect on Bragg. Polk also retraced his steps to Perryville that night to assume command of the sixteen thousand men who had so far gathered there.

The battle of Perryville began in the still, early morning hours. A reconnoissance in force had determined the exact Confederate position and the presence of water close to it. Buell ordered a brigade under Col. Daniel McCook to seize Peter's Hill and secure Doctor's Creek. At 3 A.M. on October 8, with skirmishers out in front, McCook slowly attacked along the Springfield Road, groping through the darkness. Peter's Hill was held only by the Seventh Arkansas, and after a brief but worthy resistance, it fell into Union hands just as dawn began to break. At about the same time, McCook's corps roused itself and began to move out into the growing sunlight, trying to find its assigned position on the left of the Union line and to connect with Gilbert. Crittenden's corps, which had not reached the vicinity of Perryville until about 2:30 A.M., rested until nearly seven in the morning before moving out along the Lebanon Road to its assigned position.

Nearer to town, confusion and delay characterized Confederate actions that morning. With the sun rising higher, Polk rode out to examine the ground Hardee had selected. In an officers' conference held later that morning, he told his subordinates of Bragg's order to attack whatever force was at Perryville and then to move on to Versailles. It seemed clear to Polk that not a portion but the entire Union army now faced him, and he felt it would be foolish to attack it with only sixteen thousand men. Instead, he would take a defensive position and wait to see what developed. Since most of the divisions were camped east of the Chaplin River, Polk decided to move them west, across the stream, so he could bring them into action more quickly on the rolling terrain fronting the Federal army. Buckner's division would remain in its position to the north of the Springfield Road, Cheatham's division would take position on the left of Buckner to the south of the road, and

Anderson's division would act as a reserve behind Buckner. Wharton's brigade would screen the right and Wheeler's brigade would do the same for the left.

The next clash took place, not surprisingly, along the Springfield Road. The Confederates refused to give up Peter's Hill without a fight, so the Fifth Arkansas and the Seventh Arkansas launched an assault to retake it. Daniel McCook received a brigade from Sheridan's division, and another fierce little fight took place on the eastern slope of this modest eminence. The Arkansans were forced to retreat to Bottom's Hill by 7 A.M. Ironically, both sides soon received orders to retire. Polk wanted all forces to take position closer to Perryville so Bottom's Hill was abandoned. Gilbert, who was astonished to find Sheridan's troops all the way forward to Sam Bottom's house immediately ordered them to retire to Peter's Hill. He reminded Sheridan that Buell wanted to wait until McCook and Crittenden were up before he made a general advance. The noise of battle was silenced along the Springfield Road by 9 A.M.

At about the same time, the head of McCook's corps neared a spot one mile to the north of Peter's Hill, making its way forward to the intersection of the Mackville and Benton Roads. A bit beyond, along the Mackville Road, stood an impressive, two-story wooden frame house owned by the Russell family. From here, one could get an excellent view of the surrounding countryside. Division leader Rousseau saw the Confederate and Federal forces off to the south along the Springfield Road and knew he had reached his assigned area. McCook established his headquarters at the Russell house and began to direct the deployment of his divisions north and south of that point. Crittenden's corps also came up at roughly the same time and began to deploy from Lebanon Road to Springfield Road. By noon, almost all of Buell's army had slowly crawled into position along a nearly continuous line five miles long and shaped like a crescent. But it was moving at a leisurely pace. McCook unaccountably took three hours to ride from the Russell house to Buell's headquarters to report his deployment. No one seemed to be in a hurry to push the enemy.

Equally slow movements were being made on the Confederate side. Despite his early morning decision to move all units to the west of the Chaplin River, Polk had moved virtually no one by noon. Nor had he engaged the enemy in a general way, as Bragg detected. Wondering why he did not hear the sound of artillery from his headquarters at Harrodsburg, ten miles away, Bragg mounted up early that morning and rode to Perryville, reaching the town by 9:45. There he became frustrated with Polk. Bragg still did not believe that all of Buell's army was here, and, after scouting the terrain, he decided to take charge of the available force and launch an immediate attack. He outlined his plan of action in a conference held at his new headquarters, the Crawford house on Harrodsburg Road. Wanting to keep the road to Harrodsburg open so as to maintain communication with Smith, Bragg intended to strike with his right wing and smash McCook's corps first, then to turn south and hit Gilbert in the flank. It would be a giant left wheel of almost his entire available force. Because so few men were available, Bragg could afford to keep only a small holding force on his left. Only one brigade was positioned south of the Springfield Road while the far right flank would extend as far as McCook's far left. Altogether Bragg's line would be two and a half miles long. He apparently had no idea of Crittenden's presence on the left but had no men to spare in that sector anyway. Only Wheeler's cavalry stood in Crittenden's way. The attack, which was scheduled to begin at 12:30, would start on the far right and be taken up in succession toward the left, with only a holding action along the Springfield Road. There was little difficulty in crossing the divisions over the Chaplin River, for it had little water, and their movements would be largely shielded by the rolling countryside that separated the two armies. Thus the attack would come as nearly a complete surprise to the Federals. Only the dust clouds raised by thirty-two thousand marching feet could be seen from the Russell house, but it was misinterpreted as a Confederate retreat, not an attack. Not even the opening of Rebel artillery on McCook's corps caused the Unionists to prepare for an assault.

But that attack was unfolding much more slowly than Bragg intended. Polk crossed his divisions to the west of the Chaplin River but then learned from Wharton that many more Union troops were marching toward Perryville along the Mackville Road than anyone had expected. Their obvious intention was to extend the Federal left. Bragg's tactical plan was based on the assumption that his enemy's left rested at the Russell house. If Wharton's report was true, Polk would be unable to outflank the Federals and might even be hit in his own flank when he began to wheel to the left. Bragg concluded that his corps commander was right. Cheatham's division, which was on the far right, had to move farther north. The only way it could do so was to recross the Chaplin River and reassemble at Walker's Bend, formed by the river bulging westward around a plot of mostly flat land. From here, it could cross the shallow water, ascend the sixty-foot-high bluffs, and form on a flat shelf of land. Then the Confederates could move up the higher ground that the Federals were beginning to occupy. A crude road leading from Walker's Bend had to be partially dug out to accommodate the artillery. This repositioning would take time, but it was necessary. Unfortunately for the Confederates, Bragg failed to use Wharton's cavalry to determine exactly where the forming Union line would end. As a result, Cheatham would still not be able to outflank it.

On the Union side, McCook barely had time to establish his extended line before the Confederate attack was launched. It stretched from Wilson's Creek on the left to a curve in Doctor's Creek on the right, with the Russell house and the junction of the Mackville and Benton Roads about five hundred yards to the rear of its center. The middle of McCook's position was dominated by a wide and deep branch that started only a few yards from the Mackville Road and the Russell house and ran eastward through his line at a right angle toward Doctor's Creek. All the ground on his left flank drained toward this branch and consisted of a series of low, rounded ridges. The far northern ends of these ridges were high and formed the bluff line of Wilson's Creek. All the ridges sloped southward toward the branch.

McCook positioned two brigades to hold his extreme left. Brig. Gen. William R. Terrill's brigade of Ohio and Illinois regiments and Capt. Charles Parsons's Battery, all green units, were posted on an open ridge, the second one from Walker's Bend. Col. John C. Starkweather's brigade of Illinois, Pennsylvania, and Wisconsin units was placed three hundred yards behind Parsons's Battery on the next ridge. The line continued southward from Starkweather's position to the branch but angled sharply westward to cross the branch valley. This angling was necessary because the nearest high ground to the south of the branch, an open cornfield, was some five hundred yards to the west. Thus Col. George Webster's Indiana and Ohio brigade formed a crooked line in the open valley. The Nineteenth Indiana Battery was posted near Widow Gibson's barn while the rest of the brigade turned south at Widow Gibson's cabin, some two hundred yards away.

Col. Leonard A. Harris's brigade of Indiana, Ohio, and Wisconsin units held a high, commanding position on the south side of the branch. The ground sloped eastward to Harris's front but rose to a knoll before descending toward Doctor's Creek. On his right, Col. William H. Lytle's Indiana, Ohio, and Kentucky regiments anchored McCook's right flank. Doctor's Creek curved toward the southwest in Lytle's front, placing it at the foot of the steep slope on which the Federals established their line. Lytle also straddled the Mackville Road. His troops were visible from Gilbert's position along the Springfield Road, but the two corps did not connect.

By midafternoon, Buell was about to receive a big attack from the army

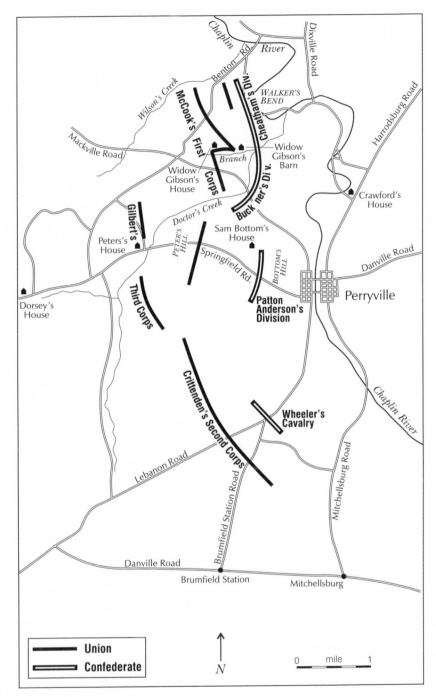

Chaplin River
Benton Rd.
Dixville Road
Wilson's Creek
McCook's First Corps
Cheatham's Div.
WALKER'S BEND
Harrodsburg Road
Mackville Road
Branch
Widow Gibson's Barn
Widow Gibson's House
Buckner's Div.
Crawford's House
Gilbert's
Doctor's Creek
Peters's House
PETER'S HILL
Sam Bottom's House
BOTTOM'S HILL
Springfield Rd.
Danville Road
Third Corps
Patton Anderson's Division
Perryville
Dorsey's House
Crittenden's Second Corps
Wheeler's Cavalry
Chaplin River
Lebanon Road
Brumfield Station Road
Mitchellsburg Road
Danville Road
Brumfield Station
Mitchellsburg

Union
Confederate

N

0   mile   1

3. Perryville, midafternoon, October 8, 1862

that he had confused and scattered during the previous week. Ironically, this complicated campaign was again turning, and the pursued was about to savagely attack the pursuer. For a change Bragg was acting decisively and aggressively, accepting the battle he had rejected at Munfordville with far fewer advantages than he had in September. The disparity of numbers between his force and the Federals was far greater. Buell had about fifty-four thousand men on the field, while, with the addition of another division that had arrived since dawn, Bragg had only twenty thousand men. The Confederates had relatively little advantage in terrain. Bragg did not even have complete information on the Federal dispositions. And, of course, Smith's force was too far away to offer any aid in the fighting to come.

Ironically, Buell was as much in the fog on October 8 as Bragg had been during the previous week. In fact, as Cheatham's division left Walker's Bend and formed its battle line, Buell had no idea that an attack was imminent. Earlier that day, he had decided to postpone his own assault until October 9, having assumed that, by the time all of his divisions were up and ready, he would have only three or four hours of daylight to crush the Confederates. It was an error of judgment that gave Bragg the opportunity to seize the tactical offensive and nearly crush a portion of the Union army.

CHAPTER FIVE

Perryville

The Kentucky campaign came to a bloody climax outside the sleepy little town of Perryville at midafternoon on Wednesday, October 8. It was the first battle the Army of the Ohio fought by itself and, even though he did not yet realize it, the only battle Buell would fight alone, without the cooperation of other armies. It also was Bragg's first engagement as an independent commander. Ironically, neither general was fully informed about the circumstances of the developing battle or completely in charge of his own forces. The outcome of the engagement was in the hands of the rank and file.

On Cheatham's far right, the Tennessee brigade of Brig. Gen. George E. Maney moved out in two battle lines over a low wooded ridge after it crossed the Chaplin River. Only three hundred yards away was Terrill's brigade, just settling into its position. The Federal infantrymen were stunned when they saw the Confederates cross the crest of this ridge, but the gunners of Parsons's Battery quickly aimed their pieces and opened fire. As Maney's men moved down the modest slope, individual battalions could shoot over the heads of their comrades in front. These hard-bitten veterans of Shiloh were blazing away as they marched. They easily sent the 123d Illinois reeling back in confusion when it was sent forward by Terrill in an effort to blunt the assault. The green Illinoisans did not stop when they reached Parsons's guns but fled in panic toward Starkweather's position on the hill to the rear, leaving only the 105th Ohio to support the artillery. Division commander James Jackson was mortally wounded while standing next to Parsons's guns, forcing Terrill to take charge of the division as well as his brigade.

Maney's first line halted for breath at a fence in the valley between the two ridges. Crouching here, the men found little shelter from the canister rounds that were fired at them from a distance of only one hundred yards.

Maney boldly walked along the line, encouraging them to rise and continue the advance. "His presence and manner having imparted fresh vigor and courage among the troops," they jumped across the fence and pushed up the slope. Parsons double-shotted his canister fire as the Rebels closed in. Atop the ridge, a soldier in the 105th Ohio glanced along his regimental line and saw a forest of twirling ramrods as his comrades fired. The Union gunners and infantrymen fought so well that Maney's Tennesseeans stopped halfway up the slope and fell to the ground. Maney estimated that, up to this point, he had suffered nearly three hundred casualties in the three regiments that made up his first line.

The surviving Rebels opened fire on the Federals. Parsons's gunners began to drop like flies. Two-thirds of them became casualties in only a few minutes of fighting, while the 105th Ohio was hit with a fire that "was terrible beyond description." It was too much for the outnumbered Yankees. Terrill issued orders to withdraw, but with so few men left and so many shells flying toward him, Parsons had a difficult time doing so.

Meanwhile, the Confederate high command began to worry about the apparent stalemate on its right. Bragg could tell that his original plan had already gone awry. He was not hitting the flank of the Federals but smashing into their left wing head-on. There obviously was no longer any hope of wheeling his force to the left. All Bragg could do now was to throw in all the men available and hope for the best. Reluctantly he committed more troops, hoping to break Terrill's command with massive force. Brig. Gen. Alexander P. Stewart's Tennessee brigade moved forward to fill the developing gap between Maney's command and Brig. Gen. Daniel S. Donelson's brigade to Maney's left. At the same time, Maney sent the First Tennessee to swing widely around his own right and try to hit the Federal line on its left flank. He also detached Col. Hume Feild of that regiment to take charge of the brigade line that had stalled on the slope of what was to become known as Parsons's Ridge and to urge it on to the crest at any cost.

Feild did his work well, forcing the men to stand up and walk into the face of their enemy. This was too much for Parsons's gunners, who were ready to retreat anyway. They left all but one of their weapons behind as Stewart's brigade came up to Maney's left in time to support his attack. The steadiness of Stewart's men awed those who saw them. "On, on they went as the volley's from the guns would mow a swath of brave fellows from their ranks," wrote an Ohio soldier named Junius Gates, "they would close up their ranks and keep on that dead run." The weakened Federal infantry withdrew. Terrill managed to reform them about fifty yards down the opposite slope, where they peppered Maney's victorious but disordered regiments, temporarily halting them on the crest of Parsons's Ridge. Yet it was a tenuous stand, for Terrill's brigade had already lost 25 percent of its strength. A Federal survivor of this contest later reported, "In less than an hour our brigade ceased to be a brigade." More Union troops were needed to save McCook's left.

The Confederates regrouped atop Parsons's Ridge, then advanced down the opposite slope. Feild easily pushed Terrill's men back to Starkweather's position, clearing the ridge of all resistance. Maney's regiments filtered through a belt of trees at the bottom of the slope and emerged into a cornfield at the foot of Starkweather's Hill. There, in the middle of the field, was the Twenty-first Wisconsin. An untried unit, it had been sent out alone by Starkweather to blunt the attack. Terrill's fleeing men ran through its ranks while short rounds from the two Federal batteries on Starkweather's Hill exploded over it. Worst of all, five regiments of Rebels, fresh from their triumph atop Parsons's Ridge, were approaching the four hundred Wisconsinites. The Twenty-first Wisconsin lost a quarter of its number in just a few minutes, and, with the Confederates easily overlapping both flanks, it was ordered to withdraw. The regiment had to cross two fences bordering the Benton Road, which ran diagonally up the bare slope of Starkweather's Hill. Maney's battle line swept this slope "with terrific effect" as the Wisconsin men scrambled up the hill.

The final struggle for McCook's left flank now began. An officer of the Ninth Tennessee put it well when he wrote that his men were "determined to die rather than to waver." Each company commander in that regiment was hit advancing through the cornfield and up the hill. The Ninth Tennessee and the Sixth Tennessee stopped, but the Twenty-seventh Tennessee made it across the Benton Road and its two fences, only about fifty yards from Starkweather's guns. This regiment was forced to withdraw but charged across the road a second time only to fall back again. Maney's attempt to outflank the Federal left also failed. The First Tennessee had completed its wide flanking march through the valley of Wilson's Creek and attacked up the northern slope of Starkweather's Hill, which was much steeper and higher than the eastern slope that Maney was trying to climb. It too was repelled by the fierce fire of the Union infantry.

This first Confederate effort to crack the anchor of McCook's left wing had failed, but Maney followed it up with a concentrated artillery barrage. Fresh batteries were brought up to the top of Parsons's Ridge and opened a heavy bombardment of Starkweather's position. That small eminence was

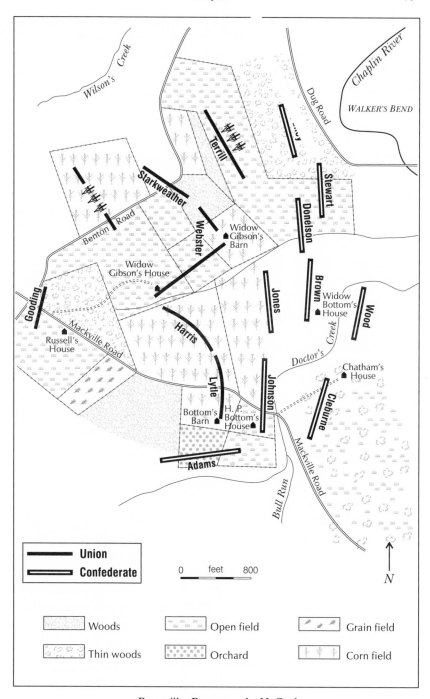

4. Perryville, Bragg attacks McCook

packed with guns and troops. An infantryman whose unit was ordered to support the Federal batteries found that the "ground was slippery with blood, many a poor dark-looking powder-begrimed artillery man was laying stretched out upon the ground around us, torn and mutilated." Terrill himself was hit by a shell as he walked up the rear slope of the hill. It literally tore his chest off, but he lived until early the next morning.

The Confederate fire so dominated the hill that Starkweather ordered his two batteries to retire. It was obvious that Maney's infantry was preparing for another attack, but the batteries would soon be shot to pieces. Starkweather could take heart in the stout support of the Twenty-fourth Illinois and the Seventy-ninth Pennsylvania on his right. These two regiments extended the line all the way to the branch valley and were holding Stewart's brigade at bay. A company of the Seventy-ninth Pennsylvania went into the battle with forty-eight men but had only eighteen left when the fighting ended. Starkweather's right flank was secure for now.

The second attack on Starkweather's Hill was more successful, mainly because of the First Tennessee, which was once again led by Colonel Feild. He rallied his men at the foot of the hill and, unsupported by artillery or other infantry, charged up the steep slope from the valley of Wilson's Creek. Feild wisely aimed his assault so he would reach the next rise of ground some three hundred yards to the rear of Starkweather's position, but the Federals had time to shift troops to this spot before he reached it. This was an open ridge covered with a cornfield. Starkweather had already begun to thin his force atop the hill by sending his artillery and some infantry units to the cornfield. The First Tennessee advanced up a gully separating the hill from the ridge and found itself caught between two enemy forces. Feild quickly decided to attack the guns and infantrymen on top of the ridge. His men took the Yankees by surprise and captured several guns, but they had to fight hard to defend their toehold on the ridge. It was a bitter struggle, "one of the bloodiest and fiercest contests of the war for the numbers engaged." Feild's men received fire from several Union regiments and faced a counterattack by the First Wisconsin Infantry. Hand-to-hand fighting broke out as a Wisconsin soldier seized and took away the Tennessee unit's flag. Finally, Feild ordered his men to withdraw. They left half their number on the ridge but had played a key role in forcing Starkweather from the hill. While they distracted the Federals' attention, Maney's line attacked the eastern side of the hill and took it. The Twenty-fourth Illinois and the Seventy-ninth Pennsylvania also were pushed back. McCook's left wing finally had to retreat, but it was not yet broken.

There still was plenty of tough fighting to do as the Confederates tried to consolidate their gains. The remnants of Terrill's brigade and Starkweather's battered units held firm on the ridge, taking shelter behind its crest, in the open cornfield. The regiments of Maney's brigade, supported by the Fourth Tennessee of Stewart's brigade, attacked to within fifty yards of the firing artillery, but the Confederates had fought themselves out. Heavy casualties and repeated assaults up and down the hills and ridges in the midafternoon sun had exhausted their strength and depleted their numbers. Maney lost 46 percent of his men in the process; Starkweather suffered 35 percent casualties. When it became obvious that there were to be no further attacks, Starkweather retired another 300 yards to a more compact defensive position only 250 yards from the junction of the Benton and Mackville Roads.

While Maney and Stewart were fighting their brigades to exhaustion on the Confederate right, other units carried the battle to McCook's center. Donelson opened the battle in this sector and was supported to his left by Col. Thomas Marshall Jones's Mississippi brigade. As these two units launched their attack, it seemed to Junius Gates of the Thirty-third Ohio as if "the whole country as far as we could see [was] covered with long heavy lines of infantry with arms at a trail comeing in on double quick." Donelson pushed aside two other regiments, his men shouting the Rebel yell, and then hit the Thirty-third Ohio head-on. They pushed up the long slope of the branch valley toward Widow Gibson's barn, which came to serve as a milepost of the surging battle on this part of the field. Just above the barn, Webster's brigade opened a galling fire on the yelling Rebels that greatly impressed Junius Gates: "Their heavy lines attacked us with the desperation of Demons. But our infantry & Artillery . . . were to the rebels what a great fire or an earthquake is to the inhabitants of a city it swallowed them up in death." Donelson's attack stalled and then was repulsed.

Jones's brigade went in to Donelson's left, on the south side of the branch valley, but it fared little better. His three regiments were supported by Capt. Charles L. Lumsden's Alabama Battery, which took post on the knoll west of Doctor's Creek and directly in front of the left wing of Harris's brigade. Jones's green troops met with a cascade of small arms and artillery fire as they traversed the rolling ground in front of Harris. They came close enough to the Federal position to fire three volleys before retiring.

The repulse of Jones led Hardee to throw more troops into the battle. Brig. Gen. John Calvin Brown's Florida, Mississippi, and Georgia regiments were ordered up. The brigade came under fire as it descended the eastern slope of Doctor's Creek valley. Brown was among the first to fall, hit in the thigh. Col. William Tucker of the Forty-first Mississippi, who was wounded in the arm, and then Col. William Miller of the First Florida took control. The brigade advanced just south of the knoll that Lumsden's artillery occupied, aiming at the center of Harris's line. It poured a hail of fire into the Federals above, dropping bluecoats at an alarming rate. "They fell on every side of me," wrote a man in the Thirty-eighth Indiana, "leaving me almost alone." Yet the Federal loss was not high enough to ensure Confederate success. Miller's men retreated. Most of his regiments had seen little fighting before this attack and now suffered terribly. The Third Florida, for example, took 247 men into the assault and came out with only 145 survivors.

The Confederate attack on McCook's right wing was pushed by Brig. Gen. Bushrod Johnson's Tennessee brigade. The Federals had a good position here. Lytle's brigade was about one hundred feet above the valley of Doctor's Creek. On his right, the Third Ohio anchored the extreme right wing of McCook's corps. Skirmishers from this regiment went forward to the valley floor and shielded themselves behind a stone fence that bordered the homestead of Henry P. Bottom, located only a few yards from the spot where the Mackville Road crossed the creek.

Johnson's four regiments descended the steep eastern slope of the valley and scrambled across the shallow stream. Here they came under fire from the Ohio skirmishers, and their attack slowed. Squire Bottom's yard became the focal point of a bitter struggle as Johnson's soldiers maneuvered and fought their way over it. They pushed the skirmish line from behind its protective fence and up the western slope of the valley. Rebel artillery and small arms fire punished the Unionists as they moved up the slope, and the main Federal line atop the crest also came under fire. As Col. John Beatty of the Third Ohio put it, "the air was filled with hissing balls, shells were exploding continuously and the noise of guns deafening."

A Rebel shell set fire to a log barn near the right wing of the Third Ohio. The hay inside fed the flames and the building blazed like a roman candle, sending clouds of black smoke into the air. The Ohioans tried to escape the choking fumes by closing the right wing in on the left, crunching the battle line, but allowing the regiment to keep up its fire. Not until they ran out of ammunition did the Ohioans pull out of line. They were replaced by Col. Curran Pope's Fifteenth Kentucky Infantry. The Third Ohio lost 175 of its 500 men.

Partly shielded by the pall of smoke from the barn, the Fifteenth Kentucky put up a spirited and tough fight. When the Confederates tried to out-flank it by crossing Doctor's Creek farther upstream, aiming their line of march directly toward the smoke, someone saw them in time to react. Just as the Rebels reached the barn, they were met with a devastating fire and had to scramble down the hill. Cutbert Slocomb's battery of the Washington Artillery moved up close enough to hit the Fifteenth Kentucky with shell fire from a distance of seven hundred yards. Despite all this, the Federals were able to pin down Johnson's men from their commanding position. They lost several color-bearers and saw their flag riddled, its staff shot in two, but they were holding firm.

In the long run, Colonel Pope could not prevent his right from being out-flanked. A new Confederate unit, Brig. Gen. Daniel W. Adams's Louisiana brigade, came from Patton Anderson's division along the Springfield Road to help. The men of Gilbert's Federal corps saw Adams move off toward the north but did nothing to stop him. They still were under orders not to bring on an engagement until the next day, and neither Gilbert nor Buell yet knew that a large battle was unfolding on the left. Sheridan chose not to violate these instructions because he remembered the reprimand Gilbert had given him early that morning for advancing so far toward Perryville. Thus Adams was able to come to the fighting along a line of march that allowed him to cross Doctor's Creek where the topography shielded him from the Ken-tuckians' view. The Louisiana brigade was in a position to hit the open flank of Pope's line.

More help now arrived for the Confederates. Hardee saw that Johnson's attack against Lytle's front had stalled and sent in Cleburne's brigade to sup-port him. Cleburne moved up with vigor and determination. He was hit in the ankle and his horse was killed under him as his Arkansas and Tennessee regiments splashed across Doctor's Creek, part of them north of the Mack-ville Road and the rest crossing the open yard in front of the Bottom house. They came up just in time, for Johnson's men were tired, disordered, and out of ammunition. Cleburne's fresh men replaced Johnson's, and, sup-ported by the fire of Slocomb's battery and the onrush of Adams's brigade, they moved on to engage Pope's command. The Fifteenth Kentucky fled in disorder, allowing Cleburne and Adams to join their flanks atop the hill just as Cleburne received his second flesh wound of the day.

Lytle scrambled to contain the damage. He formed a new line along the Mackville Road, facing south, but it was hopeless. Cleburne easily over-lapped this line and forced Lytle to retire even farther. As the Federals re-treated all the way back to the Russell house, Harris's brigade, which had repulsed Jones and Brown, saw its right flank exposed to Cleburne. McCook's right wing was not only retiring, it was crumpling in on itself, causing a great deal of confusion. A Rebel in Adams's brigade recalled: "They were in a drove like a flock of sheep and we could not miss such a dense crowd. The poor fellows fell like leaves from trees in the fall of the year." Lytle was one of those Federals who was struck down. Taken prisoner, he later died of his head injury. McCook tried to establish a defensive position around the Russell house, on the highest ground in the area. The confusion that naturally attended such a movement was intensified by the heavy artillery fire from the Rebel batteries on the east side of Doctor's Creek.

Ironically, the men of Gilbert's corps saw this terrible fighting but could do nothing to help. The III Corps contributed very little to the battle that day. Gilbert rigidly obeyed Buell's order not to engage in a general battle until October 9. Indeed, he spent much of the afternoon chatting with Buell at the Dorsey house, where the army commander was in a state of voluntary imprisonment because of his thigh injury. Buell had not yet received any information about McCook's battle and did not hear the sound of the guns, although the fighting took place only a mile or two from his headquarters. A strange atmospheric condition dampened the noise and it failed to carry in his direction. For some reason that has not been explained, McCook failed to send any message to his commander for at least two hours after the fighting began. If Buell had been willing to ride out, even if it was inside an ambulance, to inspect his army firsthand, or if Gilbert had been more energetic and imaginative, the Army of the Ohio might have taken advantage of its overwhelming numerical superiority to crush Bragg that afternoon.

The Confederate force along the Springfield Road, which was supposed to hold the Federals in place, did its job reasonably well. Patton Anderson had no real knowledge of his opponent's numbers. Neither did he know that Crittenden's corps was positioned only a short distance to the south. He sent a single brigade, Col. Samuel Powell's, to demonstrate westward. From their observation post on Peter's Hill, which was the target of Powell's advance, the Federals could see this brigade assemble a battle line south of the Springfield Road. They assumed it to be the vanguard of a much larger Confederate attack. For the time being, everyone on the front lines forgot the disturbing evidence that a major battle might be taking place to the north.

Only now, at about 4 P.M., did Buell finally get an inkling that a major battle was on. Confederate artillery along the Springfield Road opened fire. Buell had no difficulty hearing this sound at the Dorsey house, and both he and Gilbert were startled out of their lethargy. Just then, two messengers from McCook reached the house with full and accurate information of the fighting. Unfortunately, Buell found it difficult to believe them. He had not heard the sound of this battle and could not understand why McCook would wait two hours to tell him of his troubles. Nevertheless, he told Gilbert to send two brigades to help the I Corps and ordered Crittenden to advance and see what he could find on his front. Buell did not ride out to observe the situation for himself but remained at the Dorsey house, apparently assuming that McCook had exaggerated the scale of the fighting to the north.

Gilbert, however, did ride away from the house to see to his corps. He noticed Powell's brigade advancing from a point seven hundred yards south of the Springfield Road and, with Sheridan's help, began to position a large force to meet it. A gap of half a mile separated Gilbert's corps from Crittenden's left, but neither Powell nor Patton Anderson knew of it. The attack was heading for Peter's Hill into the teeth of an overwhelming Federal force, three Rebel regiments against fourteen Union regiments with artillery support from at least four Federal batteries.

Yet the Tennessee and Alabama regiments boldly marched on to a fence within easy musket range of their enemy and gamely traded volley after volley with them. The odds in this "unequal contest," as Hardee would later put it, were too great. Powell retired, having succeeded in focusing Gilbert's attention for at least a short time. His people had suffered terribly, leaving "dead and wounded . . . in swathes," according to a Federal soldier.

As soon as Powell was driven back, Sheridan and Gilbert began to turn their minds toward helping McCook. Federal batteries along the Springfield Road redirected their fire toward the Confederates on both sides of Doctor's Creek, and two brigades began to move northward to bolster McCook's crumbling line.

While these measures were being taken, Col. William P. Carlin's brigade followed up Powell's retreat. It had become painfully obvious to Patton Anderson by now that he was fighting a far larger force than he expected, and there was no recourse but to withdraw his entire division. Carlin's Illinois, Wisconsin, and Ohio regiments picked their way carefully, meeting only light resistance. Suddenly, at about 5 P.M., they ascended the last rise, only six hundred yards from Perryville, and saw the last Confederates moving through town and across the Chaplin River. An artillery duel developed with Confederate batteries on the east side of the stream. Even though Carlin was reinforced with additional brigades, there was too little daylight and he had no orders to push over the river. So the vanguard of Gilbert's corps established a defensive position here for the night.

While Carlin gave away the opportunity to press Bragg to the wall, the fighting continued its ferocious course on McCook's front, oblivious to developments elsewhere. The I Corps commander was outnumbered by Bragg and essentially on his own. Despite a veritable rain of shells falling about the Russell house, McCook managed to patch together a defensive position around the dwelling to oppose Adams and Cleburne. Units that had been driven from the Bottom house back up the Mackville Road and units from the center were repositioned on the high ground and began to slow the Confederate thrusts. Cleburne redirected his line of advance more to the north to hit Harris's brigade in flank. Harris's men, along with Webster's brigade, had served as the solid foundation of McCook's center, repelling repeated attacks by Jones, Brown, and Donelson all afternoon. Now Harris repositioned his regiments so as to deal with Cleburne. His entire brigade set up a new line at the southern edge of the branch valley, facing south, with an open cornfield stretching away from its front. When the Confederates drove across the cornfield they were riddled with fire, the field was littered with dead and wounded, and Cleburne's brigade was forced to retire.

Despite this stubborn resistance, the position of McCook's center was worsening. The retreat of the right wing had forced Harris and Webster to reconfigure their commands into a salient, making them vulnerable to a flank attack and enfilading fire. Harris and Webster ordered their men to pull back, and they did so with a great deal of confusion. The gunners of Harris's Nineteenth Indiana Battery, which had performed so well up to this point, ran up the hill in panic, leaving four of their cannon in place. The infantry regiments also retired with great difficulty, stumbling over equipment that had been piled behind their lines and trying to dodge the numerous artillery rounds that were peppering the area. Webster was killed in the middle of all this, further contributing to the chaos. Fortunately for the Federals, Cleburne was unable to continue his attacks because he ran out of ammunition. Other Confederates would have to capitalize on the tactical advantage presented to Bragg's army.

As McCook's center began to give way, Donelson's brigade launched its fourth attack of the day. Urged on by Polk, who saw a chance to crush the I Corps now that the right wing was withdrawing, Donelson pushed his tired and bloodied men into another move up this hotly contested slope. He was supported on the left by Brig. Gen. Sterling A. M. Wood's Alabama and Mississippi brigade. Wood had fresh men. He crossed Doctor's Creek and filled the gap between Cleburne and Donelson, aiming exactly at the retiring Union center. The stage was set for the final Confederate assault on

1. (*Above left*) Don Carlos Buell. Massachusetts Commandery, Military Order of the Loyal Legion and the U.S. Army Military History Institute.

2. (*Above right*) Edmund Kirby Smith. Gil Barrett Collection, U.S. Army Military History Institute.

3. (*Left*) Braxton Bragg. Massachusetts Commandery, Military Order of the Loyal Legion and the U.S. Army Military History Institute.

4. (*Opposite*) Earl Van Dorn. Alabama
Department of Archives and History,
Montgomery, Alabama.

5. (*Above left*) Sterling Price. Louisiana
Collection, Howard-Tilton Memorial
Library, Tulane University, New Orleans,
Louisiana.

6. (*Above right*) William S. Rosecrans.
Massachusetts Commandery, Military
Order of the Loyal Legion and the U.S.
Army Military History Institute.

7. Battery Robinett, Corinth. This photograph, taken shortly after the battle and published for the first time, offers a vivid view of how the parapet was constructed. The view is from inside the work looking toward the Confederate advance. The structure on the right apparently is the White House. Courtesy of Dr. William G. Jackson.

8. Confederate dead in front of Battery Robinett. This photograph is one of only two ever exposed of dead on a battlefield in the western theater of the Civil War. It shows the aftermath of John C. Moore's fierce attack on the battery. The Union soldiers standing on and near the battery give a perspective of its size. The view is toward the right wing of the work. Western Reserve Historical Society, Cleveland, Ohio.

9. (*Opposite top*) Another view of Battery Robinett. This photograph, also published here for the first time, was taken from the open rear of the battery toward Corinth. The right wing of the work ends on the left. The valley of Indian Creek lies between Robinett and the town; this is the area where many Confederates managed to penetrate the thin Union line and enter Corinth. The photograph was taken sometime between October 4, 1862, and the construction of a covered way connecting Robinett with Battery Williams to the south in the early months of 1863. Courtesy of Dr. William G. Jackson.

10. (*Opposite*) Another view of Confederate dead at Battery Robinett. This vivid photograph depicts Rebel dead in front of the right wing of Battery Robinett. Col. William P. Rogers of the Second Texas lies at the far left. Few other photographs of the dead reveal the stark brutality of war like this one. Compare this photograph to the previous view. You can fix the location of the photographer and the pile of corpses by noting the relative positions of the long warehouse in the distance, the white buildings on the left, and the small building between the battery and the town, partly hidden by the horse on the right of this view. Alabama Department of Archives and History, Montgomery, Alabama.

11. (Above) Col. Rogers' Grave. This photograph, never before published, was taken in April 1895 and depicts the grave of Col. William P. Rogers. He was buried where he fell, in front of the right wing of Battery Robinett. The site was made into a memorial park some twenty years after this view was taken. National Park Service, Shiloh National Military Park, Miscellaneous Archives.

12. Battery Robinett and the Covered Way. This view, also never before published, was taken in April 1895 from the same spot as number nine. It shows the covered way, constructed early in 1863, extending from the right flank of Battery Robinett. A similar parapet a few yards to the rear extended from the left wing so that men could walk along the high ridge between Robinett and Battery Williams while protected on both flanks. Corinth lies in the distance. National Park Service, Shiloh National Military Park, Miscellaneous Archives.

McCook, and it would come very close to shattering a third of the Union army.

The Federal position around the Russell house was a mess because of the crunching effect of many regiments retiring toward a single point. In contrast, the Confederate attack was well organized and eager to do some good. Because it was stronger, fresher, and had better ground to cover, Wood's brigade became the spearhead of this assault as it continued up the hill and smashed into the hastily assembled Union position. The Alabamans reached the crest and even crossed the Mackville Road just north of the Russell house, collapsing the Union line that had been tentatively holding there and scattering McCook's right wing over the countryside. If not for the reinforcements that Gilbert had sent, all of McCook's corps certainly would have fled just as ignominiously. But new blood had just arrived in the form of Col. Michael Gooding's brigade of Indiana and Illinois regiments. Most of these men were veterans of Pea Ridge, and they met Wood head-on. They were right in his front, having just taken position at the junction of the Mackville and Benton Roads, and opened a galling fire at short range. The two brigades became locked in a stand-up fight, the final fierce engagement of the battle, as the sun began to set. Wood was hit in the head and had to give up command to a succession of four officers, each of whom was hit. The fifth brigade commander survived long enough to finish the battle. Another Federal unit, Brig. Gen. James B. Steedman's brigade, arrived from Gilbert while the fighting was still going on and took position behind Gooding as his support.

The sun descended ever lower in the western sky, behind the Federals, as Wood's and Gooding's men continued to kill each other. Fortunately for the Confederate artillery, a full moon rose very early that evening and provided enough light for them to continue shelling the Union positions from their posts on the east side of Doctor's Creek. Into the darkening shadows marched the last Confederate brigade to go into action, across the creek and up the slope already soaked with blood. Brig. Gen. St. John Liddell's Arkansas regiments guided their advance by the sound of the firing between Wood and Gooding. Liddell hit the remnants of Rousseau's and Terrill's troops, causing the Federal left to retire farther westward, and then replaced Wood's brigade as the Alabama regiments broke off their stand and retreated. Wood's people had suffered astonishingly high casualties. The Thirty-third Alabama reportedly lost over four hundred of its five hundred men.

Liddell's fresh regiments turned the tide against Gooding's heroic defense. As his men were pushed back, Gooding himself was surrounded and captured. He had lost over 30 percent of his men but had performed magnificently, despite his confused retreat into the night. As a modern historian has written, "Truly Gooding's men had saved the day for McCook's I Corps." Steedman's brigade was 450 yards to the rear and waiting for the Rebels to strike, but it was not to be. Liddell wanted to push on, but it was already seven o'clock. Polk recognized that continuing the battle in the darkness would be as hazardous to the attacker as to the enemy, so he ordered Liddell to stay put. The battle of Perryville was over.

Without knowing it, Buell had nearly lost a third of his army. McCook's corps had been worsted while the other two corps had done virtually nothing to help. McCook took about 13,000 men into action and lost 4,211, about a third of them. One division leader and three brigade commanders had been put out of action, and eleven guns had been lost. If Bragg had been able to begin his attack a couple of hours earlier, he might have driven the corps completely from the area and shattered it even further.

Yet one must not overstate the possibility of a wider Confederate victory. Bragg took about 20,000 men into the battle and lost 3,396, about 20 percent of his force. Most of his brigades were as tired and depleted as McCook's, and he still had two more Federal corps to go through. During the night, McCook retired another mile west to the opposite side of Wilson's Creek and established a better position. The battlefield was flooded with moonlight which "lit up the ghastly faces of the dead," according to Col. J. Stoddard Johnston of Bragg's staff. The Confederates had done all they could that day and came closer to a tactical victory than could have been expected.

Buell, for his part, could not lay claim to any tactical brilliance on October 8. In fact, his performance had been dismal, bordering on the catastrophic. He had been a prisoner at his own headquarters, allowing his thigh injury to prevent him from personally inspecting his army. The battle was halfway over before he knew that it had begun. Even then, he barely sent enough help to McCook to save the I Corps. He had allowed his opponent to take the tactical initiative and paid a heavy price for it.

Buell's worst mistake was in assuming that the Confederates would allow him all the time needed to put everything in order before hitting them. This assumption set the stage for all the missed opportunities of the Army of the Ohio that day. Buell had an entire corps, one-third of his available force, in a position to enter Perryville at will and march into the rear of Bragg's attacking force. Crittenden did nothing all afternoon, knowing that Buell's orders were to postpone an attack until the next day but not aware of McCook's desperate struggle for survival. Bragg was barely aware of Crittenden's presence. He received a cryptic note from Wheeler at three o'clock that large Federal forces were out on the Lebanon Road, which prompted him to dispatch a brigade to the general area so that Patton Anderson could hold it in reserve. But neither Anderson nor Bragg knew exactly how many Unionists were to the south. Wheeler's aggressive skirmishing was enough to hold Crittenden's attention; a single brigade of cavalry blocked the movements of twenty-two thousand infantrymen. Buell did order the II Corps to move forward and develop whatever force lay before it, but this was done with such a lack of urgency that it produced nothing. Not even Thomas's presence made a difference in the operations of Crittenden's corps.

It had been a "Beautiful but bloody day," according to Mississippi artilleryman John Euclid Magee, characterized by clear weather, missed chances, and stunningly fierce fighting. It probably had been the best day of fighting done by Bragg's army in the entire war. But would it make any difference in the outcome of the campaign?

CHAPTER SIX

Good-bye, Kentucky

Most Federal soldiers went to sleep on the night of October 8 believing the battle would continue the next day. Farmhouses and churches all over the area were pressed into use as hospitals, creating horrible scenes that shocked many of the young men who had experienced their first engagement. A man in the Eighty-first Indiana saw a "yard full of wounded men lying in rows covered with blankets, shrieking with pain, some lying dead. Doctors were busy at work at tables amputating limbs. Close to the fence were piles of arms and legs. It was a ghastly sight. A short distance to the left was another house used for the same purpose. The yard was filled with dead laid in rows. Most of the dead were black in the face."

Michael Fitch, whose regiment halted at the Wilkerson house for a few minutes early in the night, saw "a sad spectacle and one never to be forgotten. There lay the sons of doting mothers, the brothers of orphaned sisters, the husbands of wives who would be left alone to buffet the world's cold neglect and fathers whose age had not prevented their responding to the call of country. A few hours before they were as strong and full of hope as those who marched by them. Now they lay hopeless and dying, far away from the loving eyes or soothing hands. Could those who looked upon them fail to think how narrowly they escaped from the same fate?"

Both commanders reassessed their plans that night. Buell still was not fully aware of the beating McCook had received. Several people had told him about it in detail, but he refused to take it in. Instead, his mind was focused on attacking first thing in the morning. Thus orders went out to Crittenden and Gilbert to prepare a dawn advance. McCook arrived at the Dorsey house later that night and finally convinced Buell that the I Corps had been badly damaged. McCook was instructed simply to hold the left wing the next morning while the other two corps attacked.

On the other side of the battlefield, Bragg held an officers' council at the Crawford house that night. It had finally become clear to him that Buell's entire army was just outside Perryville and that his battered force was grossly outnumbered. He learned of the approximate location of Crittenden's corps and knew it was in a position to cross the Chaplin River and move to cut off his retreat toward Cumberland Gap. Bragg seemed agitated, nervous, and frightened that night as he paced the floor. Although he did not precisely say so, he made up his mind to quit Kentucky altogether. The lack of support from the citizens and his exposed position far away from reinforcements and supplies from the South made him think that the prudent course was to retreat. Rather than announce this decision, Bragg simply told Hardee and Polk that he intended to retire to Harrodsburg and join Smith's army on October 9. The withdrawal from Perryville was to begin that night. Later, he dispatched orders to Smith to move his command along with Humphrey Marshall's force to Harrodsburg.

Smith had been occupied during the severe fight at Perryville with a futile attempt to crush Sill. The Federal general occupied Frankfort with his cavalry after Smith evacuated the capital, allowing Governor James Robinson to return to his office. Then Sill set out to the southwest to join Buell near Harrodsburg. Dumont's division marched east from Shelbyville to replace Sill at the state capital. Smith was kept informed of these movements by a newly raised brigade of Kentucky cavalry under Brig. Gen. Abraham Buford and saw a marvelous opportunity to cut off Sill. But by the time he formed his plan and sent out marching orders, it already was too late. The fast-moving Sill had to fight a skirmish with Allston's cavalry on October 8 and a tough fight with Brig. Gen. Jones Withers's division the next day, but he managed to avoid most of the Confederate army. After receiving Bragg's orders to concentrate at Harrodsburg, Smith called off the plan. Sill reached Perryville on October 11.

Bragg's divisions quietly and sullenly moved off the battlefield during the early morning hours of October 9, crossing the Chaplin River and camping on its east side. At dawn, bluecoated infantrymen began to walk gingerly onto the blood-soaked ground, awed by the sight of corpses stripped of their clothing by the retreating Rebels. Many dead had been piled "like cord wood and enclosed in pens made of fence rails" to protect them from prowling animals. The rolling hills and softly rounded ridges of this once pretty landscape had been transformed. "Unless something is done the country is uninhabitable," wrote a soldier in the Twenty-first Wisconsin. "It is surprising how quickly the dead become black, many lie with open eyes. One had died leaning against a tree as we passed stared at us with that wild ghastly look that you could scarcely summon courage to meet." The sights were overwhelming; bodies literally lay in rows where they fell, some of them dismembered or mutilated by shells, chests and stomachs lay open, and skulls were cracked in half. Animals and buzzards had already begun to eat some of the corpses while surgeons labored hour after hour to tend those who were still alive. "Never do I want to see another such sight," lamented an Indiana man. "It was awful to witness such a smell of human beings and the hogs eating the dead bodies."

As some Federals began the task of burying the dead, others moved on toward town. Both Crittenden and Gilbert advanced so slowly and cautiously that it was 10:30 before they entered Perryville. They found several hundred wounded Confederates and a number of frightened citizens but no army. Bragg had been given another opportunity to steal a march on his slow-moving opponent.

The Confederates marched toward Harrodsburg all morning. Most of Wheeler's cavalry moved out along the road to Danville, for Bragg believed Buell would march in that direction in an effort to cut him off from his line of retreat to the southeast. The infantry reached Harrodsburg by noon, but Bragg found no sign of Smith, whose divisions were still some distance away. Bragg's divisions moved out to the north and east of town to bivouac for the night.

Buell indeed wanted to cut off Bragg's retreat, but he did not know exactly where the Confederate army was located. His objective required a march to Danville, but a Confederate force at Harrodsburg could hit his exposed left flank as he did so. So Buell decided to advance along the roads leading to both towns.

The short-term objective of the Confederates was to safeguard the line to Cumberland Gap and shield the stockpile of supplies that had been gathered at Bryantsville and Camp Dick Robinson, some fifteen miles east and southeast of Harrodsburg. Those two places were on the east side of Dick's River, which formed a deep valley in the limestone as it flowed north to the Kentucky River. Bragg's retreat continued on October 10 as his men headed toward Bryantsville and Camp Dick Robinson.

Smith's men reached Harrodsburg that day several hours after Bragg evacuated the town. The two officers joined in a conference for the first time

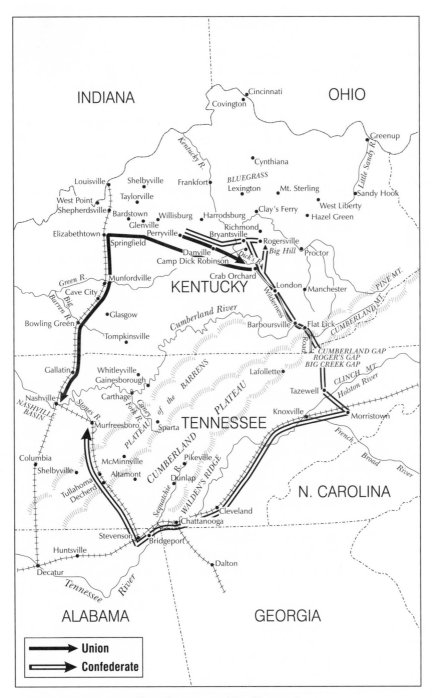

5. Bragg's retreat and Buell's pursuit

in several days to reconsider their position. It was now possible to join their strength, and the prospect elated Smith. His enthusiasm for a fight temporarily lifted Bragg's spirits. They agreed to take up a strong defensive position near town and wait for the Federal column that was reportedly coming on the Harrodsburg road. At this time, Bragg had received no confirmation from Wheeler that any Unionists were moving on the Danville road, so he felt it would be possible to fight another battle without endangering his line of retreat. But before he issued orders to bring Hardee and Polk back to Harrodsburg, word arrived from Wheeler that large Federal forces were on their way to Danville. All the fight went out of Bragg. He timidly resumed his original plan as Smith's men bivouacked in line of battle near Harrodsburg.

Bragg's composure was breaking down. He met with Smith from 3 A.M. until dawn, agonizing over his situation. While Smith continued to urge another battle before the Confederates gave up Kentucky, Bragg was convinced that course would result in the destruction of his army. Bragg finally talked Smith into retiring east of Dick's River. This was done by the evening of October 11, with Bragg placing his headquarters at Bryantsville. The two Confederate armies were finally joined, far too late in the campaign to do the cause much good. Wheeler's cavalry rode south to screen the approaches to Lancaster, which lay east of the river. If Buell moved on to that town he could outflank Bragg's left and be in a position to cut the line to Cumberland Gap.

A final, public decision to evacuate Kentucky was made by the Confederate high command on October 12. After arriving at Bryantsville, Bragg realized to his disappointment that the supply depots there and at Camp Dick Robinsin were nearly empty. Most of the stores Smith had accumulated at Lexington had been left there, while only four days' worth of food was positioned east of Dick's River. Ironically, the gathering of supplies had been a prime objective of the campaign, and a lack of food had played a pivotal role in the Munfordville incident. Now, because Bragg and Smith had delayed setting strategic plans to unite and fight for Kentucky and grossly overestimated the time Buell would waste before moving out from Louisville, nearly all of this rich prize was lost. Buell was coming on and so was wet, autumnal weather, which could hamper the Confederate retreat to Cumberland Gap. The final straw was a report that Van Dorn's army had been repulsed in a major battle at Corinth on October 3 and 4.

Bragg felt very alone. He told yet another conference of his officers that he was determined to save his army by immediately marching south. Only

Smith and Marshall, whose commands had joined the Confederate concentration at Bryantsville, objected to this course. Staff officer G. W. Brent spelled out Bragg's position: "We are outnumbered and far removed from our base. The enemy is near his, drawing ample supplies of men and subsistence. Kentucky has not furnished us men. The prime object of the invasion . . . has failed . . . nothing but retreat is left to us."

Bragg planned efficiently to achieve his goal. First, realizing that the small cavalry brigades had to play a vital role in delaying Buell, he named Wheeler commander of the mounted arm of both Smith's and his own army. Wheeler's job was to screen the route from Danville across Dick's River to Lancaster, for Buell could easily move in that direction to cut off the Confederates. The two infantry armies would separate again and retreat along different routes. The Army of the Mississippi would move by way of Lancaster to Crab Orchard, where it would enter the Wilderness Road. From there it could move quickly to Cumberland Gap. Smith would go to Lancaster too but then head east to the Richmond road, where he could retreat south by way of Big Hill and Barboursville and then follow Bragg on the Wilderness Road. Marshall's small command would move directly east toward Virginia.

Bragg had lost his last opportunity to save something from his Kentucky campaign. Once again the Confederate commander took counsel of his worst fears and opted for the safest course of action. His army had paid a dear price to reduce the fighting capacity of his enemy. An entire corps had been so heavily worsted on October 8 that Buell had to lead with his other two corps, leaving McCook behind at Perryville an extra day for rest and recuperation. Now, with Smith and Marshall by his side, Bragg had as many men as Buell in a strong defensive position east of Dick's River. There was no reason why he could not have offered battle here, risky as it would be to do so, but Bragg had lost the bold ambition that had characterized the inception of his campaign from Chattanooga. The vacillating Bragg that his subordinates would come to hate had appeared, and the optimistic, risk-taking man that surfaced ever so briefly was gone forever.

The forlorn Confederates began their retreat at dawn, October 13, with four days' worth of cooked rations in their haversacks. The wagon train went first, consisting of all manner of civilian conveyances that had been pressed into service. Included in the train, which stretched for twenty miles, were four hundred brand-new U.S. Army wagons captured at the battle of Richmond. A miscellaneous cargo of ammunition, guns, and foraged supplies filled the wagons while herds of hogs, horses, sheep, cattle, and mules moved alongside the road. Some material had to be left behind and was set afire by the retreating Rebels. Many soldiers helped themselves to what was left, sticking hams, sides of bacon, and bolts of fabric on their bayonets. Grease dripped on the men's faces as the sun beat down on this strange procession. Mixed with red clay dust, it made them look for all the world "like a bedraggled Mardi Gras" to a Louisiana soldier.

Buell crawled forward at a snail's pace on October 13. This, and effective screening by Wheeler's cavalry, allowed the Confederates to move easily beyond his reach. Bragg's two corps reached Crab Orchard that night and Mount Vernon by the evening of October 14. The next day, Bragg's men entered the western edge of the Appalachian Highlands, winding their way over the Rockcastle River. Their food began to give out, and prospects of finding any more along the line of march were few. To make matters worse, the local Unionists took potshots at the column, even throwing rocks at it from high points while shouting, "'Hurrah for the Union.'" When night put an end to this day's march, Bragg's divisions camped north of Wildcat Mountain, knowing that much more difficult terrain lay ahead.

Buell reached Crab Orchard that night and realized that Bragg had escaped. It would be foolish to pursue him into the mountains. The Confederate commander had wisely chosen a line of exit from Kentucky along a route that was not a natural line of advance for the Federals. The Wilderness Road was the best in this part of the state, but it was far rougher than any road in the Bluegrass. Buell could not hope to support his army along it, and even if he did pass the Cumberland Gap he would be isolated in the heart of eastern Tennessee. Since he had not been able to cut off and punish Bragg before the Confederates reached the western edge of the mountains, he now had to go west and restore his line of advance to Nashville on the system of railroads that penetrated Middle Tennessee. Thus Bragg was freed from the threat of an effective pursuit. All Buell intended was to send Crittenden's corps to follow up the Rebel column and make sure it was well on its way.

As Bragg continued along the Wilderness Road, Smith's army managed to retrace its invasion route into Kentucky in reverse. The route up Big Hill was a narrow dirt road that snaked up a sixteen-hundred-foot slope. Smith double teamed his wagons and assigned infantrymen to push, but his trains were only inching their way up. The delay grew so serious that Smith feared he would have to abandon dozens of his artillery and supply wagons. They were saved by, of all people, Cleburne. For some reason, he was separated from his brigade and was traveling with Smith rather than with Bragg. He took charge of this problem and ordered all of Heth's division to line both sides of the mountain road and shove. Any wagons that broke down were pushed over the side. By brute strength, the wagons and guns were forced up the hill on October 15. Smith had no trouble moving on to Barboursville and entering the Wilderness Road behind Bragg's army. Neither Smith nor Marshall was pursued by the Federals. The final skirmish between Crittenden's corps and Wheeler's cavalry took place north of London and ended the fighting associated with the Kentucky campaign.

Even though the Confederates were no longer being pursued, they suffered from a desperate shortage of food in the mountains. John E. Magee of Capt. Thomas J. Stanford's Mississippi battery complained despairingly of hunger. He had not received any rations from the commissary officer for three days, forcing him to eat parched corn until it too ran out. "The country is barren; nothing but rocks and hills, and nothing can be had. Some are very near starved now, and we do not know when we will get anything." His mess had hoarded quite a bit of flour and made biscuits that night. Other soldiers first begged, then offered to buy some of them. Magee felt insulted at the thought of selling food to a fellow soldier but offered to share what he had. "I never saw men so near starved in my life."

Bragg's men were very disgusted with their commander. Their long, hard marches from Chattanooga and their great sacrifice at Perryville had obviously gone for naught. As they trudged the rocky road up and down seemingly endless slopes and through narrow creek valleys, many a curse arose into the Appalachian air about "'Old Bragg.'"

The Army of the Mississippi crossed Cumberland Gap on October 20, a milepost on the line of march for these weary, hungry men. Smith's command passed through on October 22, followed by Wheeler's cavalrymen. From here the long gray columns marched south on the Kentucky Road through Tazewell and across Clinch Mountain at Bean Station. Here they entered the Tennessee River valley, stopping briefly at Morristown. The long, exasperating campaign was nearing its end as they marched an additional thirty miles west to Knoxville. From Chattanooga to Knoxville, Bragg's army had marched at least five hundred miles in two months. It had been the longest campaign of the entire war.

But this campaign had exacted a heavy price on the army and yielded very few gains. The men were used up, and many were badly in need of shoes and clothing. A member of the Seventeenth Tennessee was "nearly naked and starved" on the retreat. Another man and his regimental comrades received no food from the commissary for ten days. There was precious little along the line of march to make up for this starvation. Guards had to be posted to prevent soldiers from stealing corn meant to keep the horses and mules alive. "I never thought men could stand what they can until we took this march," marveled James Travis, while another Rebel reported to his sister that "I am still in a state of sanity but God only knows how long."

The campaign had been hard on Bragg's animals as well. Battery commander Henry Semple had been given only one dilapidated wagon at Bryantsville to haul forage for 125 horses and mules, and it broke down and dumped its load along the way. His draft animals went hungry for forty hours before Semple was able to beg some corn from his division quartermaster. The battery's horses and mules also suffered from the absence of any horseshoe nails during the entire campaign from Chattanooga to Knoxville, severely hampering their ability to pull cannon and caissons along the rocky roads of Appalachia. Only when he got to the Tennessee River valley did Semple get all the food for man and beast that he needed.

What had the survivors of Bragg's campaign accomplished? The verdict among the soldiers, the officers, even the Confederacy as a whole, was that they had achieved nothing. A false report of another battle, resulting in a brilliant Confederate victory, circulated on the home front by October 16. When everyone realized a day later that it was completely false, the dejection was palpable all across the South. There was no doubt by October 22 that Kentucky was lost, but the *Augusta Daily Constitutionalist* tried to put the best face on it. The editor argued that Bragg could still hold Tennessee. "There is no cause then, for despondency, or even for dissatisfaction." But Jeremy Gilmer saw it differently from Richmond: "Bragg's Campaign in Kentucky is pronouncd here a magnificent failure—big show and no result—a march up the hill and down again, and his troops, like the army in Flanders, I have no doubt 'swore terribly.'" Gilmer concluded that "the invasion policy has indeed proved a sad failure for us. Against our powerful enemy it will most likely always prove a failure."

The soldiers, who gave so much to the campaign, were absolutely disgusted. "We thought Kentucky was ours," wrote a Tennessee man, "alas, how soon the scene shifted." Many soldiers called Bragg a coward and cursed him for wasting their heavy sacrifice at Perryville.

Bragg would have to fight to keep his command, and he did a masterful job of it. He set out from Knoxville on October 31 for Richmond, obeying an order to confer personally with Davis. Bragg had the twin objectives of presenting a defense of his actions in Kentucky and of trying to secure Davis's approval for a new plan to move the army to Murfreesboro. He had already ordered Maj. Gen. John C. Breckinridge's division to occupy that town. This would allow the Confederates to secure a good portion of Middle Tennessee and offer a roadblock on the rail line penetrating the heart of the Confederacy. It also placed a sizable Confederate presence only thirty miles outside the state capital. Breckinridge reached Murfreesboro on October 28.

Bragg spent a week in the capital, engaging in day-long conferences with Davis and other officials. He soon won over the president. Davis had always believed that the only justification for invading Kentucky was to liberate oppressed Southerners. "Without the aid of Kentuckians," he assured Bragg, "we could not long occupy the state, and should have no sufficient motive for doing so." He approved of Bragg's plan to occupy Murfreesboro as a way to "recover from the depression produced by the failure in Ky," and he also decided to keep Bragg in command of the army. This was the first act of a long, frustrating drama that severely hindered the Confederate war effort in the West. Davis would consistently support his controversial general time and again. His well-meaning efforts to assuage the feelings of Bragg's critics did not compensate for the fact that, regardless of his own judgment about the wisdom of the retreat, it was folly to allow a man to command an army that did not trust or want him.

Bragg sent Polk to Richmond for a talk with the president after he returned to Knoxville. Polk had always benefited from his friendship with Davis. He was not a very good corps commander, but the president had no intention of sacking him to silence his criticism of Bragg. Like a mother caught between two beloved but incompatible children, Davis tried to talk some sense of professionalism into his friend. Polk also presented Bragg's case for unifying Smith's army with his own. This should have been done back in August. How differently the Kentucky campaign might have ended if it had been effected in time. Now Davis had no trouble with the plan. In fact, even before Polk arrived at Richmond, orders had been issued giving Bragg authority to take as many of Smith's troops as he needed.

Smith accepted this decision with sullen resignation. He had also traveled to Richmond after sending letters to Davis strongly proclaiming his desire never to have anything more to do with Bragg. Now he had no choice other than to resign his command. Smith presented his case in Richmond, frankly telling Davis what he thought of Bragg, but it did little good. He urged that Gen. Joseph E. Johnston be appointed to replace him as commander of the Army of the Mississippi, but Davis refused. The president did not get along well with Johnston, and he continued to insist that Bragg was "useful" for his administrative and organizational abilities if not for his battlefield performance. Smith returned to Knoxville having accomplished nothing toward correcting what he believed was a dangerous problem in the West.

The postmortem on Bragg's campaign was just as controversial as the reputation of the man who planned it. His critics have always judged the effort a failure, comparing its outcome to its high point, the occupation of central Kentucky by a powerful Confederate army. The true comparison should be between its outcome and its beginning. When Bragg took command of the Army of the Mississippi, it was wasting away in Tupelo, despondent and wracked with illness. Buell was on his way to consolidating Federal control of all Middle Tennessee and the important strategic point of Chattanooga, gateway to the Deep South. When the campaign ended, the Confederate army was securely in control of Chattanooga and was on its way to holding a good portion of Middle Tennessee. The Army of the Ohio had lost territory while the Confederates had reaffirmed control of an important part of their country. In evacuating central Kentucky, Bragg gave up something that he and the Confederacy never possessed.

Certainly, Bragg had conducted the middle portion of the campaign very badly. After a bold start with inadequate resources, he began to falter at Munfordville. But there were good reasons to act cautiously there in mid-September. The shortage of men and supplies loomed even larger in early October, when Buell's reinforced army advanced and Bragg's nerves grew more raw with each passing day. His vacillation after Perryville was embarrassing and counterproductive, he took greater counsel of his fears than of his ambition, and he was unable to take a great but calculated risk in opting for a second battle against Buell. Bragg had gotten as far as he did in Kentucky through marching rather than fighting, and he chose to rely on marching to relieve his army of a difficult situation. The Kentucky campaign set the precedent for Bragg's future career as a field commander. He would never again assume the strategic offensive even when it was justified, as after his one and only battlefield victory at Chickamauga. Instead, he continually fretted about the limits placed on his operations by the lack of men and supplies rather than ignoring those limits. Bragg could never again bring himself to strike out boldly to do great things. His vision would be forever narrowed by the failure of his Kentucky invasion.

Buell also came under a lot of criticism in the wake of this victorious but muddled campaign. The divided people of Kentucky were not greatly swayed one way or the other by the result of Buell's work. Newspaper correspondent Whitelaw Reid rode across the state at the end of the campaign to gauge public opinion and found no decisive shift. The hard core of pro-Union and pro-Confederate people remained committed to their respective causes, while the "shuffling middlemen" remained primarily concerned with protecting their property. Reid had an interesting conversation with a polite but frank gentleman on his way to sell mules to the Federal government. He told the newspaperman that the propertied people of Kentucky were willing to support whichever party could safeguard their financial interests. They had "found their safety with a tendency to incline gently to the party that had the nearest army." This large segment of the population failed to support Bragg because he could not demonstrate that his presence in the state was permanent. They were, as Reid put it, "pretty certain in the end to turn up enthusiastically with the winning party, no matter who may be the winners." But Reid concluded that this feeling was typical of any border territory in the midst of a civil war.

Despite saving Kentucky, Buell was targeted by many people who believed he had not done enough to punish the Confederates. Correspondent Reid talked with his soldiers at the end of the campaign and found them to be utterly disgusted. "No words were too harsh to apply to Buell," he wrote. "None differed from the general opinion about him. Major Generals and privates talked alike." Reid thought the dissatisfaction in the ranks threatened the men's combat effectiveness. "Never was a fine army less fit to fight through distrust of its commander." Treasury Secretary Salmon P. Chase became convinced that Buell's "heart is not in the war" because of his opposition to the emancipation policy. For whatever reason, Buell's halting movements infuriated the Northern public. An Indianapolis editor scored him, writing: "His career is a blank, without one vigorous action, one wise measure, one bold movement, or one patriotic impulse. The country has had just one year too much of him."

Buell's decision not to pursue Bragg into the mountains was badly received in Washington. Lincoln had long been desperate to move troops into eastern Tennessee to aid the Loyalists there, but all military commanders in the region agreed that it would be a mistake. There was little of strategic value, and the sparse population and crude roads made it impossible to subsist a large army. Buell was correct when he characterized the region as "almost a desert." "The limited supply of forage which the country affords is consumed by the enemy as he passes. . . . The enemy has been driven into the heart of this desert and must go on, for he cannot exist in it. For the same reason we cannot pursue in it with any hope of overtaking him, for while he is moving back on his supplies and as he goes consuming what the country affords, we must bring ours forward. There is but one road and that a bad one. The route abounds in difficult defiles, in which a small force can retard the progress of a large one for a considerable time and in that time the enemy could gain material advantage in a move upon other points." Buell concluded it would be "useless and inexpedient" to continue moving southeast. Instead, he proposed to move west and south to Nashville.

This cogent argument fell on deaf ears in Washington. Lincoln and Halleck did not understand the logistical and topographical difficulties in this area any better than they had understood the problems of Buell's advance toward Chattanooga the previous summer. "The capture of East Tennessee should be the main object of your campaign," wrote Halleck as he relayed the president's views. "Your army can live there if the enemy's can. You must in a great measure live upon the country . . . I am directed by the President to say to you that your army must enter East Tennessee this fall and that it ought to move there while the roads are passable. Once between the enemy and Nashville there will be no serious difficulty in reopening your communications with that place. He does not understand why we cannot march as the enemy marches, live as he lives and fight as he fights, unless we admit the inferiority of our troops and of our generals."

Lincoln and Halleck had obviously learned nothing about the practical difficulties of moving large forces into Appalachia. They were responding to a political need, not a military necessity. In some ways the individual soldier of Bragg's army was indeed a better fighter than his counterpart in Buell's army, at least in October 1862. Even Rousseau commented in his official report of Perryville, "Individually they were superior to our soldiers. . . . They loved strife and fighting for its own sake." But that disparity would even out as the Federals gained more battle experience. As for living like the Rebels lived while campaigning in the mountains, few Unionists would have preferred to share artilleryman Magee's food on the spartan retreat out of Kentucky. Bragg was able to operate in Appalachia only because he was moving swiftly through an inhospitable portion of it toward a secure base of supplies.

Buell refused to be goaded into making an unwise move. On October 22, he informed Halleck that the Army of the Ohio would begin moving to Bowling Green, the first leg in its reconcentration at Nashville. Lincoln could not stop this movement, but he could punish Buell. He relieved him of command on October 24 and replaced him with Maj. Gen. William Starke Rosecrans. The idea of a change had been brewing for months, at least since the administration became dissatisfied with Buell's slow progress in front of Chattanooga. Buell, who possessed a frustrating mixture of good and debilitating features as a commander, had ample opportunities to prove himself and failed. He had held command of the army for nearly a year. Although it was a large, impressive force, it had surprisingly little combat experience, was saddled with several mediocre corps leaders, and had adopted the slow, uncertain characteristics of its commander.

The change was widely applauded across the North. The *Indianapolis Daily Journal* rejoiced at the news, noting that "the infinite feebleness of Don Carlos Buell will . . . be spared us. His army will now have only the enemy to fight." Secretary Chase hoped that the prospect of an aggressive new commander would have a positive political effect on the country. The fall elections had gone badly for the administration, with many critics of Lincoln's radical policies winning seats in several state legislatures and a rising chorus of Copperhead sentiment filling the newspapers. Chase hoped the replacement of Buell and the relief of George McClellan as head of the Army of the Potomac a few days later would signal the "inauguration of activity in all directions" that would "paralyze the opponents & invigorate the friends of the Administration." Chase was a sponsor of Rosecrans. He urged the ambitious Ohio general to learn from Buell's mistakes and make action his hallmark. "Boldness wins where caution loses," he reminded Rosecrans.

Lincoln hoped the new leader would infuse energy into the army. Rosecrans was fresh from an impressive victory over Van Dorn at Corinth, certainly an up-and-coming commander who seemed a natural choice. Born in Ohio and graduating from West Point in 1842, he had resigned from the army eleven years later because of a nervous breakdown. This may have indicated a constitutional weakness in Rosecrans, but so far it had not manifested itself in his war record. In some ways, Old Rosey, as he came to be known, was a remarkable man. He had rejected his parents' Methodist faith while at West Point and became a fervent, almost fanatical, Roman Catholic. In a country that was dominated by Protestantism, this was bucking the trend. Rosecrans demonstrated grit and determination when he was severely burned while conducting an experiment to produce a better burning oil and had to recuperate in bed for eighteen months.

Extremely hardworking, fond of staying up into the early morning hours discussing religion with his staff members, Rosecrans had an enviable record thus far in the war. He had played a key role in the Rich Mountain campaign, which was a turning point in the Federal conquest of mountainous western Virginia in 1861. Finding his way to northern Mississippi under

Grant, Rosecrans successfully repelled Van Dorn's brutal assaults against Corinth in early October. Now he had a chance to demonstrate his abilities in a wider context, as an independent commander in what was arguably the most decisive theater of operations in the war.

Rosecrans took charge on October 30, joining the Army of the Ohio at Bowling Green that day. He immediately began to change things, beginning with the name of the army. It was now designated the XIV Army Corps and divided into three wings. This was an odd, unfelicitous name that proved to be only temporary. On January 9, 1863, after he had fought his first battle with it, Rosecrans permanently changed the name to the Army of the Cumberland.

The new commander found that the rail line from Bowling Green to Nashville was all but inoperable because Confederate guerrillas and cavalry raids had torn up most of the track. Yet in early November, reports came into Rosecrans's headquarters that Nashville was threatened. The reports were exaggerated. Actually only some cavalry units were hovering around the city, but Rosecrans could not know that. The reports probably were blown out of proportion by the arrival of Breckinridge's division at Murfreesboro as well. Rosecrans got his army moving by foot, pushing his divisions hard to save the capital. McCook's Right Wing set out on November 4 and reached Nashville on November 7. The other two wings followed. Rosecrans himself reached Nashville on November 13. His fears had been unnecessary, for the city was ably defended by a garrison under Brig. Gen. James Negley.

Rosecrans was premature in his belief that the Confederates were concentrating near Nashville, but that would soon change. With Davis's approval of his plan, Bragg began moving his own and Smith's armies to Murfreesboro in the first week of November. The divisions entrained at Knoxville for Chattanooga and rode the cars to Murfreesboro. The poor condition of the rail lines delayed the movement so that it was not until November 26 that Bragg established his headquarters in the town. It had been the final phase of a very long trip. From Tupelo to Murfreesboro, Bragg's army had traveled a total of fourteen hundred miles, five hundred of them by foot. There had been no other campaign in the war quite like the invasion of Kentucky.

CHAPTER SEVEN

The Road to Iuka

While Bragg reached for great things in Kentucky, the forces he left behind in northern Mississippi to support his invasion had enormous difficulties to overcome. They suffered from many of the same problems that bedeviled Bragg: a divided command structure and far too few troops and resources to accomplish their ambitious strategic goals. Even defining what those goals ought to be was a problem because the Mississippi forces were led by two demanding and headstrong generals. A great deal of extended, long-range debate took place between Bragg, Maj. Gen. Earl Van Dorn, and Maj. Gen. Sterling Price as to where these men ought to march and what they should attack.

Both Van Dorn and Price were men with strong personalities. Born of Mississippi planter aristrocrats, Van Dorn was forty-two years old. He had graduated fifty-second in a class of fifty-six at West Point and had seen extensive frontier service in Texas before the war. He was a dashing, romantic figure who burned for military fame and was reckless with troops. Like Beauregard, Van Dorn was given to grandiose strategic plans that were designed to win the war in one fell stroke, while at the same time he blithely ignored the fact that he seldom had the resources of manpower, wagons, or food to accomplish them. His generalship was amply evident in the Pea Ridge campaign of March 1862, when he rushed his Army of the West into an offensive against a Union force that had invaded Arkansas. He failed to acquaint himself with its personnel, capabilities, or logistical limitations. That campaign ended disastrously and led to Federal domination of the Trans-Mississippi for the remainder of the war. Van Dorn's Army of the West was then transferred to Mississippi, where it took part in the evacuation of Corinth.

Sterling Price was, in his own way, just as quixotic. Born in Virginia, he moved to Missouri at age twenty-two and made the state his lifelong home. He served in the Missouri legislature and the United States Congress, was a brigadier general of volunteers in the Mexican War, and became governor of Missouri in the 1850s. He was appointed commander of the Missouri State Guard at the outbreak of the war. Saving Missouri from the Northerners was his obsession. Price was an amateur general who captured his men's loyalty with his passionate zeal for his adopted state and his fatherly care for their welfare. Price fought at Wilson's Creek, Lexington, and Pea Ridge, leading his ragtag Missouri forces with an aggressive spirit. The State Guard was disbanded and many of its members transferred to the Confederate service after Pea Ridge. Price accepted a commission in the Rebel army, but he never lost his fierce desire to save Missouri even after his men were transferred to Mississippi with Van Dorn's army.

Indeed, Price nearly went back across the river not long after he arrived in Mississippi. When the Confederate army reached Tupelo in June, Price traveled to Richmond to confer with Davis. It was a stormy meeting. Price demanded authority to go west and resurrect a Confederate force in the Trans-Mississippi, taking his Missouri troops with him. This idea did not fit well with Confederate strategy, which now was based on the assumption that the Trans-Mississippi was lost and that scarce manpower was needed much more desperately east of the river. Price and Davis exchanged heated words and the Missourian stormed out of the room. Yet Price later cooled down and accepted his situation. When he returned to Tupelo on July 2, Bragg told him he also could not spare him or his men, but he was willing to give him command of the Army of the West. Van Dorn had already been dispatched to Vicksburg to relieve Maj. Gen. Mansfield Lovell and hold that important river city against a Federal expedition under Comm. David G. Farragut that had ascended the Mississippi. Van Dorn was given command of the District of Mississippi while Price took charge of the District of the Tennessee with instructions to hold the line of the Mobile and Ohio Railroad and to prevent Grant from sending help to Buell.

Price had two infantry divisions in the Army of the West at Tupelo, with a battery assigned to each of his brigades and a small force of cavalry. Brig. Gen. Henry Little and Brig. Gen. Dabney H. Maury led the divisions. Price had only a thousand mounted men; his other cavalry units had already been dismounted in Arkansas and were now serving as infantry. Col. Frank C. Armstrong led the mounted arm. With the addition of some reinforcements, Price's strength rose to fifteen thousand—all the Confederates had in place to defend the northern half of the state after Bragg's Army of the Mississippi left for Chattanooga. But they were excellent troops, nearly all of them veterans of Wilson's Creek and Pea Ridge. At least for the time being, Van Dorn's relatively untried soldiers in and around Vicksburg, roughly fifteen thousand in number, were unavailable either to defend northern Mississippi or to help Bragg's impending invasion of Kentucky.

The Federal position in the area was much stronger, even though the huge force that had captured Corinth had dispersed. Three armies had lumbered to victory under Halleck in May. Maj. Gen. Ulysses S. Grant's Army of the Tennessee had been temporarily commanded by George H. Thomas while Grant was made Halleck's second in command. Thomas's division of Buell's army had also been temporarily transferred to the Army of the Tennessee. Buell's Army of the Ohio was the second major field army of Halleck's force, and Maj. Gen. John Pope's Army of the Mississippi was the third. Halleck left in July to assume his post as general in chief of all Union armies, leaving Grant in charge of western Tennessee and northern Mississippi. Thomas also took his division back to Buell's army when it left the Corinth area to attempt the capture of Chattanooga.

Grant was left with roughly sixty thousand men to consolidate the Federal hold on this region, and he spread them out in garrisons located at the major towns and cities. Maj. Gen. William T. Sherman moved to Memphis and began to construct fortifications there in July. The division of Brig. Gen. Stephen A. Hurlbut also was stationed at Memphis, while the remaining troops stayed at Corinth. These dispositions were not permanent. Grant intended to move his men around at will to meet any emergencies and to fortify other towns in the area so they could be held by small garrisons. He did not have to contend with a divided command structure, having been given all the authority needed to deal with the Confederate presence in northern Mississippi. Grant would demonstrate that he was just as reliable on the strategic defensive as he was aggressive on the offensive. His troops were veterans of Fort Donelson, Shiloh, and Island No. 10, and they too could be relied on in any engagement.

Grant also received a new subordinate. William S. Rosecrans arrived at Corinth in June to replace John Pope, who had been transferred to the Virginia theater of operations. Rosecrans deserved this promotion to command of a major army in an active sector because of his sterling performance in the capture of western Virginia the previous year. He found northern Mississippi and western Tennessee to be a vastly different country than southern Appalachia. Indeed, it was very different than the landscape to be found in the Upper South as a whole. Unlike the territory that Bragg had to contend with, the region along the border between Mississippi and Tennessee was undistinguished; no high mountain ranges divided it into segments or impeded the movement of troops. Most of the country drained westward toward the Mississippi River. Just east of Corinth, however, a low ridge marked the beginning of the area that drained eastward toward the Tennessee.

The land was low and mostly level. It was covered with thick scrub timber and heavy underbrush, "dotted with clearings, farms, settlements, and little villages," as Rosecrans would later put it. The landscape was characterized by "low, rolling, oak ridges of dilluvial clays, with intervening crooked drainages traversing narrow, bushy, and sometimes swampy, bottoms. The streams are sluggish and not easily fordable, on account of their mirey beds and steep, muddy, clay banks." Water was very scarce here in the summer. Federal troops at Corinth had to dig wells as deep as three hundred feet and use ropes and pulleys to get the water out. "These matters are of controlling importance in moving and handling troops in that region," Rosecrans concluded. "Men and animals need hard ground to move on, and must have drinking water."

The area was only recently settled. Except for Memphis, most of the towns that would figure in the coming campaign were built in the 1850s to take advantage of the boom caused by the construction of railroads in the region. Corinth was at the intersection of two major trunk lines, the Mobile and Ohio Railroad that ran north to south and the Memphis and Charleston Railroad that ran west to east. There was a rawness about the landscape and a newness about the settlements that contrasted sharply with the more heavily developed portions of the Upper South which had seen so much military activity in the early part of the war.

Price found a nearly overwhelming obstacle in the Federal dispositions that were designed to hold this region. With only fifteen thousand men, he could never hope to take any of the strongly garrisoned towns. He needed Van Dorn's cooperation to have even a chance of recapturing Corinth or any other point. But he could bypass the Federal strongholds and maneuver his army into Middle Tennessee to help Bragg. Or he could so threaten Corinth and other points as to prevent Grant from sending troops to help Buell. He could even attack Corinth after reinforcements were sent off to the Army of the Ohio and have a real chance of taking the town if its garrison was substantially reduced. Price was left with several choices, but none of them held any assurance of success.

To his credit, Price tried very hard to do all he could. He planned to move

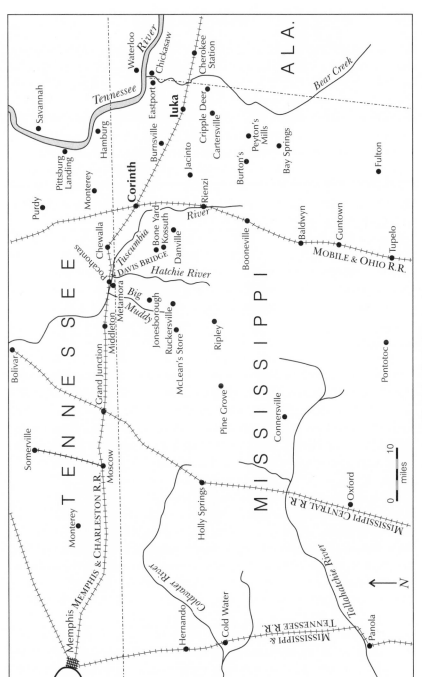

6. The Iuka-Corinth campaigns

toward Corinth immediately after Bragg's army left Tupelo. It appeared that thirty thousand Federals held the town, and he was convinced that he needed Van Dorn's help. Price dispatched a message to his colleague on July 31, telling him he could be ready "in a few days" to move northward. Price even offered to place himself and his army under Van Dorn's command as an added incentive to the Mississippi general.

But Van Dorn was far too busy to respond. He had rebuffed Farragut at Vicksburg by July 27 and then immediately ordered John C. Breckinridge to attack Baton Rouge with his division and retake the state capital of Louisiana. Rather than cooperate with Price's plan, Van Dorn actually responded with a request for a brigade of troops from Price's already small army.

Price's chief of staff, Maj. Thomas L. Snead, had already been warned that this would happen. Just before Bragg's army left Tupelo, Hardee had told him that Van Dorn would try to drain men southward to further his own strategic schemes. Hardee had already heard of Van Dorn's attempt to retake Baton Rouge and told Snead "to say to General Price, for me, that the success of General Bragg's movement into Tennessee and Kentucky depends greatly upon his (Price's) ability to keep Grant from reenforcing Buell, and consequently that General Bragg would sternly disapprove the sending of any reenforcements whatever to Van Dorn. Say to General Price that I know that General Bragg expects him to keep his men well in hand, and ready to move northward at a moment's notice."

At the same time, Price received a telegram from Bragg on August 2 informing him that Federal troops were on their way from Grant to Buell and that "the road was open for him into West Tennessee." This was, of course, an exaggeration. Some brigades were on their way northward, but Federal strength in northern Mississippi and western Tennessee was so great that formidable obstacles still stood in Price's way. This message pointed to another, more ominous, turn of events. Grant had already begun to demonstrate the ease with which he could transfer troops to Buell, given Northern control of the region. This important element of Confederate strategy had already failed.

Given all this information, Price quickly sided with Bragg and informed Van Dorn that he could not send any troops south to help Breckinridge. He also told him that the Federals were sending men off from Corinth and that the garrison there would soon be at a minimum. "We should be quick to take advantage of this, for he will soon begin to get in reenforcements under the late call for volunteers. . . . Every consideration makes it important that I shall move forward without a day's unnecessary delay. I earnestly desire your cooperation in such a movement, and will, as I have before said, gladly place my army and myself under your command in that contingency."

To better his chances with Van Dorn, Price sent a copy of his message to Bragg, who approved it. Bragg also ordered Van Dorn to cooperate with Price. Believing that all was well, Price began to work diligently to prepare his men for an active campaign. He acquired better arms for many infantry units, adequate transportation for supplies, and money from the Confederate treasury to pay the troops. On September 4, Price eagerly informed Van Dorn that he was ready to move with some thirteen thousand infantrymen, reduced by various causes from his previous strength of fifteen thousand. But Price made up for that by increasing his cavalry strength from one thousand to three thousand. He also had eight hundred artillerymen and enough food and transportation for at least seven days of campaigning.

While he was marshaling his strength, Price sent Armstrong and 1,600 cavalrymen on a raid into western Tennessee to gather information. Armstrong reached Holly Springs on August 26 and was joined there by another 1,100 cavalrymen under Col. William H. Jackson. The combined force rode to Bolivar, Tennessee, some thirty miles northwest of Corinth, where it fought a skirmish with Federal troops. Moving on, the Rebels temporarily cut the railroad between Bolivar and Jackson. They fought another small skirmish on their way back to Tupelo, losing a total of 115 men but gathering little accurate intelligence about the fluid enemy movements.

On August 5, Breckinridge attacked Baton Rouge and was bloodily repulsed. Van Dorn toyed with the idea of ordering him to try again for some time after, but he accepted the inevitable by August 24. Breckinridge's division retreated to Jackson, Mississippi, and Van Dorn informed Price that he was finally ready to cooperate with him. He needed two weeks to get ready and suggested that their combined forces invade western Tennessee, enter western Kentucky, and capture Paducah on the southern bank of the Ohio River. It was typical of Van Dorn to rebound from a failed offensive with dreams of an even more ambitious attack. The combined armies might have a chance of retaking Corinth, if luck was on their side, but the idea that they could water their horses in the Ohio River was characteristic of the absurd strategic concepts that enchanted generals like Van Dorn.

It was good for the Confederate cause that he was at least ready to work with Price, even though his strategic dreams had to be toned down to reality, for the success of Bragg's campaign into Tennessee was beginning to intensify the need for better cooperation in Mississippi. Bragg had bombarded Price with several messages, sent from August 4 through the 27, urging the Missourian to move into Tennessee before it was too late. Or, at least, Price should move more quickly and aggressively toward Grant's strongholds. On September 1, Bragg informed Price that Buell was giving up his advanced positions on and near the Cumberland Plateau and retreating to Nashville. He urged him to keep a wary eye on Rosecrans at Corinth and to pursue him if he went off to Middle Tennessee. This brought the situation to a crisis point. Price sent a telegram the next day to Van Dorn saying that he could no longer wait; he had to move in three days. Urging his army on as fast as possible, Price moved his headquarters from Tupelo to Guntown. Seven, rather than three, days after sending Van Dorn his urgent message, Price again told him that he regretted not being able to wait any longer. The army moved out of Guntown on September 11, having waited longer than it should have for Van Dorn to rush to its side.

Marching by way of Bay Springs, Price's men moved swiftly toward Iuka. Located some twenty-three miles east of Corinth, it was the easternmost point on the Memphis and Charleston Railroad that was occupied by Federal troops. Price hoped either to find it evacuated or to be able to swallow up any small garrison there. This would put him in an excellent position to determine whether Rosecrans had left Corinth for Tennessee. If so, he could also move into the state to chase him and support Bragg. If not, he could easily redirect his march westward and attack Corinth. It would all depend on what he found when he got to Iuka.

The first Confederates to reach the small railroad town were Armstrong's cavalry, who rode in on September 13. The Federals actually were caught in the middle of evacuating Iuka. With the dispatch of the last of Grant's reinforcements for Buell, Rosecrans began to draw troops from Iuka and other points east of Corinth back to that important railroad junction. This withdrawal began on September 7 but was conducted at a leisurely pace. Now only Col. Robert C. Murphy's Eighth Wisconsin was there, preparing to escort the remaining stores back to Corinth.

The first contact between Armstrong's cavalry and Murphy's infantry startled both forces. A brief skirmish ensued before the Rebels retreated from town and raced back to report to Price. Murphy reacted with just as many jitters. The Confederates had already cut the railroad and telegraph lines between Iuka and Burnsville, eight miles to the west, so Murphy decided to run as fast as possible. He abandoned all the supplies in Iuka and reached Corinth without trouble. A repetition of such an act at Holly Springs the following December, during Grant's first campaign against Vicksburg, would lead to Murphy's dismissal from the service.

Price reacted energetically to Armstrong's report. He urged his army on a night march through the bright moonlight that bathed the rugged landscape of the region. The infantry entered Iuka at 9 A.M. on September 14 and found an empty but well-supplied encampment. Tents were still standing, and commissary stores and a fully loaded train of railroad cars offered temptations that were too much for Price's hungry men to bear. Everyone feasted on "good coffee, biscuit and ham." It was estimated that as much as $200,000 dollars worth of Union supplies fell into their hands. New guns, ammunition, tea, sugar, whiskey, beer, wines, canned fruit, fish, cheese, and condensed milk lay all about. "The ragged and half-starved soldiers feasted on 'good things' for once, and had more than a 'square meal,'" wrote a member of the Third Louisiana. "The soldiers feasted, frolicked and were in high glee and spirits at the sudden change in their condition."

Price was able to clarify a great deal about the strategic picture after he reached Iuka, but he did not know that Van Dorn was scheming behind his back to control his movements even before their armies joined. When Van Dorn learned that Price was off to Iuka, he informed him that he would be ready to move out from his base at Holly Springs on September 12 but that his army needed some of Price's guns, wagons, and men. Price fired back a message making it very clear that he could not spare anything or anyone. In a huff, Van Dorn complained to Jefferson Davis and asked him to order Price to do so, telling the president that all would be well if he could only have official authority to command all troops in Mississippi. Without knowing of Bragg's earlier instructions for Van Dorn to cooperate with Price, Davis telegraphed on September 11 giving the Mississippi general what he wanted. None of this was yet known by Price.

Indeed, the Missourian had too much on his mind to deal with this order even if he had known of it. He discovered accurate information about Federal positions after reaching Iuka. Rosecrans had indeed sent a large force to Buell, three divisions, but he still had two divisions at Corinth. Major Snead recalled years later, "After some hesitation [Price] felt that it was his duty not to go to Nashville, but to look after Rosecrans and what was left of his army." So he telegraphed to Van Dorn that he "would turn back" and cooperate with him in an attack on Corinth.

Immediately after this telegram was sent, another message arrived from Bragg "urging him to hasten to Nashville." The poor man felt nearly hamstrung by indecision. He was the victim of a schizophrenic command structure, fretting over how best to deploy his small army to help the cause in a theater of operations that he would have preferred to leave altogether in fa-

vor of his beloved Missouri. Snead would later point out that, with the benefit of hindsight, it was easy to see that the best course would have been to
heed Bragg's advice. Price still had a few days of grace after reaching Iuka
before Federal troop movements could threaten him. If he could have
crossed Bear Creek six miles to the east, he would have easily made it into
Tennessee before the Unionists could catch him. Grant might have been
forced to detach even more troops from the garrisons to help Buell, and then
Van Dorn might have had an opportunity to capture Corinth.

Price was still uncertain what course to take when, on September 17, he
wired Van Dorn, "I cannot remain inactive any longer, and must move either with you against Rosecrans or toward Kentucky." Then, a member of
Van Dorn's staff arrived at Iuka on the night of September 18. He had word
of Davis's order for Van Dorn to take command of Price's army and was
there to plan a junction of the two forces. Suddenly, the responsibility for
deciding the strategic course of the war in northern Mississippi was taken
out of Price's hands. He immediately issued orders for his men to spend the
next day preparing for a march southward.

Just as Price hit Iuka in the middle of a Federal withdrawal, Grant would
attack Price as he was preparing to evacuate it. The Confederates had already stayed at Iuka as long as they possibly could without presenting a
tempting target. Grant was maneuvering two columns of troops toward the
town with the intention of catching Price in a pincers and defeating him in
detail while Van Dorn was still many miles away. The plan came very close
to achieving a dramatic success that could have altered the strategic picture
in northern Mississippi at one stroke.

Grant had been keeping a close eye on Rebel movements for many weeks
and had been repositioning his forces to compensate for the transfer of men
to Buell. If the Confederates had attacked his positions in early September,
"they would have found us very weak in consequence of the heavy drafts
that had been made on me at other points for troops, and the extended line I
was then protecting. Now however it is different. I am concentrated and
strong."

Two divisions of Rosecrans's Army of the Mississippi were still at Corinth, which also was Grant's headquarters. Rosecrans had added strength as
well. Brig. Gen. Thomas A. Davies's division and two brigades of Brig.
Gen. John McArthur's division of the Army of the Tennessee were there.
Maj. Gen. Edward O. C. Ord's division of the Army of the Tennessee was at
Jackson, fifty-five miles north of Corinth. The remaining brigade of McArthur's division was with Ord as well. As finally settled, Grant's command

was divided into three wings. Sherman led the right, headquartered at Memphis. Ord led the center, and Rosecrans commanded the left. Troops at all stations were expected to be ready to march at quick notice to any other town that was threatened. Grant put together an excellent defensive strategy that combined even distribution of his men, timely information of his enemy's movements, and flexibility in meeting any advance.

Price's move to Iuka brought Grant's defensive scheme into play. He decided to move against him early on the morning of September 15. Signs had been indicating a Confederate offensive for many days before, all of them pointing to an effort to send Price's army into Tennessee. Word also arrived that Breckinridge and Van Dorn intended to support this movement by advancing toward the garrisons in northern Mississippi. It was even possible that Price could be coordinating his movements with Breckinridge and Van Dorn so as to hit Corinth from two directions. "If I can I will attack Price before he crosses Bear Creek," Grant informed Halleck. "If he can be beaten there it will prevent either the design to go north or to unite forces and an attack here." To support this attempt, Grant moved Hurlbut's division from Memphis to Bolivar, and Ord's men marched from Jackson to Corinth.

Grant was confident that Van Dorn could not reach Corinth in less than four days, so he left only enough troops there to prevent it from falling to an advanced cavalry force. All other men were moved eastward to join in the attack on Price. "This I regarded as eminently my duty," Grant later reported. His aggressive plan was supported by everyone. Rosecrans had earlier warned Grant to be ready to move quickly against Price and take advantage of any opportunity to hit him. Grant "had better watch the Old Woodpecker or he would get away from" him. Halleck also approved of Grant's movements, telegraphing on September 17 that a "junction of Price and Bragg in Tennessee would be most disastrous. They should be fought while separate."

Just as Bragg's campaign into Kentucky was reaching its climax at Munfordville, the campaign in northern Mississippi was taking shape. Grant ordered his troops into motion on September 16. Rosecrans was to march south of the railroad from Corinth, leaving a small number of troops at Rienzi and Jacinto to warn of a possible attack on Corinth from the south. He was then to march on Iuka and attack it from the south. Ord was to march from Corinth to Burnsville, where he would move north of the railroad and attack Iuka from the opposite direction. Ord's original three thousand men were reinforced by rail with an additional thirty-five hundred troops from Brig. Gen. Leonard F. Ross's command at Bolivar. Farther west, Hurlbut was ordered to demonstrate toward Grand Junction in order to intercept any possible move by Van Dorn to bypass Corinth and rampage through the thinly defended center of Grant's defenses.

The planned offensive had every prospect of success, especially if Price could be caught napping. Rosecrans led the largest of the two columns, nearly nine thousand men. To lessen the possibility of a Rebel escape from the pincers, Rosecrans suggested that his column march along two routes. Brig. Gen. Charles S. Hamilton's division moved along the Fulton and Eastport road while Brig. Gen. David S. Stanley's division marched on the Jacinto road.

Grant estimated that Price had as many as fifteen thousand troops, so there was a possibility that the Rebels could attack one of his columns in detail with a substantial superiority of numbers. The landscape also made it more likely that this could happen. Grant found that the countryside between Corinth and Iuka was so rough and covered with thickets that it was impossible for cavalry or infantry to move off the roads and travel through fields or woods if they should need to do so. There were few secondary roads as well, which meant that the only routes over which large numbers of men could easily move were the roads his two columns were already taking. Grant conducted an examination of the countryside after the campaign and found that "troops moving in separate columns by the routes suggested could not support each other until they arrived near Iuka." Without fully knowing it, he was sending his men on a converging movement through territory that prevented them from quickly communicating with each other. It was a risky maneuver that promised either rich rewards or dismal failure.

Fortunately for the Federals, Price was completely unaware of the threat to his army, and the two columns were able to move undetected. Ord reached a point within six miles of Iuka by September 18 and captured a few Rebel pickets. Grant moved his headquarters to Burnsville so he could be closer to the action while trying to coordinate the movements of both wings. Since Ord was poised to strike the town the next day, Grant urged Rosecrans to hurry on and support him, reminding his subordinate that both columns might have to fall back to Corinth as early as September 20 to defend it against an attack by Van Dorn. Time was in short supply.

But Rosecrans's progress over the rugged landscape had been slow. He had a much longer route to march than did Ord and nearly a third more troops to handle as well. He dispatched a message to Grant, which arrived late on the night of September 18, telling him that he was at least twenty miles short of Iuka and would start his men at 4:30 the next morning. "Shall not therefore be in before one or two O'Clock. But when we come in will endeavor to do it strongly." Disappointed and a bit concerned that his carefully laid plan to catch Price might unravel, Grant reluctantly ordered Ord not to attack on September 19 until he heard the sound of Rosecrans's guns.

Hamilton's division led Rosecrans's advance that day, with Col. John B. Sanborn's brigade in the lead. The Federals began to encounter Confederate pickets when they were five miles from Iuka. A few companies of infantry were deployed to deal with them and preceded the rest of the advance. With no good maps of the area and the choking vegetation lining the narrow road, nobody knew exactly what lay ahead. Hamilton was told by his guide at 4 P.M. that Iuka lay only two miles away. He stopped his men for rest, allowing them to drop in the road. The head of Sanborn's brigade "had just finished ascending a long hill, from the top of which the ground sloped in undulations toward the front." The skirmishers, who had stayed very close to the column during the march, could see that sizable numbers of Confederates were assembled in the woods only "a few hundred yards ahead."

These Rebels were Brig. Gen. Louis Hébert's Second Brigade of Little's First Division, 1,774 men from Arkansas, Louisiana, Texas, and Mississippi, supported by two Missouri batteries. Price had ordered them sent into the woods when he realized that the Yankees were about to reach Iuka. There had been reports of pickets being driven in on the Jacinto road ever since 2 P.M., which came as a surprise to the Confederate commander. He had been busy all day supervising the preparations for a march to join Van Dorn's army and had all his available men positioned to block Ord's advance into town. The appearance of Rosecrans's column caused him to begin shifting troops southward to keep open his line of retreat. First, he ordered Little to send Hébert. The men marched nearly three miles, much of the way at double-quick. Price personally escorted the troops part of the way and oversaw their assembly in the woods astride the road. Hébert was ready to go into action just east of the hill where Sanborn stopped.

The battlefield was small and rugged. Rosecrans described it as an awful place to fight. "The ground is horrid—unknown to us, and no room for development." Narrow dirt roads snaked through a brush-entangled landscape. An open field stretched northward from the road atop the hill but not south or west. Thus the Federal column had great difficulty coming up and deploying a battle line, particularly artillery. The road crossed the hill at its highest point, with a wide and deep hollow draining northward and separating the east edge of the hill from a spur to the west. Behind, or to the west, of the spur was a more shallow and narrow hollow. To the south of the road was a large wooded area. As a member of the Third Louisiana put it, "The whole country was a succession of valleys and hills of irregular formation, covered by a dense undergrowth." Only the field to the north of the road was free of underbrush, but it was studded with blackjack trees. The eastern slope of the hill, up which Hébert's men would have to attack, was gentle.

The sudden meeting of Rosecrans and Hébert prompted both sides into action. Hamilton ordered the skirmishers to push forward and determine exactly how many Rebels confronted his division. He even rode behind them to see for himself. They advanced about four hundred yards before running into Hébert's command, and Hamilton hurriedly rode back to the column to begin deploying his men for battle. As the skirmishers retired, Sanborn's men were ordered on their feet and off the road. The first artillery in line, Lieut. Cyrus Sears's Eleventh Ohio Battery, was positioned in and just off the road, facing northeast. His gunners had to break off and tramp down a lot of hazel brush to clear an open area for the cannon. The Fifth Iowa deployed to its right, south of the road, and other infantry regiments extended the line northward. Sanborn was forced to deploy his battle line at a diagonal, his right wing extended into the thick woods south of the road and his left angled back to the northwest, behind the second, smaller hollow, and in the western edge of the blackjack field. As this was being done, Hébert's artillery opened on the Federals with canister. Even though it was at the extreme range for that projectile, canister shot sailed over and around the Ohio battery, causing one gunner to liken it to "being in a violent hail storm." Hamilton was very pleased with himself for establishing his position just as the firing began. "An earlier attack would have enveloped the head of the column," he later wrote, "and brought a disastrous rout." He believed his quick action had saved Rosecrans's command.

The Unionists had little time to catch their breath, for Hébert ordered his men to attack. The artillery ceased firing as soon as the gray infantry stepped out of the woods. Initially there were only three infantry regiments in line. The two forces quickly closed with each other and opened a raging musketry fire at close range. Sears's battery was the most exposed, and it also was in the center of the developing battle so it became the focal point of Confederate efforts. Immediately, both gunners and draft animals began to fall, but the Ohioans manfully stood by their posts and fired canister as fast as they could.

By this time, Price had brought help for Hébert. Col. John D. Martin's Fourth Brigade of Little's division came up with 1,405 men, mostly from

Mississippi. Martin put two of his regiments on Hébert's right and two on his left and pushed on to meet the lengthening Federal line. Brig. Gen. Jeremiah C. Sullivan's brigade of Hamilton's division now was up and formed a second line behind Sanborn. Sullivan deployed one regiment to Sanborn's right flank and one to his left, while keeping his other two in Sanborn's rear. Still, the Confederate battle line extended farther than the Federals', and Hamilton desperately looked for help. "Stanley's division seemed long in coming up," he later wrote. Hamilton sent a total of four aides to find Rosecrans and tell him to rush Stanley up at all speed. Meanwhile, the firing intensified. "The dead lay in lines along the regiments, while some of our troops gave signs of yielding."

Because of his head start in shifting units from Ord's front to meet Rosecrans, Price seemed to be winning the race to apply pressure and take the little hill. He ordered up the rest of Little's division, Col. Elijah Gates's First Brigade and Brig. Gen. Martin E. Green's Third Brigade. Little started them on their way and then rode ahead to confer with Price. He found the army leader sitting on his horse, talking with Hébert and another officer in the road at the edge of the battlefield. Price held his arm at a jaunty angle; his back was to the Federal lines, and Little faced him. A stray minié ball passed under Price's arm and hit Little square in the forehead. "He threw up his arms, the reins dropping to the horse's neck, and the brave man, limp and lifeless, fell into the arms of a comrade." He was taken to his headquarters, a small house in the middle of Iuka. A distraught Price now had to carry on the attack without his most trusted subordinate.

Just then the fight for the hill was reaching a crisis point. The pressure and intensity of the firing were awesome. Will Tunnard, the historian of the Third Louisiana, wrote that "the smoke enveloped both lines, so that they became invisible to each other. The lines could be distinguished only by the flash of the guns. The evening was one of those damp, dull, cloudy ones, which caused the smoke to settle down about as high as a man's head."

Sears's battery suffered horribly from the concentrated fire on its position. As the range closed, his gunners fired double canister. The infantry to his left began to give way when Col. Norman Eddy was wounded and his Forty-eighth Indiana panicked and fell back into the woods. The Fifth Iowa to its right was "cut to pieces." Lieut. Henry M. Neil later wrote that the battery "found itself facing in three directions and battling with masses on three fronts. It had a rear but no flanks. The guns were being worked with greater speed and smaller crews. Cannoneers were falling. Other cannoneers cooly took their places and performed double duty. Drivers left their dead horses and took the places of dead or wounded comrades, only to be struck down in turn." Only three of the battery's eighty horses survived the battle; of the ninety-seven men who manned it, eighteen were killed, thirty-nine were wounded, and two were missing.

This most intense phase of the battle of Iuka lasted about thirty minutes before the Federal first line gave way, including what was left of Sears's battery. As Hébert's men topped the hill, they in turn were exposed to more intense fire and took even heavier casualties. To make matters worse, some friendly units to their rear nervously fired into them as well, killing and wounding several of their comrades. But the Federal line quickly stabilized. Stanley's division came up just as Hamilton's men fell back. The forward line stopped just behind the top of the hill and stood its ground again. Sears's guns fell into Confederate hands, but several of the gunners escaped. Only three of Stanley's regiments managed to get into line in time to fire their weapons near the end of the battle, replacing some of Hamilton's regiments. The rest of Little's division, Gates's and Green's brigades, also arrived too late to take much part in the fighting or to follow up Hébert's and Martin's success, for darkness put an end to further advances.

The battle was over by 6 P.M., having lasted two hours. The men of both sides lay where they were for the night. Hébert and Martin together had 3,179 men engaged in the fighting and lost 525. Hébert bore the brunt of the losses, suffering 408 casualties out of 1,774 men. His fierce attack had saved Price's army from being caught in Grant's pincers, but tactically it was not a great victory. The Confederates had pushed Rosecrans's column back only about six hundred yards and were still greatly outnumbered. Sanborn and Sullivan had 2,800 men engaged and lost 790 of them. For Rosecrans, it had been an embarrassing end to a very successful strategic movement.

The other arm of the Union pincers movement never got into action. All day long, Grant and Ord had been waiting to hear Rosecrans's guns. Ord consulted with Grant, and both agreed that it might be some time before any attack took place. Ord was told to advance slowly toward town and drive in enemy pickets but to make no attack unless he could hear firing to the south. Even when the fighting broke out, neither Grant nor Ord heard anything. The afternoon turned into dusk with no apparent developments.

That night Grant received a dispatch from Rosecrans, written at 12:40 P.M. from Barnett's, eight miles from Iuka. Rosecrans informed his superior that the head of his column had made it this far. The courier had been forced to take a circuitous route to reach Burnsville. Grant later explained the delay: "Owing to the density of the forests and difficulty of passing the small streams and bottoms, all communications between General Rosecrans and myself had to pass far around—near to Jacinto—even after he had got on the road heading north" to Iuka. The night passed, and still neither Grant nor Ord heard anything of the battle.

At 8:35 on the morning of September 20, Grant finally received a dispatch from Rosecrans mentioning the engagement. It had been written at 10:30 the previous evening, several hours after the fighting ended, and it relayed a short report of the action. Rosecrans urged Grant to push Ord forward and attack on the twentieth. He wasted no time in putting the suggestion into effect, but the most opportune moment for action had long passed. A freak atmospheric condition, similar to the one that had deadened the sound of fighting at Perryville, robbed Grant of the opportunity to bring his pincers movement home. The wind blew steadily from the north all day, and the damp air smothered the sounds of fighting so that they carried no more than a couple of miles from the battlefield. No one with Ord's command had heard a single gun fired during the two hours of fierce fighting only six miles away.

Would there be any Confederate force left in Iuka for Ord to attack? Price's initial plan was to hold his ground and renew the assault on Rosecrans early on the twentieth. He repositioned all of Maury's division to the south for that purpose, keeping only the cavalry under Armstrong and Col. Wirt Adams in front of Ord to hold him in place. Price had to deal with Rosecrans first, for this Yankee column threatened to cut off all roads leading to Van Dorn. Price, desperately tired, went to sleep sometime past midnight after leaving all necessary instructions for the night's work with Snead.

The battlefield was a sad and dangerous place that night. When the fighting had ended, the Confederate line was a bit over two hundred yards beyond the position of Sears's battery. Green's brigade was ordered to relieve Hébert at the front shortly after dark. His men met Hébert's victorious troops rolling the captured guns down the road to the rear as they marched forward.

The moon was nearly full that night and the sky was clear, the late summer air hot and humid. Corpses and abandoned equipment lay all over the hill, gleaming in the pale moonlight. "Everything bore evidence of the bloody character of the action," wrote Ephraim McDowell Anderson of Green's brigade. "The dead were so thick, that one could very readily have stepped about upon them, and the bushes were so lopped and twisted to-

gether—so tangled up and broken down in every conceivable manner, that
the desperate nature of the struggle was unmistakable."

The scene was particularly awe-inspiring at the battery position, where
dead horses littered the ground. A caisson had overturned backward, pinning a still living horse to the earth. It rested upside down on the poor ani-
mal, which struggled vainly for hours to free itself. Badly wounded soldiers
still lay on the ground as well. Anderson found it all nearly too much to bear.
"I have been on many battle-fields, but never witnessed so small a space
comprise as many dead as were lying immediately around this battery." Anderson felt "many conflicting emotions" that night. He had already been
hardened by exposure to battle at Wilson's Creek and Pea Ridge and had always viewed the dead as a natural result of combat. But "the groans and
cries of the wounded for help and water, the floundering of crippled horses
in harness, and the calls of the infirmary corps, as it passed to and fro with
litters in search of and bearing off the wounded, rendered the scene very
gloomy, sad and impressive."

To make matters worse, the armies were so close to each other that it was
dangerous to move. The picket lines were a mere seventy yards apart, and
one could see quite a distance in the moonlight. A man in Anderson's company lit a match for his pipe and was immediately fired at by several Federals, the flashes of their guns could plainly be seen only a short distance
away. Several soldiers from both armies accidentally wandered into enemy
lines and were taken prisoner.

For some people, the saddest episode of this long night was the burial of
Henry Little. Next to Price, he was the most loved and respected general
among the Missourians. A member of Little's staff consulted Price before
the army leader went to sleep to find out what should be done with his remains. Price was inconsolable. He could only cry out, "My Little, my Little; I've lost my Little." Snead gently broached the question to Price and
came back with instructions to bury the body at Iuka that night. A grave was
dug in the garden behind Little's headquarters house and a party of seven
friends and admirers attended the burial. Each one carried a candle, and the
chaplain of the First Missouri Brigade officiated. It was midnight when the
touching little ceremony ended. A "plain piece of pine board" was erected
as a marker with the simple inscription "General Henry Little." The body
was removed by Little's family for reburial in Baltimore after the war.

Plans for resuming the engagement at dawn were upset when, after midnight, subordinate commanders began to filter in to Price's headquarters
with gloomy reports. Hébert arrived and expressed his opinion that the

members of his brigade had become badly demoralized by the heavy losses they suffered and by the news of Little's death. He was uncertain how well they could perform the next day. Maury arrived too and gave his opinion that Ord would certainly not remain idle while Price concentrated on Rosecrans, and the cavalry was obviously not strong enough to hold him back. Adams also arrived and supported Maury's views.

Snead wondered what to do. Price was already fast asleep, having left instructions not to disturb him until it was time to prepare for the dawn attack. He was sleeping at the house of a friend in town so that Snead would not wake him while working. Then a member of Van Dorn's staff arrived with messages and Snead finally decided to wake his commander. It already was nearly dawn, and the army leader assumed he was being roused to renew the engagement. Much to his surprise and disgust, Price was faced instead with an overwhelming chorus advising retreat. He tried to talk his subordinates out of their fears but failed, so he reluctantly gave the order to withdraw. Fortunately, the trains were already packed from the previous day's work, so the infantry began pulling out of town at dawn. Maury's division, assigned to cover the rear, left Iuka at 8 A.M., the cavalry following behind.

Thus, when Ord pushed ahead that morning, he found nothing to impede his way into town. Grant received word from one of his staff officers that Price had gone, and he immediately rode into Iuka to discover that the Confederates had withdrawn by the Fulton road. This came as a great surprise, for Grant assumed Rosecrans was covering all roads leading south. The truth was that Rosecrans had done virtually nothing all night and still was not ready to push forward rapidly or to pursue the Rebels. If that road had been blocked, then the only route for Price would have been east, across Bear Creek. It would have been immensely more difficult but not impossible for him to escape by that route.

The Federals sent only a small cavalry force along the Fulton road to locate Price; no pursuit was attempted. The infantry wandered through Iuka or examined the battleground of the day before. Hamilton's men, in particular, were just as amazed by the scene on the hill as Anderson had been the night before. Sears's guns had been left near the eastern base of the hill by the retreating Confederates. All of them were spiked, and the carriages were cut and splintered. Parties covered the small battleground to retrieve the remaining wounded and to bury the dead. They found eighteen dead horses in one tangled mass at the battery site. Three teams had tried to escape the day before but had "swung together and died together." Henry Neil's horse had been hit with seven balls but survived and was taken by one of Rosecrans's staff officers before Neil managed to retrieve it. The horse died two years after the war while standing in its stall because a ball it had carried since September 19 finally "worked its way into an artery." Neil was ordered by Rosecrans to rebuild the battery because Sears had been put out of action by a wound the day before. He set to work unspiking the tubes, repairing the carriages, and finding more harness and horses. The battery was back in action within two weeks.

The campaign thus far had resulted in little good for the Confederate cause. Because he was torn between two contrary commanders, Price's indecision and delays had failed to prevent the transfer of reinforcements to Buell. He had also failed to add to Bragg's strength or to take advantage of any opening in Grant's defenses caused by the reduction of Union strength in western Tennessee. He nearly suffered a devastating defeat at Iuka; if Grant's pincers movement had worked a little more efficiently, Price's army might have been neutralized. Price's men had once again shown their mettle by saving his reputation in a short but terrible little battle. It was an infantry fight, primarily. Only one battery on each side managed to play a role in the fighting, and one of them was nearly annihilated by musketry.

The only thing settled by September 20 was that a union of Price and Van Dorn was inevitable. There no longer was any chance of moving into Tennessee to help Bragg, who by now was moving northward from Munfordville. After Iuka, Van Dorn would provide the decisive leadership that Price had failed to show, but it would be a very rash leadership. Van Dorn had already demonstrated in the Pea Ridge campaign that he could ride off into uncertain and ill-prepared offensives. Although the two armies would make a formidable force, they had to contend with equally strong opponents. The strategic course of the war in northern Mississippi would shift into high gear as bloody October dawned on the horizon.

CHAPTER EIGHT

Corinth

Price, his mind made up to join Van Dorn, pulled away from Iuka with speed and efficiency. He gained a head start of at least three hours on the Federals, and with the narrow roads providing the only route through this rough country, that was all he needed to escape Grant's two columns. Federal cavalry caught up with his rear guard on the afternoon of September 20 but were repulsed by waiting Confederates who lay in ambush. No further tailing of the column was attempted. Price reached Baldwin on September 23 and was firmly astride the railroad leading to Holly Springs.

Van Dorn received word from Price two days later that his army was safe and ready to join his own. The two had earlier discussed the possibility of a rendezvous at Ripley, twenty-five miles west of the railroad and twenty miles south of the state line. The two armies finally came together there on September 28.

Without hesitating, Van Dorn proposed an offensive for the newly enlarged force he now commanded. He informed his subordinates that he wanted to move boldly into Union-held Tennessee to the west of Corinth. This would allow him a shorter line of advance that took his army between the detachments of Federal troops at Corinth and Bolivar. Van Dorn also was motivated by a realization that his goal was not only to aid Bragg's invasion of Kentucky by causing as much havoc as possible in western Tennessee but also to liberate as much Southern territory as he could. He even hoped to regain control of the Mississippi River. A less ambitious but more practical plan was to advance west of Corinth to deceive the Federals and then to turn quickly eastward and attack the railroad town. Recapturing Corinth would allow the Rebels to reclaim the railroad junction and possibly its attendant lines north and south. Mansfield Lovell liked the idea of attacking Corinth, but Price strongly opposed it. One of his staff officers, Maj. John Tyler Jr., reported that his commander objected to the attack because Federal troops could converge on the army from Memphis and Bolivar and hit its rear. Price suggested that the campaign be postponed until the exchanged prisoners who had been captured at Island No. 10 and Fort Donelson could be reclaimed and brought into the field. This was typical of Price's uncertain grasp of strategy. While he tended to be aggressive on the battlefield, he could never quite get the hang of planning larger movements. Price had earlier proposed an attack on Corinth, but now, when the opportunity presented itself, he hesitated. By the time those exchanged prisoners could be repatriated and distributed to their regiments, Bragg's campaign in Kentucky and any chance that Corinth might be vulnerable would slip away.

Van Dorn ignored Price's opinion. "I determined to attempt Corinth," he wrote a few weeks later. "I had a reasonable hope of success." Of course, striking one of the most heavily defended posts in the region, even with his bigger army, would be hazardous. It would have to be done decisively and result in an immediate success. Any delay would give other Federal garrisons time to concentrate and cut him off from his base to the south. His newly christened Army of West Tennessee was barely large enough to attempt this campaign. It was divided into three divisions with Price commanding two of them, Hébert's First Division, consisting of four brigades, and Maury's Second Division, with three brigades. Lovell commanded the First Division of the District of the Mississippi, consisting of three infantry brigades and a brigade of cavalry. Van Dorn had twenty-two thousand men. The garrison of Corinth alone would be equal in strength to his entire army.

Brimming with confidence, Van Dorn issued orders for an advance on the night of September 29. The next morning, the men left Ripley on the thirty-mile march toward Pocahontas, located only five miles north of the state line and about twenty miles northwest of Corinth. Van Dorn intended to threaten Bolivar and then to turn "suddenly across the Hatchie and Tuscumbia" to attack Corinth "without hesitation." As he had during the Pea Ridge campaign, Van Dorn moved quickly and decisively. He was forced to rebuild Davis's Bridge over the Hatchie River, burned by watchful Federals. Located near Matamoras only two miles south of Pocahontas, this bridge would have to be guarded as Van Dorn's only certain crossing of the river in case he needed to retreat. After crossing on the morning of October 2, he left behind Adams's brigade of cavalry to guard it. The rest of the army moved an additional four miles eastward and crossed the Tuscumbia River. Van Dorn positioned his wagon train on the west bank of the river so it would not be in the way when he hit Corinth. Lieut. Col. E. R. Hawkins's First Texas Legion of infantry and a battery of artillery were left behind to guard the train and support Adams if he was harassed by any force coming from Bolivar. Van Dorn reached Chewalla, Tennessee, ten miles northwest of Corinth, before nightfall on October 2. Lovell's advance was near Cane Creek, only five miles from downtown Corinth, and Price's command was stretched along the road as far back as the Tuscumbia River. All the men bivouacked along the road, tired from the hard marching in the hot and humid weather that was settling over the region. But Van Dorn was optimistic. His rapid marching had brought his daring plan to the verge of success.

The Federals would be ready for him, for they had been readjusting their defensive posture ever since the battle of Iuka. That town was evacuated and troops were started toward other points. Rosecrans and Grant were back at Corinth by September 26, the day that Rosecrans received his promotion to major general of volunteers. Grant also decided to move his headquarters to Jackson that day. He slightly reorganized his District of West Tennessee, with Sherman commanding 6,880 men at Memphis, Ord commanding 17,884 troops at Jackson and Bolivar, and Rosecrans leading 23,077 men at Corinth. A fourth division in the district encompased 6,243 men scattered in various posts across western Kentucky and northwestern Tennessee.

Rosecrans worked hard to ready his command for an attack because the union of Price and Van Dorn seemed to make one inevitable. Corinth was "mainly on low, flat ground . . . flanked by low, rolling ridges, except the cleared patches, covered with oaks and undergrowth for miles in all directions," he recalled. It had three lines of defenses. The old Confederate Line, built by Beauregard in April and May, was two and a half miles from town on the east, north, and northwest. It had deteriorated, and Rosecrans called it merely "a line of light defensive works." In June, Halleck ordered the construction of a second, shorter line one and a half miles from town. It was a series of detached artillery emplacements stretching from the Memphis and Charleston Railroad to the south so as to cover the quadrant left exposed by the Confederate Line. There were not enough men to hold Halleck's line after Buell left Corinth for Chattanooga. Rosecrans also pointed out to Grant that it was too far out of town to protect the stores there. When Grant asked him what should be done, Rosecrans suggested "a line of light works" on the outskirts of town, anchored on College Hill to the southwest. Grant, Rosecrans, and Capt. Frederick E. Prime scouted the ground, and work was started.

The College Hill line, which would serve as Corinth's main defense, was mostly finished by early October. It consisted of a series of five batteries for artillery covering the south and west sides of town. Rosecrans ordered connecting infantry trenches and abatis to augment the batteries. Most of the labor was performed by squads of freed blacks headed by officers detailed either from the infantry regiments or the Quartermaster Department. Rosecrans wanted the line extended to the north too, but only Battery Powell was finished by the time of the battle. An abatis made "from the scattering trees" fronted the College Hill line, but only the batteries on the left had connecting infantry trenches when Van Dorn attacked. The northeast and southeast approaches to Corinth remained open except for the degraded Confederate Line.

The forces available to Rosecrans totaled twenty thousand men divided into four infantry divisions and one cavalry division. The Army of the Mississippi contained Stanley's division, Hamilton's division, and Col. John K. Mizner's cavalry division. The Army of West Tennessee had Davies's and Thomas McKean's divisions. Only Davies and McKean were at Corinth. Stanley and Hamilton were stationed at Jacinto and Rienzi watching for the Confederates. The two outlying divisions moved closer as more reliable word arrived from a Union sympathizer, by way of Hurlbut, that Van Dorn was near Pocahontas. It was not yet possible to tell if Corinth, Bolivar, or Jackson was the target, but Rosecrans guessed Van Dorn would cut the Mobile and Ohio Railroad north of Corinth and force his men out of their defenses for a decisive fight. His cavalry patrols to Pocahontas brought back word of Rebel infantry moving eastward on October 2. Grant had already come to the conclusion that Corinth was Van Dorn's target, and now Rosecrans seemed to think so too. He pugnaciously suggested to Grant on October 2 that he take all but six regiments out of Corinth, advance toward the Hatchie, and "push those fellows to the wall." That suggestion met with no response, so Rosecrans simply moved Hamilton's division to the northern outskirts of town on the Purdy road to watch for any Rebel movement.

Rosecrans also sent Col. John M. Oliver's brigade of McKean's division to Chewalla, Tennessee, ten miles northwest, in case Van Dorn decided to take a more direct route to Corinth. Oliver would make the first contact early on the morning of October 3. Rosecrans was forced to play a wait-and-see game all morning, knowing that the skirmishing along the Chewalla

Road could be a feint. He had to see what developed and hoped he could control events so as to receive the Confederate attack at the College Hill line. Thus he placed his troops at all possible posts to detect any Confederate advance. Hamilton was on the north, Davies was positioned between the two railroads northwest of town, McKean was to Davies's left, and Stanley's division was placed in reserve on the far left. Each command was to delay the enemy if a major attack began on their front while Rosecrans would try to shift troops accordingly. Rosecrans also dispatched Brig. Gen. John McArthur's brigade of McKean's division to help Oliver on the Chewalla Road.

The sun rose bright and early on the morning of Friday, October 3. The sky was clear and the temperature already was on its way to the ninety-degree mark. Price's men cooked bread on a stick before setting out, the only food many of them would have for three days. When the column started directly for Corinth, the members of the Third Louisiana were stunned, "their hearts misgave them," for they recalled their own earthworks there with a heavy abatis in front and were certain the Yankees had strengthened them even further. The Chewalla Road branched five miles from Corinth, and Price crossed the Memphis and Charleston Railroad to march north of it while Lovell took the route south of the line. When both wings concentrated at Cane Creek, a short distance in front of the Confederate Line, they found Oliver's and McArthur's men on the east side. After some brisk skirmishing, the Rebels pushed across the creek at 8 A.M. Lovell then deployed in battle line, and the Federals fell back to the Confederate works.

After this initial success, Van Dorn moved his headquarters up to the Murphy house on the road taken by Price and held a conference of his division leaders. He ordered them to deploy in an arc from the Mobile and Ohio Railroad to Smith Bridge Road, covering the entire northwestern and western approaches to town. Armstrong's cavalry would be stationed on the left and Col. R. A. Pinson's cavalry would screen the right. On Van Dorn's left, Price's two divisions covered the area between the two rail lines. It took a while for the men to form and move out over this "irregular ground, covered with timber," especially when Federal artillery began to open, but the opposing lines were fully defined by 11 o'clock. Maury deployed two brigades on Price's right, holding one in reserve, while Hébert did the same on the left. On Van Dorn's right wing, Lovell put all three of his brigades in line, stretching south from the Memphis and Charleston Railroad. Van Dorn hoped to push his main assault in the center and right, noting that Hébert's division on the far left faced a high wooded ridge. Hébert was instructed to

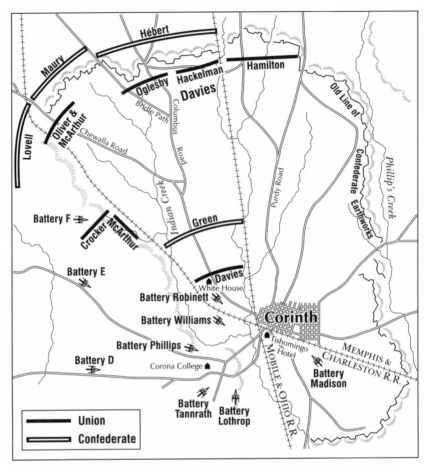

7. Corinth, October 3, 1862

delay his advance in the hope that the Federals would detach troops from the ridge to reinforce other threatened points.

Van Dorn had gained an advantage over his opponent. He now had deployed his entire army against only a portion of Rosecrans's force and could win a decisive victory if he pushed ahead with vigor and certainty. But the Confederates did not yet know how many Federals lay before them, and they had to contend with a broken and heavily wooded terrain in boiling hot weather. Instead of the decisive breakthrough he needed to take the town, Van Dorn would struggle all day trying to push his eager but heavily burdened men into a difficult assault. The Federals fought a long delaying action, exhausting the Confederates and making them pay a heavy price for closing in on the College Hill line, where they had an excellent chance of securing Corinth. The fighting on October 3, and the campaign itself, would hinge on whether Van Dorn could break through this newly constructed line of works before night fell.

Price had the task of attacking Davies's outnumbered division, which had deployed behind the Confederate works between the two rail lines. Brig. Gen. Pleasant A. Hackleman's brigade formed on the right, and Brig. Gen. Richard J. Oglesby's brigade aligned to the left. Col. Silas D. Baldwin's brigade was dispatched to help Oliver and McArthur on the Chewalla Road. Davies also positioned the Eighty-first Ohio and a section of artillery several hundred yards to his left to cover a bridle path that crossed the Confederate works.

Davies could not hold this advanced position when Price attacked because he was not only outnumbered but outflanked. The Eighty-first Ohio was hit by five Confederate regiments and was driven off. Oglesby also was heavily pressed, but Hackleman was spared because of Hébert's order to stay put. While the two brigades were beginning to withdraw from the Confederate works, Oliver's outnumbered contingent was nearly overwhelmed by Lovell farther to the south. McArthur took command when Oliver was wounded. He was forced to retire fighting along the Chewalla Road just as Davies withdrew from his position. Price carried the Confederate Line by noon, having lost a considerable number of men. But his "soldiers stood once more within the works their own hands had erected," according to John Tyler Jr. Lovell seized the Confederate Line at about the same time. His Ninth Arkansas and Twenty-second Mississippi took a high hill where the fortifications crossed the Chewalla Road.

The first stage of the fighting on October 3 ended with a relatively easy Confederate victory, but Van Dorn would have difficulty taking advantage of this success. The Federals retreated stubbornly and in order. Baldwin's regiments fought their way back along with the rest of Oliver's and McArthur's men. Farther to the north, Oglesby and Hackleman temporarily halted their retreat down the Columbus Road about a thousand yards south of the Confederate Line to delay the Rebels, but their men pulled out before receiving an attack. Farther south, they did the same thing at the junction of the Chewalla and Columbus Roads. These delaying actions, along with the heat and the rugged, forested terrain, helped to slow down Price's advance and buy valuable time for the Federal cause that day.

Davies hoped to make a final stand at a large, two-story white house nearly 1,000 yards south of the intersection of the Chewalla and Columbus Roads and 725 yards in front of Battery Robinett, which was on the College Hill line. The ground there allowed for a compact position, close in to town, and from there it would be easier to cover the roads that approached Corinth. Davies could not count on the assistance of Baldwin's brigade or the rest of McArthur's contingent because they had already gone off to reinforce McKean south of the Memphis and Charleston Railroad, so he ordered Oglesby and Hackleman to retire to the White House.

Even with the addition of McArthur's and Baldwin's men, McKean had a tough fight with Lovell's division. His men had deployed to Davies's left at dawn, occupying a section of Halleck's line with their right flank near Battery F, just south of the Memphis and Charleston Railroad. McArthur led his men to the north of the railroad to extend McKean's right flank. But the Federal effort to hold there was sabotaged when Davies fell back to the White House, exposing their flank. McArthur was unable to prevent the Confederates from turning McKean's position. He fell back to the south side of the railroad, and Battery F became the anchor of McKean's embattled line. It was one of six redans on the Halleck line, measuring forty yards wide and open to the rear, with four gun embrasures and a ditch in front. Moderate slopes surrounded the work. Lovell, however, considered it "a strong redoubt, well flanked with infantry and with an abatis of felled timber half a mile in width extending around it in one direction but with no obstructions to the north." Lovell believed it could be taken if the Confederates could coordinate their attack. He relayed all the information he had to Van Dorn, who ordered an immediate assault. Brig. Gen. John C. Moore's brigade of Maury's division hit it from the north, and Brig. Gen. John C. Bowen's brigade of Lovell's division turned its left flank.

The Yankee troops to the south of Battery F fought hard to hold on against Bowen's assault. Cyrus F. Boyd of the Fifteenth Iowa was stationed on a "naked ridge with nothing to protect" him when the Rebels attacked at 2 P.M., "all advancing in the most deliberate manner at *bayonets fixed*." He could hear Rebel officers shouting orders, but Lieut. Col. William W. Belknap rode along the line and cautioned the men to hold their fire until ordered. Boyd and his companions kneeled on one knee and fired, not knowing exactly where to aim because the Confederates were on lower ground than they occupied and smoke soon engulfed the battlefield. Bowen outflanked the Fifteenth Iowa as confusion began to ripple through the Union ranks. "The battle raged fiercely for a time and men fell in great numbers," recalled Boyd. As they retired, the Federals were pressed so closely they could not carry off their wounded. Boyd fired ten rounds altogether in this short but close fight. Battery F fell, and McKean was forced to retire fighting toward the College Hill line.

Lovell paused after taking the battery to resupply his men's cartridge boxes, then continued to advance slowly and deliberately with Brig. Gen. Albert Rust's brigade as a reserve. McKean was aware of Davies's concentration at the White House and tried to join him there, but he received orders from Rosecrans to pass by and occupy the College Hill line. His men were pressed so heavily that Col. Marcellus M. Crocker's brigade had to counterattack and stall Lovell long enough to allow the division's artillery to escape. McKean was safely behind the earthworks and holding the town by dusk, but he was of no help to Davies's badly outnumbered and isolated division.

Davies was left at the White House to hold most of Van Dorn's army at bay. He had a good chance of repelling a frontal attack, with an excellent position in the edge of a woods and an open field in front. A swamp helped to protect his right flank, and the guns of Battery Williams and Battery Robinett could help protect his left. Davies's field artillery also had its first chance of the day to deploy on advantageous ground and command the Chewalla Road. Davies called it the only position "where the small force under my command had any hope of meeting the enemy with success. At all other points it could have been flanked and surrounded by the host in the field before us."

Hackleman with 1,211 men was on the right, Oglesby with 576 men deployed on the left, and Maj. George H. Stone commanded eleven guns that reinforced the line. "The day was intensely hot," reported Davies, "and, the men having been twelve hours underarms, many had fallen from sheer exhaustion, sun-stroke, and other casualties." Yet they gave an excellent account of themselves. The Federal guns opened up as soon as Price's infantry appeared on the other side of the field and "poured a steady stream" of fire for an hour and a half. Brig. Gen. Martin E. Green's brigade of Hébert's division bore the brunt of this fire, but many shells overshot his men and hit those in Gates's brigade two hundred yards to the rear, even though they were lying flat on the ground. A few Confederate guns fired over Price's men, but they had no good positions from which to do any damage. On two occasions, Stone nearly ran out of ammunition and dispatched a six-mule team and wagon to Corinth for more, but it was not enough. When his guns fell silent, Davies ordered them back to town. "The artillery filed slowly to the rear, men looking more like coal-heavers than soldiers," Davies thought, "with perspiration streaming down their faces blackened with gunpowder, and the wounded horses leaving a stream of blood in the road." The eleven guns had fired over fifteen hundred rounds and had played a major role in stopping Price's two divisions dead in their tracks.

Davies sent word to Rosecrans that his little band desperately needed help, either reinforcements or an attack by Hamilton's division on Van Dorn's left and rear. As soon as the artillery retired, Price sent Green's men across the field "in steady line, firing as they advanced." Hackleman's command "rose from its concealment" when the Confederates came within close range and fired. Davies wrote, "They fell like the leaves of autumn, staggered for a moment, closed up their openings, and advanced again." Oglesby began to open an oblique fire into Green's flank and the Rebels retreated. Green reformed and attacked a second time, only to be repulsed by a counterattack. It was nothing less than foolish of Price to employ only one brigade in this piecemeal effort, but it was a great boon for Davies. Green's walking wounded were streaming to the rear by this time, shouting to Gates's men, "We are hard pressed in front, and need you there." A regiment was sent up to support Green as a third assault was launched.

This attack resulted in the most deadly exchange of infantry fire that day. Lieut. Col. John S. Wilcox of the Fifty-second Illinois, in Hackleman's brigade, vividly recalled the fight. "We opened on them and their lines melted away into death and confusion as quickly almost as I can write it." Yet the Rebels held on tenaciously. Union reinforcements came up in the form of Col. Joseph A. Mower's brigade of Stanley's division, but the men were panicked by the blast of battle when they began to deploy into line and became confused. Hackleman and Oglesby rushed about to rally them and both were hit. Col. Thomas W. Sweeny took over Hackleman's brigade and continued fighting. "The guns became so hot," he reported, "the men could scarcely hold them and the cartridges prematurely exploded in the guns from heat." When subordinate officers asked Sweeny what to do about it, he replied, "Let them burst, there is no time to cool off now."

Illinois officer Wilcox was enraged when he learned that Hackleman had fallen. He "felt malice & hatred. I did not swear but I shouted & screamed 'damn them, boys give them hell.'" He looked to the left and saw Oglesby's men waver and told Sweeny about it. The ammunition was almost gone as well. Fortunately, the Confederates broke and fled just before either Oglesby's brigade or the cartridges ran out. Yet it was obvious to Davies that the enemy were massing to outflank his left. After holding at the White House for two hours, he ordered a withdrawal.

This move ended the fighting of October 3. Davies's division easily made it back to the safety of the College Hill line, arriving there by 5 P.M. It was not harassed by Price. Stone's guns refilled their caissons and rejoined the division, and the infantrymen also were able to resupply their ammunition. Wilcox found something even more helpful in this hot weather. His men had no water so he scrounged up a half barrel of whiskey for them. "You may be sure I was nearly used up," he reported to his wife. "I had had nothing to eat since morning."

The Confederates were just as exhausted and thirsty. Price's men paid a heavy cost to drive Davies from the White House. One company of the Sixth Missouri, of Green's Brigade, lost thirty-seven men of fifty-two engaged that day, while another regiment lost twenty-six of twenty-eight commissioned officers. When the fight ended, "scores of our men sank down exhausted by heat & nearly famished for water," reported John Tyler Jr. Price rode among them to cheer their spirits, sending his bodyguard to find water. He wanted to go on, crying, "*Now is the time to push into Corinth! Now is the time to assure the victory.*"

Price might better have thanked his stars that the apparent victory did not turn into a rout, for Rosecrans had been trying for several hours to turn Hamilton's division onto his flank and rear. The Federal commander had come to the conclusion after noon that Van Dorn was indeed attacking along the Chewalla Road with his main force. As Davies and McKean pulled back, the Confederates advanced past Hamilton's position without seeing his men, who were in thick woods east of the Mobile and Ohio Railroad. About 3 P.M., Rosecrans sent Col. Arthur C. Ducat, his acting chief of staff, to instruct Hamilton to help Davies. Hamilton found Rosecrans's written order unclear. It told him to move by the flank and go to Davies's left. Hamilton correctly thought it should have instructed him to move to Davies's right. Rather than assume any risk, he wrote, "I cannot understand it," on the back of the order and handed it to Ducat, who had to ride back to Rose-crans for clarification. The army leader hurriedly scribbled a message to the effect that Ducat would explain the order verbally and sent the staff officer on his way. It was 5 P.M. before this confusion was straightened out. Ham-ilton was to "file by fours to the left, and march down until the head of his column was opposite the right of Davies's, then to face his brigades" to the southwest and advance. They were to move en echelon so as to hit the Con-federate left and rear. Ducat had had to run a gauntlet of scattering rifle fire from some Confederates who had worked their way east of the railroad to deliver this order.

Hamilton was further delayed by the singular action of Brig. Gen. Napo-leon B. Buford, who led one of his brigades. A few Confederates appeared in Buford's front just as the division began to move, and he impetuously ad-vanced toward them. Sullivan's brigade was already executing the flanking movement and soon the two commands were half a mile apart. Hamilton had to send two orders to Buford before he stopped his wild goose chase and followed Sullivan, but another hour had been wasted. The men maneu-vered through a dense forest and had only reached a point opposite the Con-federate left when darkness put an end to any hope of attacking the Rebels. Rosecrans blamed Hamilton for the delay, writing afterward that if he had moved on time, "we should have crushed the enemy's [left] and rear." He noted with irony after the war that Van Dorn had pined in his report for one more hour of daylight so he could conclude his victory. Rosecrans too wanted an extra hour of sunlight, for it "would have brought Hamilton's fresh and gallant division" into play.

The Federals had a lot of repositioning to do that night. Rosecrans held a council of his four division leaders and gave them their orders. McKean would hold the left, centering his position on College Hill; Stanley was to center his line on Battery Robinett and hold the center; Davies would cross the Mobile and Ohio Railroad and stretch his small, exhausted division as far as Battery Powell; and Hamilton was to deploy to Davies's right. Miz-ner's cavalrymen were to secure both flanks. Rosecrans inspected the new positions that night and returned to his headquarters at 3 A.M. His line was one mile long and at the edge of town. The men were not permitted to build fires and "were too tired to intrench." Whatever digging had already been done would have to suffice.

Davies rode into town to visit his injured soldiers after tending to the re-positioning of his command. He found the Tishomingo Hotel packed with wounded. Hackleman died in one room while Davies was present. Oglesby "was undergoing excruciating pain" next to him, but he would survive. Baldwin, who had also been hit, was in the same room. All three of Davies's brigade leaders were down. He had lost one-third of his men that day but saved Corinth. About eighty-five hundred Federals and about fifteen thousand Confederates had been engaged in the fighting.

"I had been in hopes that one day's operations would end the contest and decide who should be the victors on this bloody field," reported Van Dorn, but his men had marched ten miles and then fought a tough battle in dense undergrowth and thick forests with no water. He ordered three batteries to concentrate that night on the western bluff of Indian Creek, intending to open an artillery barrage at 4 A.M. He fully meant to continue pushing the offensive at dawn. Hébert's division was to cross the Mobile and Ohio Railroad at daybreak and attack Corinth from the north along the Purdy road, while Maury would attack Battery Robinett. Lovell's division would attack on the right, following Hébert's start, and try to enter Corinth from the west. The hard fighting at the White House had been only a prelude for what was to come.

CHAPTER NINE

Bloody October

The fighting on Saturday, October 4, began at 4 A.M., when three Confederate batteries opened fire. Fourteen guns split the early morning silence with salvo after salvo. They were about six hundred yards from Corinth on the western bluff of Indian Creek near the cleared space fronting the Federal line. The gunners frequently overshot their targets, sending shells into Corinth and hitting houses. The Tishomingo Hotel was damaged, killing a soldier who had been wounded the day before. In the darkness, Capt. Oscar L. Jackson of Company H, Sixty-third Ohio, found that "the scene was a grand one, a real display of fireworks," but the Federals lost much needed sleep.

The artillery barrage woke Rosecrans, who had slept only half an hour. "I had no time for breakfast," he later recalled. Union artillery sprang into action as Battery Robinett opened fire with three guns under Lieut. Henry C. Robinett of the First U.S. Infantry. Battery Williams opened too with three guns under Capt. George A. Williams of the same regiment. Battery Phillips added its weight to the counterfire with a howitzer and two field batteries. The Federal guns enfiladed the Confederate artillery and silenced it in thirty minutes.

The Rebel batteries withdrew at dawn. One of them had already lost a gun when skirmishers of the First U.S. Infantry pushed forward and found it placed too far in advance and captured it. From then until the time of Van Dorn's attack, only the skirmishers of both armies were active. Price had received and issued orders to advance at sunrise. Hébert was supposed to attack first, followed by Maury and Lovell. The infantrymen managed to get some breakfast at dawn before they were set to waiting for what everyone could guess would be a fierce assault. But time began to slip away with only the sound of skirmish fire disturbing the stillness along the Confederate line. Hébert was ill and decided that he could not effectively command his division that day, but his late decision meant that it would take some time to inform Green of his new duties and allow him to take in the situation.

Rosecrans took this time to inspect his lines. "The air was still and fiercely hot," he wrote, but the sky was clear. He visited the entire line, including Battery Robinett. The reserve artillery was parked in the town square because the Federals already had plenty of guns on the line. Rosecrans was riding behind Sweeny's brigade of Davies's division when columns of Rebel infantry suddenly emerged from the woods at 9 A.M. He could not help but admire their appearance as they "advanced splendidly to the attack."

Rosecrans saw Green's division open the Confederate assault. Green had received a note from Hébert just before dawn that he was too ill, and, soon after, he also received an order from Price to take charge of the division. Col. William H. Moore of the Forty-third Mississippi had to take over his brigade. The division was positioned in an L-shaped formation. Moore's brigade was on the right, connecting to Brig. Gen. Charles W. Phifer's brigade of Maury's division, with his left ending at the Mobile and Ohio Railroad. Gates's brigade angled the line northward, facing east and fronting the railroad. Col. Robert McLain's brigade and Col. W. Bruce Colbert's brigade continued the line northward. The division's skirmishers continued to parry with the Federals while Green positioned his units. They were on a tangled bit of ground just east of the railroad, covered with vines, trees, and weeds, firing at the Union skirmishers at ranges of seventy-five to one hundred yards.

Finally, Green's men moved out. Colbert and McLain had farther to march than Gates and were ordered to attack en echelon, "throwing their left forward, so as to come to a charge at the same time of the right." Green expected to meet heavy resistance so he requested reinforcements as soon as his brigades started. They crossed the railroad "slowly and steadily" but cheering as loudly as they could. The woods extended a quarter of a mile east of the railroad with cleared ground beyond except for "a few scattering trees," some logs and brush left there to trip up an attacker. Fences had already been removed. When Green emerged from the timber, he could see the Federal line only six hundred yards away. The ground was irregular and undulating, with dips and rolls about thirty feet deep.

When Gates's brigade emerged from the woods, his skirmishers, who

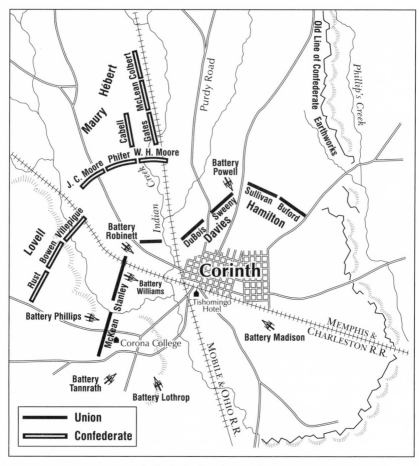

8. Corinth, October 4, 1862

had preceded the advance in the timber, rejoined the battle line. Everyone paused, now that Gates could see what lay between him and the Federal line. All eyes searched for the best point to hit. Suddenly, Col. Francis M. Cockrell of the Second Missouri Infantry waved his sword and yelled for everyone to head for Battery Powell. The men moved out and broke into a double-quick only two hundred yards short of the Federal line.

Gates hit the Unionists before any other of Green's brigades and quickly began to push them back. Cockrell had accurately pinpointed the key to the line that Davies and Hamilton held. Battery Powell was the apex of a chevron and had to be taken if that line were to be collapsed. Davies's division was far weaker than Hamilton's, having been exhausted by the fighting of October 3 and drained of manpower. With the detachment of several hundred men to guard duty in town and elsewhere, Davies had only 1,877 infantry in line, with 406 in reserve. Yet his division had to cover a space that was a half mile long over open ground. He should have had at least 5,000 men for this job. The division line failed to go all the way to the railroad, leaving a gap of 250 yards. In addition, Stanley's division west of the railroad also left a similar gap, creating a hole in the Union position that was 500 yards wide straddling the tracks. It was, as Davies put it, "an irregular line." His division faced northwest, its right resting just behind Battery Powell and its four guns. Capt. Henry Dillon's Sixth Wisconsin Battery was divided so that two cannon were placed to the front and right of the earthwork and two guns were put in the middle of the division line. Sweeny's brigade was positioned on the right just behind the crest of a gentle slope that offered no cover. Col. John DuBois, who had arrived at Corinth that morning, was given charge of Baldwin's brigade to Sweeny's left. Col. August Mersey led Davies's other brigade, formerly commanded by Oglesby, but it was broken up to provide guards for various points and a picket line that stretched behind the Federals to catch any stragglers. DuBois's men managed to find some slight shelter, rolling a few logs into place along their front to compensate for the level ground they occupied.

Davies was in poor shape to resist a vigorous assault. He even saw a few of his men fire their muskets wildly into the air and run away as the Confederates closed in. Gates's brigade had no difficulty taking Battery Powell for it was poorly supported. The Federal infantry was positioned a few yards behind it rather than guarding its flanks. Some artillerymen were shot down at their guns, all of which were captured, but the rest fled to the rear when the Rebels were only twenty yards away. The guns of Dillon's battery that were posted outside the battery were also taken, but the gunners escaped, running their teams, limbers, and caissons pell-mell through the ranks of the Twelfth Illinois and Eighty-first Ohio, injuring twenty-one men and throwing each regiment into confusion.

For the men of Sweeny's brigade, waiting just to the left of Battery Powell, it was a very tense moment. They had waited patiently ever since dawn for the Rebel attack, listening to the skirmishers at their work. Then an "ominous silence" ensued and the Confederates "burst from the woods in front and to the right." The Federal skirmishers retired at the double-quick, firing as they ran. Gates's men and the other Rebel brigades marched out of the woods. "It was a terribly beautiful sight to see the enemy's columns advance," reported Sweeny. His men were told to lie down for safety, and the Fifty-second Illinois fixed bayonets. It was on the right flank of Sweeny's line, and its commander had managed to scrounge up a few gabions to offer some protection for his men. As the Confederates closed "in perfect swarms" they opened a heavy fire. Lieutenant Colonel Wilcox of the Fifty-second Illinois described it as "one continuous humming about our ears. It was wonderful, thick and close they flew, the men lay like snakes on the ground." Wilcox kept up a patter behind the line to inform his men what was taking place, cautioning them not to rise until he gave the order.

When the artillery abandoned Battery Powell, Sweeny shouted the order to stand up and "give them hell and they did it." Wilcox's regiment fired eight volleys before he looked to the right and saw that Sullivan's brigade of Hamilton's division, to the east of Battery Powell, had retreated. One of his captains rushed to his side and yelled, "In the name of God do you see they are on our flank." Wilcox could plainly see it. He also clearly saw that Battery Powell was filled with Confederates. Wilcox considered ordering a bayonet attack when he noticed the Second Iowa still holding firm to his left, but before he could make up his mind to do it the Iowans fell back. Wilcox immediately ordered his men to do the same; Sweeny's right flank crumbled and fell back at least 175 yards. DuBois also fell back about 75 yards.

Fortunately for the security of Rosecrans's army, the fall back was short and brief. Gates's men essentially stopped after taking Battery Powell; no one seemed able to rally them to keep going. Only a few scattering soldiers advanced another fifty yards south of Powell, the rest waiting at the work for orders. This delay gave Davies enough time to rally his brigades and send them forward again. Sweeny's men counterattacked and retook the battery. Wilcox claimed to be the first man to reenter the work although he was "completely exhausted." After sitting a bit on a gun named Lady Halleck, he ran off to rejoin his men, who had advanced 150 yards forward in pursuit of the Rebels. The chase was cut short because Union artillery did not have enough time to receive word that friendly troops were advancing in front of the line. Several men in Sweeny's and DuBois's brigades were killed and wounded by Lieut. Fletcher H. Chapman's Battery B, Second Illinois Artillery, of McKean's division. The Federals were forced to retire and be content with holding their gound. They opened a long-range musket fire at the last Rebels who were struggling to pass the fallen timber, even loading a Parrott rifle and firing it at them.

Off to the west, Brig. Gen. William Cabell's brigade of Maury's division joined in the attack. Its commander had been sheltering his men from Union artillery fire behind a hill, waiting to help either Maury or Green, when an order arrived from Maury at 11 A.M. to support Gates. "This order was received with a shout by the whole brigade who had stood this terrible cannonading for more than an hour," Cabell reported. The brigade moved in column at double-quick across the Mobile and Ohio Railroad tracks under a "terrible fire of artillery," then faced to the right and attacked. By now Gates had already fallen back and Cabell was forced to attack unsupported. The men had been under artillery fire ever since they started the march, so Cabell ordered a charge at the double-quick. The men shouted and drove back the Union skirmishers. Cabell hit DuBois's small brigade of only a thousand men with about twelve hundred troops. Most of the Confederates were stopped by heavy musketry and enfilading artillery fire, but part of the Twentieth Arkansas broke through, probably by moving past DuBois's unsupported left flank, and got into Corinth. They were driven out of town by the Federals. When Cabell retired from this unwise assault, he could count only 550 men left in his brigade.

Hamilton's division also was heavily attacked by McLain and Colbert. Hamilton could plainly see the two columns emerge from the woods and cross the Purdy Road west to east, only half a mile north of his position. One brigade deployed into a battle line on the crest of a ridge and the other crossed the ridge to the east, and then it also changed front to the right and formed a battle line. Skirmishers ran out in front, and the two brigades attacked, their combined fronts covering all of Hamilton's line. Just as with Davies's division, the vulnerable point of Hamilton's position was Battery Powell. When Gates's men took it, some of Hamilton's artillery opened fire, killing the remaining battery horses in the work to prevent Gates from withdrawing the guns. Sullivan's brigade then fell back in some disorder, beginning the breakdown of the infantry position around the battery.

On the center and right, Hamilton's men held firm. Henry Neil's Elev-

enth Ohio Battery was by now back in service from its terrible mauling at
Iuka. Neil could see "Masses of rebels, screaming the familiar yell" as they
approached. He shouted, " 'Boys, there are the same troops that fought us at
Iuka; are you going to let them touch our guns today?' " With a yell, the gunners opened fire at six hundred yards. Neil proudly reported that his men
"worked like tigers." The Confederates attacked three times, getting close
enough so that the Ohioans doubled their canister charges, but each time
they were repulsed. This time, Neil's men got the better of their opponents,
firing 214 rounds and losing only four gunners wounded.

The attack on the Confederate left came to a bloody failure despite tantalizing evidence of success. The Federal line had been cracked but not broken, while Rebel soldiers had run through the streets of Corinth but could
not secure the town. Price had been unable to bring any artillery support to
bear because of the rough nature of the ground and the fact that Federal artillery dominated all the cleared area fronting the Union line. Although
Cabell came up to support Green, it was too late. The Confederates were
forced to withdraw to a hill west of the Mobile and Ohio Railroad. By 1 P.M.,
the fighting was over here. Rosecrans put in an appearance when he rode to
Hamilton and instructed him to move Sullivan's reassembled brigade forward. It advanced to the left of Battery Powell and found no Rebels nearby.
Losses on this part of the battlefield had been heavy. Sweeny's brigade took
126 prisoners and four colors, while John Wilcox found a horrible sight
when he walked over the battlefield that afternoon. In front of his regiment's
position were "boddies, bones, blood, brains, limbs, everywhere." His
Fifty-second Illinois had lost eleven killed and sixty wounded.

Yet even worse fighting was taking place on Rosecrans's center, the area
that lay between the two railroads. Maury could use only two of his own brigades in the assault, for he held Cabell's in reserve and it later was shifted to
the left, but William H. Moore's brigade of Green's division was available.
Phifer's brigade was on Maury's left, its flank resting four hundred yards
from the Mobile and Ohio Railroad, and Brig. Gen. John C. Moore's brigade was to Phifer's right. Skirmishing continued until after 10 A.M., when
the sound of Green's firing at close range with Davies's division became
clearly audible.

The focus of Maury's assault was Battery Robinett. It sat on a ridge about
one hundred feet above the flat, wide bottom of Indian Creek to the east. Although the terrain on this ridge was irregular, with dips and rolls at random
intervals that were as much as fifty feet deep, it was an excellent stage for a
battle, visible from a wide distance around. The battery was built of two

levels of gabions, a horizontal row of fascines on top, and raised artillery platforms for three guns. It was a detached work fully open to the rear.

With a bugle call as their signal, the three Confederate brigades started through the woods, which shielded them a bit from the rain of artillery projectiles. John C. Moore's men marched 250 yards and crested a low ridge. There they saw as in a panorama the town of Corinth, the Union earthworks, and long lines of bluecoated infantrymen in full view. The men shouted and began crawling through what J. A. McKinstry of the Forty-second Alabama called "the most obstructive abattis" he had ever seen. McKinstry and his comrades climbed "over the tops, under the limbs, around the stumps, along the fallen trunks of the trees . . . like squirrels." Halfway through the abatis, the guns in Robinett switched from shell to canister. "Our yells grew fainter, and our men fell faster," moaned McKinstry. They finally got through the tangled timber and still had one hundred yards of cleared land to tackle.

Here they began to receive musket fire from the infantry to each side of Robinett. With few obstructions to hinder them, the men of John C. Moore's brigade moved quickly. "I saw men, running at full speed, stop suddenly and fall upon their faces, with their brains scattered all around," wrote Lieutenant Labruzan of the Forty-second Alabama, "others, with legs and arms cut off, shrieking with agony. They fell behind, beside, and within a few feet of me. I gave myself to God and got ahead of my company. The ground was literally strewn with mangled corpses. One ball went through my pants, and they cut twigs right by me. It seemed by holding out my hand I could have caught a dozen. They buzzed and hissed by me in all directions, but I still pressed forward."

The Federal troops holding this part of the line were Stanley's division. Stanley did not think much of his position. Robinett formed an angle in the Union line, perched on a prominent ridge. The Rebels had the opportunity of firing on it from several angles and could attack both sides of the battery. There were no earthworks to either side of Robinett, forcing the supporting infantry to stand or lie on the ground. Yet Battery Williams was within easy supporting distance to the south. Stanley placed the Forty-third Ohio to the left of Robinett and the Sixty-third Ohio to its right. The Eleventh Missouri was held in reserve behind the redoubt. The Sixty-third Ohio did not stretch all the way to the Mobile and Ohio Railroad, leaving a gap near the rail line.

Stanley had already engaged the enemy that morning. At 8 A.M. Rosecrans had ridden by and ordered him to deploy skirmishers on both sides of the Chewalla Road to feel out the Confederate position. Col. Joseph A. Mower took two regiments out, ran into Maury's division, and was bluntly repulsed. Mower himself was wounded in the neck.

Soon after that ill-advised probe, the Confederate attack "burst . . . from the wood." The artillery in Battery Williams increased its fire as Phifer's brigade hit the Federal line. All four of Phifer's regiments were deployed in columns and heading straight for the Sixty-third Ohio. Captain Jackson of Company H could see the columns coming from a long distance away, at a "firm, slow, steady step. . . . In my campaigning I had never seen anything so hard to stand as that slow, steady tramp. Not a sound was heard but they looked as if they intended to walk over us."

This wait was a real test of Jackson's men. He observed with a great deal of interest as one soldier checked to see if his gun was properly primed and another man stood "a while on one foot then on the other." Still others "pulled at their blouses, feeling if their cartridge boxes or cap-pouches were all right, and so on, but all the time steadily watching the advancing foe." Jackson steadied them by shouting, "We own all the ground behind us. The enemy may go over us but all the rebels yonder can't drive Company H back."

The Federals lay down, partly screened by the undulations of the ground. As soon as Jackson saw Rebel heads appear above a rise only thirty yards in front, he ordered his men to stand up and told them to fire just over a short bush that was immediately before his line. The first volley stunned the head of Phifer's column, leaving "a mass of struggling bodies and butternut clothes." The Rebel formation seemed to "reel like a rope shaken at the end." To another observer, it seemed as if the head of Phifer's columns melted away and the rear immediately retreated and took shelter in the tangled abatis. From there, they opened a harassing fire at the Union line but never resumed the attack.

While Phifer's men retired, John C. Moore's brigade came up and began a fierce struggle for control of Battery Robinett. The Second Texas, under Col. William P. Rogers, attacked the left wing of the Sixty-third Ohio, shattering a company that was supporting two Parrott guns placed outside Robinett. Company H was ordered to relieve its comrades. Jackson felt as if it was a death sentence, but he positioned his twenty-four men in two lines just in time to receive about one hundred Texans who had broken off from Rogers's column to take the guns. Jackson could even hear a Rebel officer order his men to shout, and "it almost made the hair stand up on my head." Jackson's men fired furiously, dropping many Rebels, as the unknown officer in gray tried to bring the few men who had bayonets to the front of his formation, "doing the thing among and literally over his dead and wounded comrades." Jackson ordered his own men to fix bayonets and charge so as to meet the Rebels with momentum on their side. "It reminded me of a man cutting heavy grain, striking at a thick place," but it worked. The attack was blunted and repelled, although Jackson had only eleven men left and a retreating Rebel took a potshot at him that smashed into his face and inflicted a dangerous but not fatal wound.

But Jackson's heroics could not save Battery Robinett, which was assaulted by the Forty-second Alabama. Even from a distance, an observant Union soldier could see and hear this column attack with "the most terrific yells." The Alabamans found it difficult to climb the steep exterior slope of the parapet, lengthened as it was by a deep ditch. About forty of them got into the ditch and began to claw their way up. A man only three feet from Lieutenant Labruzan was shot in the head at close range by artillerists who had forsaken their cannon for muskets. His brains were "dashed in a stream over my fine coat, which I had in my arms, and on my shirt sleeves. . . . Several were killed here on top of one another and rolled down the embankment in ghastly heaps."

Seventeen-year-old J. A. McKinstry had a similar experience on the slope of Robinett. The Federals threw a few hand grenades over the parapet, and McKinstry and his comrades began throwing them back before they exploded. Then someone shouted, "Over the walls, and drive them out." McKinstry tried to do that, but a man to his left was killed and grabbed him as he fell. Both tumbled back down the slope into the ditch, but other Alabamans managed to get into the battery.

Rebel possession of the work would be short-lived. Captain Williams had prepared for this emergency, arranging with Robinett's gunners beforehand to seek shelter in an angle of the work protected from his fire. Two Parrotts in Battery Williams opened up, exploding their shells above Robinett and helping to clear the slope of Confederates. More important, the Eleventh Missouri sprang into action. Maj. Andrew J. Weber had been instructed to have his men lie down forty paces behind the Sixty-third Ohio, to attack with bayonets if the Ohioans faltered but not to fire unless all friendly troops were cleared of his front. The Sixty-third Ohio was so heavily pressed by Phifer's harassing fire from the front and by John C. Moore's enfilading fire from the left that it was forced back. The Federal regiment had done all it could, losing 45 percent of its strength and nine of its thirteen line officers.

This retreat gave Weber his opportunity, and he ordered his Missourians to stand up and charge. The Twenty-seventh Ohio came up and joined Weber's attack. The two regiments met the exhausted Confederates in and near the battery with irresistible force. J. A. McKinstry ran around the work when he heard shouts of "Victory! Victory!" but was mortified to see two blue regiments approach a group of Rebel officers, Colonel Rogers among them, only "a few paces from the fort." McKinstry instinctively raised his musket and fired, causing the Federals to return fire. Rogers fell dead; he apparently was preparing to surrender before McKinstry foolishly fired his musket. McKinstry was hit by a ball in the left hip, one in the right shoulder, and a third in the left shoulder. All fifteen men in Rogers's group were down "in a heap." McKinstry escaped to the rear, bleeding all the way, but he spent three months in bed recovering from his wounds. His company had only eleven men left of thirty-three engaged. Lieutenant Labruzan also survived the Union counterattack by hiding behind a stump twenty yards from the fort. He was temporarily shielded from the hail of bullets although the stump was shattered and splintered. Labruzan gave up after a half hour of this and was taken prisoner.

Battery Robinett was cleared by members of the Forty-third Ohio in hand-to-hand combat. Positioned to the left of Robinett, this regiment temporarily wavered when it received fire to its rear from the Rebels who had come around the right flank of the work. Lieut. Col. Wager Swayne moved the regiment to the left so he could refuse the right wing and fire into the battery's open rear and to its right. Then his right wing attacked the few remaining Rebels who were trapped inside, several of whom were killed. An observant soldier near Battery Williams recalled that he "could see men using their bayonets like pitch forks and thrusting each other through."

The fight for Robinett had been the most vicious of the battle. An awe-struck observer saw 126 men lying within forty feet of the work, "with the most unearthly look on their dying faces." Lieutenant Robinett was wounded and thirteen of his twenty-six men were lost, preventing him from reclaiming his guns and firing on the retiring Rebels.

Despite all the obstacles, William H. Moore's brigade managed to bypass the bulk of the fighting and slip through the gap between Stanley and the railroad. His men easily entered Corinth, but they were confronted by the Federal guards and pickets established there before the battle. At times the fighting grew tough, with street-to-street action. Some Rebels managed to penetrate to the town square, at the intersection of the two railroads, where they temporarily came into the possession of Rosecrans's reserve artillery. This gave rise to the erroneous report that Price's men had captured forty guns. A call to Stanley brought reinforcements, and soon the Rebels were swept out of town without taking off any of the unused artillery.

Maury's attack had been a magnificent failure. Like Green's assault, it produced tantalizing results but no breakthrough. The superiority of the Union artillery and the stout defense of the infantry, plus the fortifications, defeated the Rebels. Maury had taken 3,900 men into action on October 3 and lost 2,598 by the end of the fighting on October 4. Stirman's Sharpshooters of Phifer's Brigade suffered 323 casualties out of 640 engaged in the battle. All but one member of its color guard was killed or wounded, and the flag had sixteen bullet holes in it. Yet the unit's commander, Ras Stirman, remembered years later that he had "never witnessed anything so grand as the charge made by the 7 brigades of Gen. Price."

In contrast to Price's men, Lovell's division did almost nothing to help the Confederate cause that day. Its three brigades advanced at dawn for a mile and a half, John C. Bowen's on the right, Brig. Gen. John Villepigue's on the left, and Albert Rust's in reserve. They came within two hundred yards of the Federal line at College Hill, where Corona College stood. The hill was heavily fortified, and all three brigades of McKean's division were concentrated in the area. The Rebels were impressed with the "formidable-looking breastworks" of Battery Phillips. The ground in front of it was cleared, and the brush and trees made a very strong abatis. No order to assault was given, so officers puttered around, placing and replacing units. Villepigue was sent off to reinforce Price, and Rust came up to replace him.

Bowen tried to feel the Union line by ordering a battery to open up, which touched off a heavy exchange of artillery fire that killed or injured fifty of his men before he retired for safety. Lovell finally appeared late in the morning, riding up to Bowen's command. He did not immediately order an attack, but one of his staff members asked Bowen if it was possible to take College Hill. Bowen replied that it was too late to try it, for the element of surprise was lost. Even if it had not been too late, the prospects of success were bleak. "Suppose General Lovell orders you to take it?" queried the staff officer. Bowen grimly replied, "My brigade will march up and be killed." No attack was ordered.

Lovell's reluctance to press home an assault was widely criticized after the battle, but there is no reason to believe that he could have been more successful than Green or Maury. Van Dorn ordered him to cover the retreat of his army. He quickly pulled away and assigned Rust the task of establishing a defensive position where the old Confederate Line crossed the Memphis and Charleston Railroad. Rust deployed a skirmish line three-quarters of a mile in front, stretching it one mile wide to cover two wagon roads as well as the railroad.

Van Dorn had given it his best shot and meant to pull out quickly. Price's two divisions were utterly exhausted from the fighting and their lack of water. Villepigue's brigade arrived too late for Price to use it, and thus it retired with his division. Cabell had the presence of mind following his drubbing by DuBois to take along all the blankets and knapsacks he could find before pulling out. At first, many Confederate units retired in disorder because of the heavy losses of officers, their thirst, fatigue, and the rough nature of the terrain. But after they passed Indian Creek and were out of immediate danger, order was quickly restored. Rust waited forty minutes after the last unit passed his position, then he too retired, unmolested.

The Confederate disengagement and withdrawal went very smoothly, but some officers were disturbed when Van Dorn ordered the army to halt for the night at Chewalla. John Tyler Jr., of Price's staff, believed they should have marched another four miles to reach the train and protect it or an additional four miles to secure Davis's Bridge over the Hatchie. The men needed all the food, water, and security they could get. But Van Dorn had not yet given up the idea of taking Corinth. Astonishingly, he proposed attacking it from another direction. That night he ordered Armstrong's and Jackson's cavalry to sieze Rienzi, some twelve miles from Corinth, for he intended to march the army there the next day and attack from the south. Price put his foot down, telling Van Dorn that his men were too cut up to try the impossible again. Van Dorn reluctantly changed his plan and ordered a march to Ripley and then to Oxford.

It took some time for the Federals to realize that the battle was over. By midafternoon Rosecrans was convinced that no further attacks were coming, and he collapsed in relief. The army leader had had only thirty minutes of sleep the night before and was exhausted by the stress of two days of complicated fighting. Soon after he lay down in the shade of a tree, he saw "three bursts of smoke" and concluded that the Rebels were blowing up their ammunition, preparing to withdraw. He remounted and rode along the line, telling the men that he could let them rest for the remainder of the day, as they were exhausted, but they needed to prepare five days' rations and be ready to pursue the next morning. Just at sundown, reinforcements arrived from Jackson in the shape of four regiments under Maj. Gen. James B. McPherson. They bivouacked in the town square and provided fresh troops for the morrow's march.

All along the Federal line, different units slowly came to the realization that the day was theirs. John McArthur led a reconnaissance from McKean's division as far west as the Halleck line on the Kossuth road and then northward, encountering only a few Confederate stragglers. Joy mixed with relief was the prevalent emotion throughout the army. When Rosecrans rode among the Fifteenth Iowa at nearly sundown, he "was almost taken from his horse by the soldiers," according to Cyrus Boyd. *"The wildest enthusiasm* prevailed and every man seems ready to pursue the enemy."

The battle of Corinth had been fierce and costly, making for a bloody October in Mississippi. Each side had about 20,000 men engaged. Van Dorn's Army of West Tennessee lost 505 killed, 2,150 wounded, and 2,183 missing, totaling 4,838. Rosecrans's force lost 355 killed, 1,841 wounded, and 324 missing, for a total of 2,520.

The fighting on October 3 had been a long delaying action, the engagement at the White House being the only sustained, bitter fighting. Rough terrain greatly delayed the Confederate attack and also allowed the Federals to slip away easily from one defensive position to the next. On October 4, the Confederate artillery played no role despite its spectacular introduction of the fighting. There was no good position for it because of the same difficult terrain and vegetation that had bedeviled Confederate operations the day before. In contrast, the Federals had quickly and effectively prepared their defenses before the battle. The College Hill line had good artillery emplacements, cleared fields of fire, and an excellent abatis. The Federal artillery played a key role in repelling Van Dorn's attacks. The Confederates could not take advantage of their opportunity to catch exposed angles in the line, such as Battery Robinett, in a crossfire. Even when Rebel infantry did capture Powell and Robinett, they could not hold them because they lacked enough men. If Van Dorn had had an adequate reserve and employed it promptly, he might have been able to exploit any advantage. Finally, the Federal infantry fought as well as the Confederates. Even though their line had holes in it, reserves to the rear could deal with any Confederates who broke through.

Van Dorn would not escape without having to fight his way out, for Grant was preparing to block him. For several days before the battle, scouts had brought reports that Van Dorn was aiming at either Corinth or Bolivar, forcing Grant to delay shifting forces until he knew for certain where to send them. By September 30 he guessed it was Corinth and warned Rosecrans to draw in his outlying detachments and send back all the cars and locomotives he could from Corinth to Jackson to save them from capture. He also ordered Hurlbut to be ready to move out of Bolivar at a moment's notice to hit

Van Dorn's men near Pocahontas. Hurlburt received the order to go on October 3. Grant also tried to help Rosecrans by sending McPherson with four regiments and informing him of Hurlbut's advance. Grant wanted Rosecrans to pursue the Rebels right after they retired. He later regretted that Rosecrans did not do so on the fourth, but he understood the pressing need for rest. Still, if Van Dorn could have been hounded, he might have been forced to abandon much of his artillery and wagons.

Hurlbut started from Bolivar with eight thousand men at dawn on October 4. A battalion of the Fifth Ohio Cavalry preceded his march and began to skirmish with Rebel pickets at Middleton before dark. The Ohioans, however, pushed forward so rapidly that they were able to capture the bridge over the Big Muddy before the Rebels could burn it and to secure the levee there before a strong defensive position could be established. Brig. Gen. Jacob Lauman's brigade crossed the Big Muddy before dark, having marched twenty-three miles that day, and camped on the hills east of it, while Brig. Gen. James Veatch's brigade camped west of the creek.

Veatch crossed the creek early on Sunday, October 5, bringing Hurlbut's force back together again. Major General Ord arrived that morning and, as Hurlbut's superior, took command of the expedition. He advanced the troops five miles along a road that was "narrow and winding, through swamps and jungle." Veatch's brigade was in the lead with Lauman a short distance behind him. Veatch's men deployed into a battle line when Confederate cavalry resistance grew stiffer and plunged ahead over very broken terrain covered with dense woods and thickets. Then the line came upon the western bluff of the Hatchie, about forty feet high, and the small town of Metamora. Ahead was the flat, wide valley of the river and Davis's Bridge, only six hundred yards to the east. As they approached the bluff, Confederate artillery began to fire at Veatch's men. Capt. William H. Bolton's Battery L, Second Illinois Light Artillery, deployed at the road while Capt. Silas A. Burnap's Seventh Ohio Battery set up to the right. The "morning sun was shining brightly," according to gunner Albert Martin Forbes of Bolton's battery, "not a cloud was to be seen there was a pleasant breeze blowing from the south & all was calm & beautiful while the plain below us was filled with the enemy the bright steel sparkling in the sun." The battle of Davis's Bridge, or, as some preferred to call it, the battle of the Hatchie, was about to be fought just three miles north of the state line in Tennessee.

Van Dorn began the morning with the knowledge that Federal forces from Bolivar might try to dispute his crossing, so he ordered Hawkins's First Texas Legion to move as quickly as possible to the bridge. Hawkins's men were dismounted and ran at the double-quick, arriving at 8:30 to relieve Adams's tired cavalrymen who had been battling Hurlbut. They established a line in the bottomland west of the bridge, three hundred yards from the bluff. Then Adams sent word to Van Dorn that he needed much more help. The army leader was riding beside Maury when the dispatch arrived. He turned to him and said, "Maury, you are in for it again to-day. Push forward as rapidly as you can and occupy the heights beyond the river before the enemy can get them." John C. Moore's brigade was at the head of the column and rushed forward. Moore had only three hundred men, all of them weak from hunger, but he crossed the bridge in a column of fours and deployed to the right of Hawkins, surrounded by flat and mostly open ground. Bolton's battery opened fire as soon as Moore took position and silenced Capt. William E. Dawson's St. Louis Battery of four guns, which Moore had brought with him. In addition, there were two guns on the field that the Rebels had captured at Corinth. None of them could withstand Bolton's well-aimed fire.

Veatch followed up this duel with an order to advance, and his whole battle line moved out at noon on the double-quick, two regiments on the left of the road and the rest of the brigade on the right. Even Bolton's guns joined in the charge. The cry was, "Forward forward everything forward down the hill." Veatch widely outflanked the Confederates on both sides and delivered a heavy fire of musketry into both flanks. Moore's men retreated pell-mell toward the river. They abandoned the artillery, which fell into Federal hands unspiked. Veatch's left flank reached the river before the Rebels and cut off and captured about one hundred Confederates. The rest of Moore's and Hawkins's men crossed wherever they could find room, though many of them lost their guns and their units.

But help was on the way. Phifer's brigade had gotten up in time to establish a defensive position on the bluff east of the Hatchie. Cabell's brigade also came up. Still later, Price himself arrived to take charge of the defense. Green's division was delayed by the trains, but it eventually came up. The Rebels had an excellent artillery position on the bluff two hundred yards from the bridge and a sizable force of infantry to support the guns.

The reinforced Confederate line made Ord pay dearly for his next move. He pushed Veatch's men across Davis's Bridge to follow up their success, but they became perfect targets for Price's well-placed artillery. With projectiles raining down on them, a section of Bolton's battery and three regiments crossed and found the ground east of the river to be poorly suited for deployment. Thick woods crowded the road on both sides and the river bent sharply eastward just south of the bridge, leaving very little room on the right side of the road. Veatch could deploy the Fourteenth Illinois to the left and the Fifty-third Indiana to the right, but there was little room for any other units. Bolton's guns were forced to stay in the road for a while, suffering from the Confederate fire, until a place could be carved out for them.

The confusion grew as Lauman's brigade came up and began to cross the bridge. His men went in regiment by regiment, and it took more than an hour for the entire brigade to cross. The crush of men and animals east of the river, particularly south of the road, was tremendous, and it offered a marvelous target for the Rebel artillery. The Third Iowa lost fifty-seven men crossing the bridge and deploying in the crowd, even though it ran at double-quick, shouting all the way. There was considerable mixing of units as well. Ord himself was hit and had to retire, but Hurlbut took his place and ordered the intermixed brigades to extend northward into the middle of the river bend. This move reduced the confusion and crowding. Then Hurlbut ordered an attack. On the left of the road Veatch advanced over an open cornfield up the bluff. He halted just below the crest, for the Confederates were posted in the edge of the woods near the top. Veatch did not want to waste men in such an exposed position so he simply waited, his men crouching for cover. Fortunately, Lauman's brigade on the right had better cover and managed to pressure Price into retreating three-quarters of a mile east to the top of a ridge. Hurlbut's men followed up cautiously and opened what Albert Martin Forbes called a "regular artillery duel for about two hours, magnificently terrific."

Neither side was willing to push the engagement further, giving Van Dorn enough time to find another way across the Hatchie. Armstrong's cavalry had scouted another crossing at Crum's Mill, six miles south, and sent word that it was usable. Ironically, Van Dorn had earlier ordered the troops to destroy the wooden bridge there. Now he realized he would need it to save his army, and orders went out for Armstrong to prepare the way. There was no time to rebuild the bridge, so two companies of the Seventh Tennessee Cavalry quickly laid logs and rocks on top of the mill dam to improvise a crossing. Van Dorn started his five hundred wagons on the Boneyard Road, which branched off to the southwest from his route, the State Line Road. The Mississippi general also ordered Lovell to send two brigades to Davis's Bridge and leave one to guard the crossing of the Tuscumbia against Rosecrans's pursuit. Villepigue replaced Price at 3:30 as his men were greeted with a shout of joy from their harried comrades. Price's two depleted divisions filed out of position and headed for Crum's Mill following the train.

Rust's brigade covered their rear, and Villepigue joined them after holding Hurlbut a while longer.

Bowen's brigade had a brief fight at the Tuscumbia with the advance of Rosecrans's army. McPherson started out just after dawn on the Chewalla Road with four companies of the Fifth Ohio Cavalry and a battery added to his four regiments. He could hear the sound of Ord's battle at Davis's Bridge when he was still six miles east of Chewalla, and his cavalry began to skirmish with Rebel horsemen as soon as it reached the town. Bowen was posted atop high ground covered with trees and underbrush east of the Tuscumbia crossing so the Federals were forced to deploy and feel their way gingerly. It was almost dark when the Federals closed in, but Bowen stopped them with artillery fire and a limited advance by the Fifteenth Mississippi. He then crossed the river, burned the bridge, and obstructed the nearby ford. Bowen rejoined Lovell's division before it crossed the Hatchie, having lost three killed and ten wounded.

The crossing at Crum's Mill was precarious, but it saved Van Dorn's army. When Gates's brigade crossed at 9 P.M., Ephraim McDowell Anderson saw Price personally supervising the constant repairs to the crossing. Passing wagons and careless soldiers frequently knocked a part of it out of place, and Price, who stood on the west side, had to call on his men to help replace parts of it. He even helped them to throw rocks back into place. "His whole soul seemed to be in the work, and when it was done, he straightened himself from his stooping posture, remarking 'well done, boys—now stand back and let the train pass.'" All of the army was over by 1 A.M. of October 6 and stopped for rest late in the night only five miles short of Ripley. It had marched for twenty hours "nearly famished with hunger" but had lost only thirteen wagons on the way.

The battle at Davis's Bridge failed to trap and destroy Van Dorn's army. The Confederates had about 2,000 men engaged, with an additional 2,000 in close support. They lost at least 200 prisoners and left 32 dead on the field, but no full accounting of Rebel losses was ever made. The Unionists had 8,000 men available on the field, most of whom came under fire at some point in the action, and lost 570 casualties. As Maury would aptly put it, "Never did an army more narrowly escape than did Van Dorn's from the forks of the Hatchie."

The Federal pursuit petered out after the battle at Davis's Bridge. Hurlbut did not even attempt to follow Van Dorn, citing a lack of adequate transportation and food. He received an order from Grant to return to Bolivar on the night of October 6. McPherson pushed ahead early that morning. His engineers repaired the bridge over the Tuscumbia, part of which was still burning when they began to work on it. McPherson found much abandoned equipment, clothing, and tents, and a short stretch of the Boneyard Road was obstructed with felled trees. He found both the mill and the makeshift bridge at Crum's Mill on fire when he reached there at noon but immediately set his engineers to work repairing the crossing. The infantry began to cross at 4:30 P.M, and McPherson bivouacked near Jonesborough that night.

The rest of Rosecrans's army made only a halfhearted attempt to join the chase. All units started early on October 5, but there was enormous confusion about the best roads to take, causing a traffic jam when all four divisions came together on the same route. They were far behind McPherson's vanguard all day on October 6 and dallied at various points from Corinth until about October 12, when it became fully evident that no Rebel forces lurked anywhere near the town. Rosecrans's army marched about a hundred miles on this futile effort.

His men did encounter the stark evidence of battle and retreat. John Wilcox marched over the battleground of October 3, two days after the fighting, and reported that "we saw sights to make the soul sick. The blackened swollen decaying bodies of the dead, festering in the hot sun, poluting the air with a foul sickening stench." He found some bodies that had been robbed of their boots and clothes and passed corpses for four miles as Davies's division tramped out of Corinth.

Evidence of a hasty retreat was found all along the road to Crum's Mill. "The hills were steep and wagons had struck trees and rolled over and over," reported Cyrus Boyd of the Fifteenth Iowa. "Some had been loaded with Corn meal and some with flour and others with cooking utensils and all kinds of stuff was scattered like some great whirlwind had overtaken the retreating army. Artillery caissons had struck trees and the ammunition had exploded tearing everything to pieces around. Many places the cannoniers had cut the *traces* and gone leaving their load behind. The hillsides were white with corn meal and flour and the dust in the road fully one foot deep." Several stragglers found in the woods easily gave up. "Glad to do anything to save all they had *left* and that was their *lives*."

Only McPherson persisted in the chase. He skirmished with the Rebel rear guard on October 7 and found Ripley empty of Confederate troops that night. While his infantry camped there, a cavalry brigade that had joined his column moved another twenty miles farther but made no contact. McPherson tarried at Ripley, where Stanley's and McKean's divisions joined him, and then he retraced his route back to Corinth by October 12. Grant had decided to call off all pursuit as soon as Van Dorn crossed the Hatchie, but McPherson was already at Ripley when the word reached him. Grant realized that no one could catch Van Dorn before he found safety behind the fortifications of Holly Springs.

The Confederates retreated well but suffered a great deal. They left many stragglers behind, and everyone was "worn out with fatigue, sadly depressed, almost demoralized." The army marched by way of Roxbury, Hickory Flats, and Connersville, crossed the Tallahatchie, and reached Holly Springs on October 11. It had a chance to rest for the first time since the battle. The Third Louisiana was, according to Will Tunnard, "in a terrible condition. Worn out with fatigue, sick, ragged, filthy, and covered with vermin, it was not strange that even their brave spirits should give way under the accumulated disasters, sufferings and hardships which had so rapidly befallen them. Human endurance is not composed of cast-steel, and they felt, as well they might, depressed in spirits, disheartened in mind, prostrated in body."

The man most intimately responsible for the campaign and its outcome soon lost his job. On October 14, Lieut. Gen. John C. Pemberton assumed command of the Department of Mississippi and East Louisiana. Van Dorn was reassigned as chief of cavalry, "his proper sphere," thought Ephraim McDowell Anderson of Gates's brigade. Pemberton visited Holly Springs for a few days to inspect the troops, then moved on to establish his headquarters at Jackson.

Criticism of Van Dorn's handling of the campaign began to circulate immediately after the army's return. John Tyler Jr. wrote a long letter to William Lowndes Yancey, an influential Confederate politician, pointing out his faults as a commander. Capt. Edward H. Cummins, inspector general of Maury's division, wrote similarly to Beauregard, but the most serious efforts came from Bowen. He brought formal charges against Van Dorn, accusing him of neglect of duty for failing to acquire proper maps of the fortifications at Corinth; failing to reconnoiter Union positions properly; failing to supply his men with adequate food, "depending entirely upon captures from the enemy"; marching his men "in a hastily and disorderly manner, hurling them upon the enemy"; and delaying the attack on the inner line of Union works on October 3. Bowen also accused Van Dorn of "Cruel and improper treatment of officers and men" on the retreat, claiming that a trainload of wounded was delayed at Water Valley for no reason, causing unnecessary suffering.

Van Dorn requested a court of inquiry to exonerate himself. It convened on November 10 at Holly Springs with Price acting as president and Maury and Brig. Gen. Lloyd Tilghman as members. Van Dorn opened the inquiry by pleading for his reputation. "I have been a soldier for nearly a quarter of a century . . . this is the first time I have been called upon to defend myself against allegations of any kind, though my career has been an eventful one." He had no wealth, hence "my reputation is all that belongs to me, without which life to me were as valueless as the crisp and faded leaf of autumn."

The testimony from a variety of witnesses produced no consistent evidence of incompetence. Van Dorn's chief commissary swore that he had secured enough food for Lovell's division until October 9 and for Price's two divisions until October 3 or 4. Price's men were resupplied as they crossed the Tuscumbia on the retreat. In addition, he had accumulated four hundred thousand rations at Holly Springs just before beginning the campaign. Price testified that food shortages were circumstantial, a result of provision trains being so far from the scene of battle and that Van Dorn did all he could to make up for that lack. Price also swore that he had an excellent map. Bowen's testimony was the most damaging. He spoke of the shortage of wagons and explained that Lovell's division had only a half day's ration when the attack began on October 3. No one else spoke as tellingly about the faults of his commander. The result was a mixed bag of evidence, some apparent covering up by friendly witnesses, and no consensus as to guilt. On November 22, the court ruled Van Dorn innocent of all charges. He forwarded the findings to President Davis with an impassioned letter defending his character against accusations of a nonmilitary nature. Rumors had been flying for months that he had seduced innocent young women and married ladies alike, and he fiercely defended himself. "I am unfortunately not a good Christian," he admitted, "*but I am not* a Seducer, nor a drunkard."

The impact of Van Dorn's campaign among the Southern people was dreadful. Everyone's spirit was dampened by the lack of success and the heavy casualties. Josiah Gorgas called it a "disaster" with a "mournful result, risked without an object." In the eyes of the public, the campaign reflected very badly on the generalship of both Price and Van Dorn. Editorial response varied. The *Augusta Daily Constitutionalist* was determined to steel its readers with the thought that defeat would only make the people fight harder. The *Savannah Daily News* was more bluntly accusatory: "It is not our purpose here to comment upon the facts related. They are too painful to dwell upon, and call loudly for prompt and searching investigations by the Government."

Corinth had little impact on the Northern public, obsessed as it was with the results of Buell's campaign in Kentucky, Lee's repulse in Maryland, and the growth of Copperhead sentiment in the looming fall elections. It was taken as a proper follow-up to the larger victories west and east. The campaign also had no impact on foreign relations. Britain and France were influenced principally by military developments in the Virginia theater, not by the comparatively small movements in Mississippi. If Van Dorn had been successful in crushing Rosecrans's force and capturing Corinth, more people in the North and overseas would have taken notice.

As it was, the results of Price's and Van Dorn's campaigns in northern Mississippi failed to contribute to Rebel strategy. Price was unable to prevent Grant from sending troops to Buell, nor did he reinforce Bragg in Kentucky. At best, his muddled maneuvers only prevented the further transfer of aid to the Army of the Ohio, if any was contemplated. On the level of regional strategy, Van Dorn's attempt to crack the Union hold on northern Mississippi and western Tennessee was a bloody failure. He did not liberate any territory or redress the balance of power in the area. As at Perryville, aggressive Confederate tactics led to heavy losses and close calls for the defending Federals but no strategic gains. The utility of well-planned fortifications was vividly demonstrated on October 4, and the value of establishing a series of troop concentrations at different towns that could converge on an attacker was also demonstrated at the Davis's Bridge battle. For the second time, Grant attempted a pincers movement and again came close to making it work. The Union position in western Tennessee was too strong to be broken by the artless bungling of Price and Van Dorn.

While Van Dorn lost his army command and had to fight for his reputation, Rosecrans's career skyrocketed after Corinth. He was quickly promoted to command Buell's army in Kentucky, eventually renaming it the Army of the Cumberland and taking it on two of its bloodiest campaigns, Stones River and Chickamauga. The impact of Van Dorn's attack was just as significant for Grant's career. Ever since May, Union forces had busied themselves with occupation duties in the territory won during the previous winter. Now that the only Confederate force in northern Mississippi was reduced in size and morale, Grant decided to resume the offensive down the Mississippi Valley that had been put on hold ever since the fall of Corinth. He planned and initiated a bold campaign in November involving a two-pronged approach to Vicksburg. Sherman would lead a column down the Mississippi by boat to hit the town from the riverside, while Grant would advance down the railroad line into central Mississippi to approach the stronghold by land. The tumultuous summer of 1862, which had seen important Union victories mixed with startling Confederate offensives, was over. The results of these efforts represented the passing of a unique opportunity for the Rebels to seize the strategic initiative and redirect the flow of events in their favor. Never again would they have such a good chance to save the West.

CHAPTER TEN

On to Murfreesboro

Van Dorn's failed attack on Corinth ended the Mississippi phase of Bragg's offensive into Kentucky and also set the stage for Grant's drive into the Deep South. This was the first of several Union offensives that gained steam in November and December 1862, the first simultaneous campaigns that the Union army had launched since the war began. Grant's drive also represented the continuation of the offensive that had stalled in June following the capture of Corinth. For the first time, a major Federal army was attempting to penetrate the Lower South. The war to destroy the Confederacy entered a new phase.

Farther west and east, other Federal forces also launched moves in the Upper South. In northwestern Arkansas, a Confederate army under Maj. Gen. Thomas C. Hindman met an army of Yankees under Brig. Gen. Francis Jay Herron and Brig. Gen. James G. Blunt at Prairie Grove. The resulting fierce battle on December 7 was a tactical draw, but Hindman felt compelled to retreat southward, leaving the field and northern Arkansas in Union hands. In Virginia, the Army of the Potomac moved swiftly toward Fredericksburg under its new commander, Maj. Gen. Ambrose E. Burnside, who succeeded George B. McClellan following the repulse of Lee's invasion of Maryland. Burnside's plan to cross the Rappahannock River at Fredericksburg and outflank Lee was stymied by a delay in bringing forward pontoons, forcing him to wait for nearly a month on the eastern bank of the river while Lee assumed a strong defensive position on the heights west of the stream. Despite that setback, Burnside still was determined to move on before severe winter weather put an end to the campaigning season.

Indeed, it seemed as if all Union armies were on the move that late fall except the Army of the Cumberland. William Starke Rosecrans was repeatedly urged by his superiors to move forward and fight Bragg's army at Murfreesboro, but he took his time preparing his new command. The Army of the Cumberland had arrived at Nashville by the middle of November and needed rest, reorganization, and a boost in morale before it could commence a new campaign.

Rosecrans began by asking permission to cashier incompetent field officers. Men who had demonstrated their inability to measure up to Rosecrans's exacting standards were sent to other assignments or dismissed from the service. Charles C. Gilbert was relieved of his corps command, and others felt the sting of the ax as well. Rosecrans strictly enforced discipline in the camps to bring a sense of order to the army. Then he attacked supply problems with personal inspections of the regiments, urging men who lacked material to bother their officers until the spare canteen or cartridge belt was issued.

Rosecrans hoped to rejuvenate the support arms of the army as well. He appointed Brig. Gen. David S. Stanley as chief of his cavalry. Stanley had had a great deal of experience in the mounted arm on the pre–Civil War frontier, and worked energetically to reorganize the army's horsemen. Rather than scatter the regiments about by attaching them to infantry units, he recommended that they be concentrated into brigades. Rosecrans also felt he did not have enough cavalry regiments and that those he did have were not properly armed, a deficiency he could not remedy before the coming campaign got under way. As his chief engineer, the army commander selected Capt. James St. Clair Morton, a regular officer who was young and brilliant. He organized a larger and more efficient engineer force than existed in any other western army, blue or gray, with a brigade of some two thousand men detached from the infantry regiments. These soldiers would be used to build fortifications, bridges, and roads. This engineer work had largely been done on an ad hoc basis in the past by detailing infantrymen as needed. Now, a full brigade under the control of an energetic engineer was dedicated to the task. This was the beginning of a professional engineer force that the Army of the Cumberland would need as it continued to advance into the South along a single rail line.

The entire army had been reorganized even before Rosecrans had taken it to Nashville, a result of his earlier assignment to its command on October 24. George H. Thomas was given charge of what Rosecrans designated the Center, with 29,337 men. Alexander McCook led the Right Wing with 15,832 men, and Thomas L. Crittenden commanded the Left Wing with

14,308 soldiers. Rosecrans was not impressed with either McCook or Crittenden, but he had no political leverage to replace them. Thomas was so widely respected among the men and the authorities in Washington and so well liked by Rosecrans himself that he was given the biggest "corps." Although he continued to call his army the XIV Army Corps for the duration of the coming campaign, Rosecrans had gone a long way toward revitalizing the tired and somewhat abused force that would become known as the Army of the Cumberland.

His campaign would take place at a time when the home front was nearing a point of political crisis. The startling success of Copperhead candidates in the fall elections created a sense among the authorities in Washington that the war had to be pushed harder than ever, even if that meant a series of winter campaigns. The Copperheads, Democratic critics of Lincoln's policies, had gained enough seats to dominate the legislatures of several states, including Lincoln's own Illinois. They were widely viewed by the Republicans as traitors to the Northern cause, but in reality they were a loyal opposition, critical of the emancipation policy and Lincoln's other bold moves but not in favor of a Confederate victory. The Copperheads' primary threat was to the continued domination of the Republicans and their vigorous prosecution of the war effort.

Senator John Sherman was convinced that the main reason for the growth of Copperhead sentiment among the voters was the muddled way the war progressed. "The slow movements on the Potomac and worse still in Kentucky dissatisfied and discouraged people," he wrote to his brother. The team of McClellan and Buell had employed cautious strategies to the detriment of the Union's political future. Lincoln had to pay for this because he had "put and kept in these slow generals and we shall be punished for it by having an organized opposition limiting appropriations." Sherman also cited the suspension of the writ of habeas corpus and the emancipation policy as major features in the Copperhead phenomenon. The only way to counteract this wave was to fire slow generals and speed up the war effort by urging their replacements to move.

Lincoln was pressed by other issues as well in late fall. An effort by loyal mountaineers in the occupied counties of western Virginia came to a climax in late December with an application to enter the Union as a state. Both houses of Congress passed a bill approving the application, and Lincoln asked his cabinet members for their opinions on its constitutionality and political expediency. The jury was evenly split, but the president signed the bill admitting West Virginia on the last day of the year. A more difficult task lay in reviewing the cases of dozens of Sioux Indians who had been condemned to death by a military tribunal for their part in the great Sioux uprising of 1862 in Minnesota. It had been one of the more brutal Indian wars in American history, leading to hundreds of deaths. The president wanted "to not act with so much clemency as to encourage another outbreak on the one hand, nor with so much severity as to be real cruelty on the other." He determined that only thirty-nine of the condemned had been involved in committing an atrocity and approved their sentencing. All but one of them was executed on December 26; the remaining Sioux was pardoned by Lincoln a year and a half later.

In the middle of these trying times the president delivered his annual message to Congress on December 1. It was a momentous time. The Emancipation Proclamation was due to go into effect in one month. The military offensives he had urged to compensate for the reverses of 1862 were unfolding, and the Copperheads were preparing to take their seats in governmental bodies all over the North. He spent a great deal of time with matters that, in peacetime, would have been banner issues but now seemed mundane compared to the war. Lincoln supported the laying of a transatlantic telegraph cable and the construction of a transcontinental railroad. He also announced the creation of a new department to handle matters relating to the agricultural economy. But the most memorable part of the long address dealt with the revolutionary significance of his emancipation policy. Lincoln tried to prepare the Congress and the electorate for this watershed event in American history. After 250 years of slavery, the nation was on its way to becoming wholly free. "The dogmas of the quiet past, are inadequate to the stormy present," Lincoln warned the legislators. "The occasion is piled high with difficulty, and we must rise with the occasion. As our case is new, so we must think anew, and act anew. We must disenthrall ourselves, and then we shall save our country." Lincoln demonstrated his genius for grasping the moment and urging others to follow his course when he said that the "fiery trial through which we pass, will light us down, in honor or dishonor, to the latest generation. . . . In *giving* freedom to the *slave*, we *assure* freedom to the *free*. . . . We shall nobly save, or meanly lose, the last best, hope of earth."

Jefferson Davis had no such invigorating issue to revolutionize his war effort in the South. In fact, he gave no annual message to Congress that December. But the Confederate president did make a long address to a crowd in Jackson on December 26 while visiting his home state of Mississippi. For ninety minutes he took stock of the war and commented on his government's actions. Davis reminded the audience that he had predicted war would result from the South's secession, but even he was stunned by the length and ferocity of the conflict. This was attributable to the North's "lust of power and of aggrandizement." The Yankees had no respect for the traditional customs of warfare, and Davis wondered how his native section had lived so long with them because they had "a government rotten to the core." "There is indeed a difference between the two people," Davis concluded. "Let no man hug the delusion that there can be renewed association between them." The president refused to apologize for the conscription policy, which was becoming more unpopular as the war demanded able-bodied soldiers. He claimed that the men who had volunteered in 1861 and who had been forced to stay in the army a year later when the draft was passed responded positively to the measure. There was "no disgrace to anyone" in being drafted.

Davis noted all the radical moves Lincoln had already begun, especially the emancipation policy, as clear signs of the degraded character of the North and the tyrannical tendency of the United States government. "The issue before us is one of no ordinary character," he told his audience. "We are not engaged in a conflict for conquest, or for aggrandizement, or for the settlement of a point of international law. The question for you to decide is, 'will you be slaves or will you be independent?' . . . will you consent to be robbed of your property; to be reduced to provincial dependence; will you renounce the exercise of those rights with which you were born and which were transmitted to you by your fathers?" The radical course of the Northern war effort had sealed the commitment of many Southerners to their cause, at least in Davis's view. There was no turning back, if ever there had been a time when the Confederates wanted to turn back.

Davis also alluded to the stale hope of foreign intervention. By December 1862, the prospects of that glittering possibility had faded nearly into nothing. Emperor Napoleon III of France had pushed a plan for joint intervention with Britain and Russia, which had as its goal the signing of an armistice between the North and South, during the month of November. But the scheme failed when the British government showed no interest. England was still not convinced it was an opportune move. Davis steeled himself with the idea that the South must fight alone. "This war is ours," he reminded the crowd in Jackson, "we must fight it out ourselves, and I feel some pride in knowing that so far we have done it without the good will of anybody."

Davis could more easily afford to rest that December as Union military moves began to unravel, and defeat on the battlefield loomed to haunt the North's holiday season. First, Grant's campaign into northern Mississippi was turned back. Sending Sherman down the Mississippi while leading the rest of his army overland, Grant made excellent progress until Earl Van Dorn led a cavalry raid to destroy a depot of supplies at Holly Springs, behind Grant's advancing army. This action compelled the Federals to return to Tennessee. Sherman continued south and attacked a strong Confederate position at Chickasaw Bluffs, just north of Vicksburg, during the last days of December. He was rudely rebuffed and forced to retire a few miles up the river and wait for Grant's instructions. The Union effort to capture Vicksburg was not over, but the first round had not helped Lincoln's political cause among the voters.

The worst disaster that season occurred in Virginia, where Burnside suffered a crushing defeat at Fredericksburg. Demonstrating a foolishness beyond comprehension, he sent his powerful Army of the Potomac across the Rappahannock River and assaulted Lee's strong position just west of the town on December 13. It was a slaughter. The heaviest fighting took place at Marye's Heights, where the Rebel line was strongest. Divisions wrecked themselves trying to attack up a gentle, open slope against several ranks of Confederate soldiers packed behind a stone retaining wall. Burnside lost 12,600 men and failed to exploit the modest success he had gained on another part of the line. His battered army retreated across the river and waited for the next move from their bumbling general. There was nothing for Northerners to do but mourn the heavy losses and pin their hopes on Rosecrans in Tennessee.

Lincoln felt the pressure more than anyone in Washington. He knew that another defeat would be a crushing blow to morale and began to send testy messages to Nashville. Impatient to see the Confederates pressed hard in Middle Tennessee, he and Halleck even threatened to take away Rosecrans's new command if he continued to refit in Nashville. The army commander did not panic at this threat to his career, but he continued to believe that delay was necessary. He tried to convince Washington of something that Buell could not drum into the heads of his superiors, that a field army had to be properly fed and supplied before it could fight. The rail line north of Nashville remained broken until November 26, and it took some time after that for the quartermaster to accumulate supplies at the Nashville depot. "I have lost no time," Rosecrans tried to convince Halleck, and he continued to follow his own timetable for advancing rather than that of his superiors. It was too reminiscent of Buell, however justified Rosecrans's arguments may have been. He would have to move soon and decisively, regardless of the limitations of the Louisville and Nashville Railroad in supplying his army.

The strategic problem confronting Rosecrans was simple. Bragg's army lay only thirty miles to the southeast, at Murfreesboro. Both armies relied on the railroad as their line of communication. The terrain in this region was mostly level and supported numerous farms that produced significant amounts of food and fodder. In contrast to the Kentucky campaign, when both armies had marched long distances over mountains, this campaign would be short and easy. The greatest strategic difficulty confronting Rosecrans was the Confederate army itself. Bragg had as much time and opportunity to rest and rejuvenate his men as did Rosecrans. Although the march to Murfreesboro would be simple, the confrontation there promised to be brutal.

Finally, by the Christmas season, Rosecrans began to plan his advance. The quartermaster had time to accumulate enough supplies to last for more than a month. Also, reports had filtered in that Bragg had detached a division of infantry to Mississippi to help defend Vicksburg against Grant's invasion and that large forces of Rebel cavalry had ridden from Bragg to conduct raids on isolated posts in Tennessee. It seemed as if the Confederates did not expect Rosecrans to make a winter campaign, and thus, in his own words, "the moment was judged opportune for an advance on the rebels."

Rosecrans based his plan on inaccurate reports of Confederate troop positions. He believed that Bragg had placed his army along Stewart's Creek, which flowed on a southwest-to-northeast line about ten miles northwest of Murfreesboro. Thus he planned to move his three corps along widely divergent roads. Crittenden's Left Wing would move along the Murfreesboro Pike, which paralleled the Nashville and Chattanooga Railroad, at least as far as Lavergne. McCook's Right Wing would march along the Nolensville Pike to Triune, twenty-eight miles south of Nashville and fifteen miles west of Murfreesboro. Rosecrans believed, incorrectly, that most of Hardee's corps was positioned there. Thomas's Center would move still farther west, along the Franklin Pike and the Wilson Pike. Thomas would be nearly six miles west of McCook's line of march, but he was instructed to move east before McCook reached Triune and fall in to his rear. Thus he would be able to support McCook, whose wing was to move farther forward than the other two portions of the army. Rosecrans hoped that by threatening Hardee with overwhelming force he could force him to withdraw or be defeated in detail. Then McCook and Thomas could move eastward to hit Bragg's left wing behind Stewart's Creek. Crittenden's job was to hold Bragg's attention while this movement was taking place, and Stanley's cavalry would act as a screen ahead of the advancing army. Col. Robert Minty's brigade would ride ahead of Crittenden, and Col. Lewis Zahm's brigade would cover the front of Thomas's column. Zahm also was to screen McCook's left flank. All in all, it was a sensible plan, although it was based on erroneous information; much of Bragg's army was still in its winter encampments outside Murfreesboro. Only Hardee's corps was dispersed in the countryside west of town, with just a few small units near Stewart's Creek.

Rosecrans outlined this plan to his wing commanders in a conference on Christmas night. As each regiment tried to celebrate the holiday with whatever food and gifts were at their disposal, the army's high command worked hard into the early morning. Finally, the plans were absorbed and approved. The advance would begin at dawn, and brandy was served to everyone. There was at last a few minutes of fond conviviality on the eve of this trying campaign as generals and staff celebrated the holiday with liquor and traded good-hearted jibes. McCook, whose corps had nearly been wrecked at Perryville by the Confederate army he was soon to confront, seemed particularly jolly as day approached. He bragged that he "would be under the painful necessity of defeating his old friend, Hardee." But Rosecrans put a stop to the festive mood and signaled the end of both the party and the conference when he put on a fine display of the exaggerated bravado that associates often remembered. Forcefully hitting the table, he shouted, "We move tomorrow, gentlemen! We shall begin to skirmish, probably as soon as we pass the outposts. Press them hard! Drive them out of their nests! Make them fight or run! Strike hard and fast! Give them no rest! Fight them! Fight them! Fight, I say."

Such behavior was odd, even for a Civil War general. Rosecrans had cautiously prolonged his refitting in Nashville, and now that he was ready, he put on a great show of resolve and decisiveness. It was symptomatic of the mercurial disposition of the man. His temperament often took him to the heights of energy and resolve, but it also took him to the depths of despair and inaction. This was about the only flaw in an otherwise admirable general. Grant would never have given such a display to his subordinates or waited so long to settle his preparations, and Buell was incapable of stage-managing such a show. Whether or not they were infused with enthusiasm by Rosecrans's performance, the wing leaders of the Army of the Cumberland certainly were ready to give their commander a chance to prove himself.

Bragg's army would be ready to meet them. He had been able to let his men rest since they reached Murfreesboro in the first week of November. Food was relatively abundant in the countryside around town, and Bragg's men foraged liberally to fill their commissary stores. Shoes, clothes, and blankets were shipped in from army depots to the south as the weather began to turn chilly and then cold.

Bragg also reorganized his available force and accomplished something that should have been done back in July before the onset of the Kentucky campaign, the consolidation of his Army of the Mississippi and Edmund Kirby Smith's Army of Kentucky. Smith had slyly resisted such a move for months to protect his independent status, which was a major factor in Bragg's defeat in Kentucky. Now Bragg had wrested authority from President Davis to concentrate command in Tennessee. The newly merged units were designated the Army of Tennessee, and three corps were organized. Polk's corps had divisions led by Benjamin Franklin Cheatham, Jones Withers, and John C. Breckinridge. Hardee's corps had divisions led by Simon B. Buckner, who was replaced by Patrick R. Cleburne before the coming campaign began, and by Patton Anderson. Smith's corps was small, consisting only of two weak divisions commanded by Carter L. Stevenson and John McCown. Smith was so disgusted by the consolidation of his and Bragg's armies that he did not appear in Murfreesboro to assume his command until early December. Joseph Wheeler was retained as chief of Bragg's cavalry. He had performed well, especially on the retreat from Kentucky. Each of his three brigades of horsemen was assigned to an infantry corps. Knowing the value of both Nathan Bedford Forrest and John Hunt Morgan as hard-riding cavalry leaders, Bragg wisely allowed them to command their own brigade-sized forces for independent operations.

Bragg even helped to reshuffle the larger Confederate command structure in the West. Throughout this sprawling theater, Confederate forces had long suffered from a breakdown of coordinated movements, a surplus of crotchety subordinates, and far too many independent-minded commanders. Bragg was pressured by John C. Pemberton for reinforcements to help him block Grant's campaign into northern Mississippi. He strenuously resisted doing so, knowing that he needed every man to oppose Rosecrans. There was a great deal of confusion about the command structure. Pemberton assumed that Bragg was not only in charge of Middle Tennessee but of his own force in Mississippi as well, a responsibility that Bragg did not want to assume. But Bragg did try to take charge of Earl Van Dorn's and Mansfield Lovell's forces in northern Mississippi, a move that Van Dorn strongly opposed and which made little sense. Bragg was too far away in Murfreesboro to direct the movements of either commander, and it also was illogical for him to take over Van Dorn's and Lovell's commands without supervising all of Pemberton's men in central Mississippi as well. This muddled situation was ostensibly solved on November 24 with the appointment of Gen. Joseph E. Johnston as commander of the Confederacy's western forces, putting him over both Pemberton and Bragg.

But Davis and Johnston could not agree on a proper strategy for the West. The president saw Vicksburg as the key and expected Johnston to drain Bragg of men, if necessary, to save it. Johnston knew that to do so would mean the loss of Middle Tennessee, and even then it might not guarantee the safety of Mississippi. Davis decided that a personal inspection of Bragg's army would give him the opportunity to assess the opinions of Bragg's subordinates. He reached Murfreesboro on December 12 and reviewed the troops of Polk's corps the next day. His visit was capped off by a lavish dinner with the army's principal commanders. Everyone was on his best behavior. Those officers who had been loudest in their denunciations of Bragg remained discreetly silent, giving the president the impression that the army was united with a positive spirit behind its leader. The debilitating dissension that followed the Kentucky campaign seemed at an end. Also, Davis got the impression that the army believed Rosecrans would not move before spring and that Middle Tennessee would be quiet throughout the winter. The president left Murfreesboro on December 14 with all the wrong ideas. He stopped at Chattanooga to confer with Johnston and then ordered Bragg to send reinforcements to Pemberton. On December 16, Stevenson's division of seventy-five hundred men moved out for Mississippi.

Only one division remained in Smith's corps, opening the opportunity for Bragg to transfer McCown's division to Hardee and eliminate Smith's command altogether. Bragg was finally rid of the man who had, in many ways, let him down in Kentucky. Smith left Murfreesboro for eastern Tennessee and eventually was elevated to command of the Trans-Mississippi region. Further reorganization of the army took place as Breckinridge's division was shifted from Polk's to Hardee's corps, and Patton Anderson's division was disbanded and its regiments divided between Polk and Hardee. The reorganization made the Army of Tennessee a more efficient force, but the detachment of Stevenson's men seriously weakened Bragg on the eve of an important campaign. Stevenson's addition to Pemberton's army would prove, through no fault of the division commander, to have no effect on the outcome of the Vicksburg campaign.

Not expecting an immediate attack, Bragg dispersed his men to several points in the countryside. While Polk's corps built winter quarters near Murfreesboro, McCown's division was stationed twelve miles east at Readyville. Hardee's corps moved to Eagleville, twenty miles southwest of town. One of his brigades was dispatched to Triune, fifteen miles west of Murfreesboro, while a battalion of John A. Wharton's cavalry brigade was placed at Franklin, thirty miles to the west.

Bragg also felt secure enough to send off a good portion of his cavalry on a spectacular raid. John Hunt Morgan took 2,100 infantry and cavalry some fifty miles north to Hartsville, Tennessee, crossing the Cumberland River and surprising a garrison of 2,400 Federals. In a sharp fight on December 7, the Yankees were beaten in quick order; 1,834 of them surrendered and another 58 were killed and 204 were wounded. The total Federal casualties of 2,096 men far outweighed Morgan's loss of 139 soldiers. The Confederates evacuated Hartsville and easily reached safety before Federal reinforcements arrived in the area. It was a small but impressive display of daring, resourcefulness, and tactical success at little cost to the Confederates, but it made no difference in the strategic course of the war in Tennessee.

The Confederates celebrated Christmas with a feeling of relief that a quiet winter seemed at hand. A ball at the Rutherford County courthouse in Murfreesboro was sponsored by officers of some of the Louisiana regiments in the army. The principal guests were the unmarried women of the town. Federal flags captured at Hartsville were put on display, and the building was festooned with cedar boughs and enlivened by chatter, good cheer, and hundreds of dancing feet. The enlisted men of Bragg's army made do with whatever they could buy or scrounge from the countryside. Some of them managed to find geese or turkeys, and liquor was a favorite holiday beverage for anyone lucky enough to find it. Considering what these men would have to endure in just a week, no one could begrudge them a few moments of quiet celebration.

Soon after dawn on December 26, everyone realized that the warm, balmy weather of the past two weeks was gone. Instead, the campaign began under dark, low clouds and chilly winds. A cold rain set in later that day, reminding the men that winter had begun. But McCook's Wing set out on schedule at six o'clock. Jefferson C. Davis, back on duty following his shooting of William Nelson the previous September, started his division first. Wharton's isolated outposts along the Nolensville Road did not offer much resistance. Under orders only to delay the Federal advance, they fired a few shots now and then before pulling out for the south. By nightfall, Davis was within striking distance of Triune and the rest of McCook's divisions bivouacked at Nolensville.

Thomas also started early, only an hour later than McCook, and encountered no opposition all day. Franklin Pike and Wilson Pike were turned into a "very thick paste" by the cold rain that fell nearly all day, and Thomas's divisions were scattered over the Center's line of march by nightfall. Brig. Gen. James S. Negley's division rushed eastward to the Nolensville Road as soon as the sound of Davis's skirmishing with Wharton was audible, but the other divisions bivouacked along the Wilson Pike to the west.

Crittenden's advance was equally successful. Minty's cavalry preceded the infantry along the Murfreesboro Pike, hitting Wheeler's first outpost only eleven miles from Nashville. Bragg's cavalry leader hastily deployed his brigade, and just as dusk began to fall a sharp fight broke out between Minty's men and Brig. Gen. John M. Palmer's infantry division. The Confederates, heavily outnumbered and certain that a full-scale advance was under way, retired into the night as the Federals settled down to sleep just outside Lavergne.

It continued to drizzle all night, worsening the roads and making it difficult for Rosecrans's men to rest. The army commander could not afford to sleep, for he had to assess the progress of the day and plan adjustments for the morrow's march. He worried most about the right, for no definite news had yet arrived to indicate whether Hardee had given up Triune. Rosecrans decided to ride hard to Nolensville and talk with McCook. It was a vintage Rosecrans moment. Into the wet night impulsively rode the army commander and his staff, getting lost in the matrix of pikes and small country roads that crisscrossed this part of the Nashville Basin. He had to stop at several houses to ask directions before finally hitting Nolensville and stumbling on McCook's headquarters. Confederate prisoners had told McCook that Triune was empty save for S. A. M. Wood's infantry brigade and Wharton's cavalry. This report was accurate, although the prisoners did not tell him that Cleburne's division and Daniel Adams's brigade were eight miles south of Triune at Eagleville. Rosecrans directed McCook to push on the next day and see if any of Hardee's men were in the area. With that matter settled, Rosecrans and his staff mounted up for an even rougher ride back to his headquarters at Hamilton's Church. Frustrated with the congested roads, Rosecrans struck out across country into the darkness, ignoring all impediments, and reached his destination by 1 A.M. He had been in the saddle fretting over his divisions all day and nearly all night.

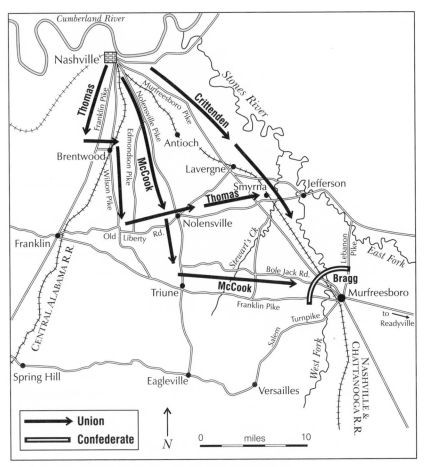

9. The Stones River campaign

The Confederate commander was fully aware of Rosecrans's advance on December 26. Wheeler's report of Crittenden's movements reached him by midday, and, only a short time later, the sound of the firing at Lavergne could be heard by many of Polk's infantrymen near Murfreesboro. McCook's advance along the Nolensville Pike was also reported by Wharton. Bragg decided to concentrate his army at Murfreesboro immediately and hoped that the cavalry could delay Rosecrans long enough to make this happen. McCowan moved out from Readyville, and Hardee was instructed to move all his units eastward that evening. Only Wharton's horsemen and Wood's infantrymen dallied at Triune to delay McCook.

The morning of December 27 was even wetter and foggier than the previous day. This meant that the Confederates had to struggle with soggy roads, but it also delayed Rosecrans's advance. The fog did not burn off until early afternoon, creating such a blanket around Triune that when McCook went forward, his skirmishers accidentally fired into the cavalry screen that preceded them. It was a decisive break for Hardee, whose corps now had a great opportunity to plow eastward without fear of the kind of hot pursuit that had brought on the battle of Perryville in Kentucky. When the fog lifted, sleet and hail began to fall, forcing McCook to halt his advance even longer. The storm more effectively delayed the Federals than either Wharton or Wood so they retired under its cover. As a result, McCook managed only to move one mile south of Triune before night's falling temperatures deposited a layer of ice on the roads.

Thomas's men had an equally difficult time on the miry roads and made little progress in positioning themselves to support McCook. Crittenden had slightly better weather and pushed down the Murfreesboro Pike late that morning. His advanced units had no difficulty passing through Lavergne and marching five miles farther to Stewart's Creek. They found the bridge on fire and Wheeler's cavalrymen falling back, but quick-thinking Federals ripped the floor planks off in time to save the structure. The van of Crittenden's Wing camped only eight miles from Murfreesboro that night.

With all signs pointing to a confrontation near town, Bragg began to prepare for it on December 27. All of his outlying units were on their way to him. Polk's men set to work cutting open roadways and shoveling the banks of Stones River to prepare for the rapid movement of artillery and troops across the stream. Bragg and his generals surveyed the terrain north and west of Murfreesboro to lay out a line of battle. By evening, Hardee's men had arrived and Bragg had decided where to place his army. He issued orders after nightfall for Polk to form the left wing two and a half miles north of Murfreesboro and west of Stones River. Withers's division would constitute Polk's first line and Cheatham's division the second, some eight hundred to a thousand yards behind. Hardee would form the right wing east of Stones River with Buckner's division in front and Cleburne's division in rear. While Polk's line ran mostly north and south, Hardee's line ran west and east and extended far enough to cover the Lebanon Road. McCown's division and Jackson's brigade would form a reserve, with Wharton's cavalry brigade to cover the left flank and Wheeler to screen the right.

The Army of Tennessee marched out early on the morning of December 28 to form a line. The position was controversial from the beginning, perhaps because Bragg himself had selected it. Hardee questioned the wisdom of straddling a significant stream. Even though Stones River was currently shallow and easily forded, the recent rains could quickly swell its current and cut one wing off from the other. Also, there were a few points of ground just in front of the line that were a bit higher than the Confederate position. By far the most serious point was Wayne's Hill, located to Hardee's front and just east of Stones River. If the approaching Federals crossed the stream and occupied this swell in the terrain with artillery, they might be able to drive the right wing from the field. Also, as the brigades deployed along the line, a few gaps developed between them which no one took the responsibility to fill. Much was made of these faults in Bragg's disposition, but the criticism must be tempered. The faults would have been serious if Bragg had intended to remain on the defensive, but, as his actions would soon prove, the army commander had no intention of waiting for Rosecrans to hit him first. Also, the line he chose was the only available position because of the configurations of the road and river that were the key features of the battle area. To have deployed along the Nashville Pike (as the Murfreesboro Pike became known near town), without straddling Stones River, would have required Bragg to move many miles away from town, all the way to Stewart's Creek, where he could be easily outflanked by McCook and Thomas. Or he would have had to deploy only a half mile outside town, where Murfreesboro itself would have been in his way when he wanted to move divisions laterally behind the line or if he had to retire his army under fire. As long as Bragg could get the jump on Rosecrans, once the Federal army deployed opposite his line, he need not worry too much about the defects of his position.

Most of the Confederates were content merely to lay out and occupy their place in the line, but two of Bragg's brigades decided to dig in. James R. Chalmers's men were posted astride the Nashville Pike in relatively open ground. Remembering how bitterly they had been repulsed when attacking fortified Yankees at Munfordville the previous September, they constructed rough entrenchments of logs and earth. Patton Anderson's brigade to Chalmers's left also dug in. Otherwise, Bragg felt no need to ensure that all of his line was fortified.

The Confederates could take their time preparing, for Rosecrans decided that Sunday, December 28, ought to be a day of rest. His men seemed to need it, but really the decision was attributable to the army commander's intense devotion to his Roman Catholic faith. The only Federal activity that day involved a brigade that McCook sent out toward Eagleville. It advanced far enough to assure McCook that Hardee had retreated to Murfreesboro, relieving Rosecrans's mind of a nagging burden. Rosecrans sent out orders for all his divisions to concentrate there. McCook would move east along the Bole Jack Road, while Thomas would continue to march directly toward the Nashville Pike. Crittenden was to push across Stewart's Creek the next morning.

Nearly everyone expected the Rebels to hold at Stewart's Creek, but Crittenden soon found that theory wrong when he advanced on December 29. Wheeler's men annoyed the Yankees as they waded the waist-deep water and burrowed into the cedar thickets. They reached Overall Creek by noon and were only six miles from Murfreesboro on the northern edge of what would become the battlefield of Stones River. They crossed Overall Creek too and came close enough to see Hardee's wing east of the river. This was as far as they would go, within two miles of town, without further orders. Crittenden posted his arriving brigades in a line that stretched from McFadden's Ford at Stones River, south along McFadden's Lane and across the Nashville and Chattanooga Railroad and the Nashville Pike. A wooded area known as the Round Forest straddled these two routes, and the Federal line went right through it. Then the line entered a dense cedar thicket where Thomas's left connected with Crittenden's right.

The only fight that occurred that day, December 29, resulted from an impromptu advance by Col. Charles G. Harker's brigade. His men scrambled across Stones River just after nightfall, pushed back the Rebel skirmishers, and headed for Wayne's Hill, which was held only by a battery of Kentucky artillery. Harker nearly took this important spot, but infantry reinforcements came up just in time to repel him. Harker was ordered to retire across the river at ten o'clock.

Rosecrans was very fortunate that nightfall prevented Bragg from taking the offensive on the twenty-ninth, for only a third of his army managed to concentrate along the partially filled line he was making in front of the Confederates. McCook's brigades bivouacked where Wilkinson Pike crossed Overall Creek a mile and a half from Negley's exposed right flank. He had been slightly delayed by Wharton's cavalry but mostly by his own lack of energy. Even after reaching Overall Creek, he delayed so long in pushing forward to find Negley that it became too dark to complete the concentration. A frustrated Rosecrans sent for McCook well after midnight to impress upon his wing commander the importance of closing up as early as possible the next day. McCook agreed and rode back to his command, having promised to start very early, but it was nearly dawn before he reached his headquarters.

Bragg was unaware of the gap between McCook's and Negley's positions, but Wharton's report of McCook's presence on the west side of Overall Creek led him to fear for the safety of his left. His only movement on December 29 was to send McCown's division from its reserve post in the rear to extend the left wing across Franklin Pike.

McCook dallied in the early morning hours of December 30, the last day of preparation. It was 9:30 before his wing moved out and crossed Overall Creek, with Philip Sheridan's division in the lead. It had no trouble until the advance neared the Gresham farm and the Harding homestead, where it encountered skirmishers from McCown's division. At times the fighting became very intense, although limited to a regiment or two, as the different divisions of McCook's wing fell into line and extended Rosecrans's formation across the partly open landscape of Harding's farm. McCook continued to deploy units into the woods until his right ended at the junction of Gresham Lane and Franklin Pike. On the Federal left and center, Crittenden and Thomas remained in place all day in a steady rain, their men preparing for battle by bringing up ammunition, food, and medical supplies. All of the army was up and ready by dusk.

Bragg watched the signs of McCook's deployment with increasing concern. It seemed to him that McCook was extending so far that Rosecrans could outflank the Confederate left if he launched an early morning assault. His only recourse was to extend his flank as well. Bragg ordered Hardee to strip the right wing and help McCown. Hardee sent Cleburne's division west, leaving only Breckinridge's division to hold the area east of Stones River. Breckinridge had to reposition some units, sending more infantry and artillery to hold Wayne's Hill and deploying a strong skirmish line to watch Federal movements. Cleburne and Hardee moved onto unfamiliar ground on the far left and thus had to spend several hours deciding how best to post their men. McCown had located his brigades on the south side of

Franklin Pike, only three hundred yards from McCook's men, the day before. Now Cleburne deployed in the darkness some five hundred yards behind him. The men were forbidden to build fires because the Federals were so near. The Arkansas soldiers of Brig. Gen. Evander McNair's brigade had neglected to bring their blankets along, and they shivered in the cold, wet night.

Bragg wanted to attack before Rosecrans had a chance to do so. His first thought was to hit the Federal left and center. If Rosecrans had weakened this area to extend the Union right, Bragg might be able to drive him from his line of communication and scatter the Federals into the countryside. But Polk correctly pointed out that the Confederate right was now far too weak to undertake such an action. With McCown and Cleburne extending the left, Polk suggested that the Confederates attack with that wing and roll up the Union line. It would mean that Rosecrans's army would be pushed toward, not away from, its line of communication, but to redeploy divisions from the left to the right would exhaust the troops and delay a dawn advance.

Bragg readily agreed. He issued orders for Hardee to attack with two divisions and Wharton's cavalry brigade. They would swing around the Federal flank and tear into the rear. Polk would begin his attack later, and all units were to "wheel to the right." It was an extremely difficult maneuver, to say the least, and one that was similar to Bragg's tactical plan at Perryville. The ground was broken by cedar thickets and limestone outcroppings. A section of the Confederate battle line nearly three miles long would have to move out in successive order and keep uniform pacing, like a giant gate swinging on its hinges. Even if no enemy troops stood in their way, it would have been a tough assignment. At the very least, Bragg's tactical plan maximized the potential for confusion on the battlefield and guaranteed that individual brigades would largely have to attack and maneuver on their own with little coordinated support to their flanks.

Ironically, Rosecrans was busy that same night planning his own dawn attack against Bragg's right. Crittenden was to push Brig. Gen. Horatio P. Van Cleve's division across McFadden's Ford and attack Breckinridge's men. He would be supported on his right by Brig. Gen. Thomas J. Wood's division, whose task was to occupy Wayne's Hill with artillery and enfilade the Confederate line west of Stones River. Thomas would advance along the Nashville Pike in the center, and McCook was to hold Bragg's left wing in place so it could not reinforce the right. It was a clear, methodical plan that probably would have worked if Bragg had been content to remain inert with his current dispositions.

As Rosecrans explained his plan to the wing leaders, Thomas informed him of indications that Bragg was preparing to attack McCook. Rosecrans paid little worry to this warning hoping to hit the Confederates first as soon as daylight allowed. He did order campfires to be built far beyond the right flank to fool the Rebels as to his real deployment. But other than this, no one in McCook's Wing did anything special to prepare for an assault. After interviewing a civilian who knew where the Rebels were, McCook placed a brigade under Brig. Gen. August Willich to extend and slightly refuse the extreme right. Willich posted his men parallel to Franklin Pike, facing south. The men in the ranks, all along the front of McCook's Wing, could hear the sounds of moving troops and artillery in the night as the Rebels continued to prepare for an attack. When informed of this, McCook simply replied that Crittenden's planned assault would nullify any gray strike in the morning.

Most Federal troops ate their rations and made their separate peace to prepare for the storm ahead. Their nerves and spirit were on Rosecrans's mind as he sat down to compose an exhortation that was distributed to all units, advising them that "the eyes of the whole nation are upon you, the very fate of the nation may be said to hang on the issue of this day's battle. . . . Be cool! I need not ask you to be brave. Keep ranks. Do not throw away your fire. Fire slowly, deliberately; above all, fire low, and be always sure of your aim. Close steadily in upon the enemy, and, when you get within charging distance, rush on him with the bayonet. Do this, and the victory will certainly be yours."

Bragg also tried to encourage his men, but in a very different way. He searched for St. John Liddell to apologize to him for the action of a staff member who had earlier refused to let Liddell have some ambulances the brigade leader needed. Bragg spoke familiarly with Liddell, who had been a West Point acquaintance, and assured him that he was not the ogre so many men in the army thought. Liddell was impressed. "My indignation was gone. I had done Bragg an injustice." Liddell stated, "No man needed friends more than Bragg." The army leader "said to me feelingly, 'General, I have no children. Hence, I look upon the soldiers of my army as my own— *as my* children.'" Bragg repeated this again and said, "General, I wish you to tell this to your men. I am in earnest." Liddell wrote it down and distributed it to his regiments that night. "There was some manuevering in answer to this paternal speech. Men were heard to say, 'He has a very large family and sometimes causes his boys to be shot.'"

Few men in either army were moved by these appeals. Perhaps the only solace for many soldiers that night was the sound of a regimental band playing a familiar tune. Along both lines the strains of patriotic songs filled the air. Both armies could hear each other's music, and soon the bands were competing. Favorites such as "Dixie" and "The Bonnie Blue Flag" provided a counterpoint to "Yankee Doodle" and "Hail Columbia." After some time, the sentimental song "Home Sweet Home" was played by first one band and then another. It was an instant reminder of what was ultimately important to all soldiers, North and South. The competition ended, and soon all bands picked up the song and gave it one of the most poignant of all performances during the Civil War. Even when nearby bands finished it, the bittersweet strain could be heard off in the distance until everyone had a chance to hear it. After this all too brief moment of peace, the only thing left was the killing of the morrow.

On the evening of December 28, several Federal and Confederate pickets had talked with each other along Stewart's Creek, before Crittenden had forced his way across that stream. They were from units that had met before on another battlefield and thus felt a sense of familiarity with each other. When a Unionist told his counterpart that Rosecrans intended to take Murfreesboro, he heard in reply, "Well, you-ens'll find that ar a mighty bloody job, sho." Only forty-eight hours later, the sounds of "Home Sweet Home" were dying away into the forested darkness as forty-four thousand Federals and thirty-four thousand Confederates were finally facing off for a winter battle for control of the rail line that penetrated the heart of the Confederacy. The "mighty bloody job" was about to begin.

CHAPTER ELEVEN

Stones River

As dawn approached on the morning of Wednesday, December 31, the battlefield was covered with mist, and a gray overcast hung overhead. The temperature was very cool as the men of McCook's Wing woke up and began to cook their morning meals. A strange lethargy characterized the actions of all Federals on the right flank. Taking their cue from McCook, who spent a leisurely time shaving at his headquarters tent near the Gresham farmhouse, officers and men alike failed to prepare for the coming attack. Everyone assumed that Rosecrans's left would launch its assault while they simply held their ground. It was an odd parallel to the battle of Perryville nearly three months before, when Bragg's army caught McCook's corps by surprise and nearly crushed it.

On the far Federal right, Willich's brigade was fairly well set for a battle. Its regiments faced south, covering the intersection of Gresham Lane and Franklin Pike, taking cover in the trees with an open field in front. But the brigade next to it, led by Brig. Gen. Edmund N. Kirk, was poorly placed in the middle of a thicket. Kirk's pickets moved out to the wood's edge and found an open field, but no one ordered the battle line to move forward and take advantage of this excellent field of fire. Because Kirk's right rested on the Franklin Pike and the rest of his brigade spread out to the northeast, he joined Willich at an obtuse angle. The brigade of Col. Philip S. Post continued the Federal line inside the woods to Kirk's left.

The Unionists were caught by surprise when McCown's division attacked at about 6:30 A.M. Three brigades of North Carolina, Tennessee, Georgia, Texas, and Arkansas regiments moved briskly across the open field, straddling the Franklin Pike as they marched nearly due west toward the angle where Willich joined Kirk. Only five hundred yards behind them

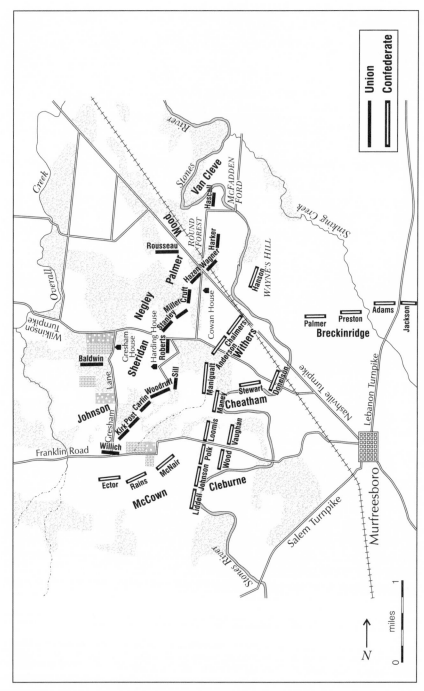

10. Stones River, 6:30 A.M., December 31, 1862

was another tough division of Rebel infantry, Cleburne's men. Both divisions were ready for a fight, having grown tired of marching, maneuvering, and waiting for Rosecrans during the past several days in very uncomfortable weather. They had stripped themselves of all excess baggage, drank a small ration of whiskey to make up for the fact that they had no breakfast, and went on the attack.

Success came almost instantly. The Federal picket line fired a shot or two before racing back to the main line, where confusion quickly set in. An Ohio battery supporting Kirk's infantry fired only a few rounds of canister and then realized it could not withdraw because many of its horses had been sent to the rear for water. In an act of desperation, Kirk ordered the Thirty-fourth Illinois forward to give the gunners a chance to retire, but it was futile. The Illinois regiment was quickly stopped by Brig. Gen. M. D. Ector's Texas brigade and sent reeling. It made a brief effort to rally at the guns, but by then all of Ector's Texans and McNair's Arkansas brigade had closed with Kirk's infantry line, and the Federals fled for their lives. Every gun fell into Rebel hands as Kirk was badly wounded in the thigh and lay helpless on the ground. He was captured and held prisoner for seven months, later dying at his home in Illinois.

The Confederates were jubilant following this quick victory. They found coffee pots still simmering on campfires and breakfasts still frying in the skillets. Only the Seventy-seventh Pennsylvania managed to put up a good fight, stopping the First Arkansas dead in its tracks and driving it back. But the rest of Kirk's brigade was already on its way to the rear, so the Pennsylvanians retired to their neighboring brigade, Post's, to continue the struggle.

Willich's brigade was well posted to meet any trouble coming from the south, but McCown's division was approaching from the east and southeast. Willich was not present when the Rebels arrived, having gone to the rear to talk with his division leader, Brig. Gen. Richard W. Johnson. Col. William Gibson of the Forty-ninth Ohio would have to deal with the enemy as best he could, and his prospects could not have been worse. When Kirk's brigade collapsed, it left Gibson's left flank completely exposed. Gibson was badly outnumbered, unsupported, and in danger of being cut off from the rest of the army within a few minutes after the battle was joined. Many of Kirk's men ran in front of and through Gibson's formations, masking his fire and disrupting his lines. The Thirty-ninth Indiana and Thirty-second Indiana crumbled and quickly ran away, while the Forty-ninth Ohio did not even manage to retrieve its stacked, unloaded guns before Ector's brigade hit it. An Ohio private later recalled that men were "running every way and no one knew where to go but to try and get out of danger." The Eighty-first Illinois stood its ground for a while and traded volleys with Ector at a range of only fifty yards, then it too fell back.

McCown's division had achieved a signal triumph. It had utterly routed two brigades, scattered Rosecrans's right flank, and captured eight guns in only half an hour. There was no stopping the Confederates. McCown's division pushed on through the woods and open fields after the fleeing Unionists. All regimental organization disintegrated; each man ran by himself or with whatever small groups he could catch. When members of the Fifteenth Ohio hit a post and rail fence bordering the Smith farm, about one hundred of them simply surrendered to the oncoming Confederates rather than try to climb over or burrow through it. The rest of Gibson's and Kirk's men headed west to find safety on the opposite side of Overall Creek.

The Yankees' retreat toward the west was the logical direction to take, for their pursuers were approaching from the east and southeast, and this inadvertently aided the Union cause. Two of McCown's brigades, led by Ector and Brig. Gen. James E. Rains, pushed westward after them instead of angling off to the north as they should have done to comply with Bragg's right wheel. McNair lost contact with both brigades because he had already begun to oblique to his right and now his men were advancing to the northwest. All of this served to separate McCown's division from the rest of the army, at least temporarily, and to create a gap between his men and their supporting units to the right. Cleburne filled that gap by accident, not design. He ordered his brigades to right wheel from the very beginning of the attack and thus moved into the area where McCown should have been. It was not easy to do this, for in the mist that still covered parts of the field, Cleburne had lost sight of McCown's men. He assumed they were still in his front as Liddell's brigade, his left wing, literally ran a half mile while Brig. Gen. Bushrod Johnson's brigade in the center walked so as to make the right wheel work properly. Brig. Gen. Lucius Polk's brigade on the right saw that Cheatham's division, to his right, was delayed in its advance, thus exposing his own right flank. Fortunately, S. A. M. Wood's brigade came up to cover Polk. Cleburne did not realize that McCown had advanced away from his division until he hit the woods and found Federals instead of Confederates posted in large numbers there.

These Unionists were better prepared than either Gibson's or Kirk's men. Alerted by the noise of firing off to the right, Jefferson C. Davis had partly realigned his division. Post's brigade was detached and moved to the right and rear so that it straddled Gresham Lane, facing south, with a cleared field to its right and front. The Seventy-seventh Pennsylvania from Kirk's brigade and a Wisconsin battery supported it. Another brigade, under Col. Philemon Baldwin, had earlier been posted by Johnson four hundred yards to Post's right and rear.

The Confederates soon appeared in Post's front. Bushrod Johnson's Tennessee brigade straddled Gresham Lane and hit the Federals head-on. His men moved up under heavy artillery fire until they were only one hundred yards away, then they fell to the ground and opened fire. An artillery duel began as Johnson brought up the Jefferson Flying Artillery of Mississippi. In a rare victory for Southern gunnery, the artillerymen managed to punish the Wisconsin battery so heavily with shell that the Federals had to withdraw. Johnson's infantrymen now attacked, hoping to capture the battery before it escaped, and a bloody short-range fight broke out between the Seventeenth Tennessee and the Twenty-second Indiana. Confederate rifle fire brought down so many battery horses that members of the Fifty-ninth Illinois had to be detailed to pull five guns out of danger before the right flank of Post's line collapsed, leaving only one cannon to the Confederates. The Seventy-fourth Illinois and Seventy-fifth Illinois, both brand-new regiments, held firm on Post's left. The Confederates had a thick wood to advance through east of Gresham Lane, rather than the open field to the west, and this helped the green Illinoisans to stall their attack. It was the withdrawal of Post's right wing that forced them to retire.

A short distance to the west and north, Liddell's brigade joined McNair's Arkansans in an attack on Baldwin's brigade. The two Rebel units advanced northward over open fields with Liddell on the right. Baldwin's Federals deployed in depth in a cornfield, the front line taking shelter behind a rail fence that bordered the southern side. They had the support of a four-gun battery. To the west, some fragmented parts of Gibson's and Kirk's brigades hastily assembled to cover Baldwin's flank.

The fight was joined at 7:30 A.M. Liddell gave a pep talk to his Arkansas soldiers, telling them "in few words that we were about 'to go in,' and that I did not wish them to stop to take charge of prisoners, which would weaken our strength by escorting them to the rear, but that every man must stand to the front, for we needed all." Liddell's line could be plainly seen by the Federals, Liddell himself riding in front waving his hat. When his men crossed half the 150 yards that separated them from the rail fence, Liddell saw a volcano of fire shoot out from between the rails. His men had already lost connection with McNair's brigade, which had fallen behind, and they instinctively fell to the ground and returned fire. "I tried to move them forward and ordered the charge sounded repeatedly—all to no purpose. They had deliberately set themselves to work to kill all they could." So Liddell and his aide dismounted and let their men fire away for about an hour. Some of them were accidentally hit by their own artillery firing from the rear in a futile effort to support the attack.

Meanwhile, McNair's brigade came up to Liddell's left and easily scattered the remnants of Gibson's and Kirk's brigades to the northwest, capturing two more cannon. McNair then began to outflank Baldwin's command. This was the right moment for Liddell's stubborn Arkansans to rise from the ground and continue their attack. Baldwin's position collapsed unit by unit as Liddell's regiments advanced. All Federal soldiers west of Gresham Lane now made their way north toward the Wilkinson Pike, where they tried to establish a defensive line. To the west, Rains's and Ector's brigades finished their chase after the Federals who had escaped to the opposite side of Overall Creek and redirected their advance due northward to find more fight to pitch into. The far Confederate left was doing a splendid job in these early morning hours.

To the east, the remaining brigades of Cleburne's division, led by Polk and Wood, marched boldly into the thick cedar growth that stretched from the Harding homestead to the Franklin Pike, assuming that McCown's division had already dealt with any Union force there. They were stunned to receive fire only a few hundred yards into the thicket. The vegetation was so thick no one could see more than a few yards, so the Federals had the initial advantage in this contest. They fired at nearly point-blank range into Wood's men, and the Confederate brigade pulled back out of the woods. William P. Carlin's Federal brigade lay in front of Polk, and it was posted on and around a limestone outcropping with artillery support. But Post's brigade to the west was gone, and Carlin suddenly found himself holding the Union army's right flank. Wood attacked a second time as Polk moved west and outflanked Carlin's position. He was hampered more by the vegetation than by Federal fire. It was time to retreat, but Carlin was shot along with all of his staff members before he could organize a withdrawal. His regiments pulled out one by one as their commanders, or the rank and file, decided they had had enough. It was impossible to do this in an orderly fashion; "everything was perfect confusion," recalled an Ohio soldier, with "men and horses running in every direction and Rebels after us, firing upon us and yelling like Indians." The Fifteenth Wisconsin, an immigrant regiment composed of Germans, Norwegians, and Swedes, was the last of Carlin's units to leave. It stayed long enough to allow a Minnesota battery to take off all its guns. Then the immigrants withdrew, peeling yet another layer of Rosecrans's right wing off the line and sending it piecemeal to the rear.

All of Johnson's division and most of Davis's division had been beaten, outflanked, and sent on their way by McCown's and Cleburne's men. Farther to the east, Sheridan's division on and near the Harding farmstead offered stiffer resistance, but the retreating units of the other two divisions were being driven north. They tried to make a stand at the Wilkinson Pike, but it was done in a very haphazard way, with only fragments of regiments able to gather together. Several Union field hospitals fell into Rebel hands. Liddell's men came across one and stopped for rest. Here Liddell learned of the mortal wounding of his son Willie, which made him "deeply distressed." He could not abandon his victorious brigade but sent an officer to help him.

The Confederates paused at Wilkinson Pike to regroup. While resting, Rains, Ector, and McNair ordered their men to refill their empty cartridge boxes. McCown realized, to his pleasure, that all three of his brigades were once again together in one place on the battlefield. After they had caught their breath, he redirected the advance eastward in an effort to follow Bragg's right wheel. The scattered Federals who were still making their way northward had taken themselves out of the battle and need not concern McCown anymore. Only Liddell's brigade set off after them, crossing the Wilkinson Pike and getting lost in the thick woods. The distraught Liddell and his men drifted off to the northwest, separating themselves from the rest of the Confederate army.

Wharton's cavalry brigade now hounded the fugitives of Johnson's and Davis's divisions. His horsemen had to ride a distance of two and a half miles in a wide arc to clear McCown's left flank, and then they ran into Zahm's cavalry brigade, covering McCook's right. Wharton pushed the Federal horsemen back and to the north side of the Wilkinson Pike and then began to round up bluecoated infantrymen. Hundreds of sweating, frightened soldiers were taken, but many of them managed to escape as Confederate captors lost track of them in the confusion that reigned supreme south of the pike. McCook's ordnance train also became vulnerable, its seventy-five wagon loads of ammunition offering a tempting prize for Wharton's men. Capt. Gates P. Thruston, who was in charge of the train, had a terrible time trying to pull enough reliable troops from the chaos to protect his wagons. It had to be done in "a scene of strife and confusion that beggars description," remembered Thruston. "Stragglers from the front, teamsters, couriers, negro servants, hospital attendants, ambulances added to the turmoil. Wounded and riderless horses and cattle wild with fright rushed frantically over the field." After several hairbreadth escapes, Thruston managed to pull the train to Nashville Pike and safety.

By 9:30 A.M., after three hours of combat, the far Union right was shattered and taken out of action. But this Confederate victory was not cleanly won. All Rebel brigades had suffered losses and wandered over the countryside, barely keeping contact with each other because of the tricky wheeling maneuver Bragg asked of them and the cluttered terrain of the battlefield. And as the battle continued to roll along the Union line, resistance grew fiercer. The Federal right center, consisting mostly of Sheridan's division, began to put up a far tougher fight, refusing to break up its formations or to flee wildly into the forest.

Sheridan was greatly aided by the tactics used by Cheatham, whose division was responsible for continuing the Confederate attacks. Cheatham sent his brigades into the assault one by one, beginning at 7 A.M., instead of bringing his full weight to bear on the Unionists. First, the brigade of Col. J. Q. Loomis marched over a wide open cornfield toward Col. William Woodruff's brigade, the only unit of Davis's division that was not yet engaged. Woodruff had an excellent position, his regiments posted in the edge of the thicket behind a fence atop a distinct rise of ground. Woodruff's left joined Sill's brigade in a meadow that bordered the Harding farmstead. Loomis had to contend with a great deal, but his Alabama and Louisiana regiments moved over the deadly ground, right wheeling as they marched.

Surprisingly, Loomis's left wing gained a quick success. He pushed back two of Woodruff's regiments but was forced to stop because there was no support to his left. At this time Carlin's Federal brigade still held its original position, just before redeploying to meet Polk's attack, and it was able to fire into Loomis's flank. His left wing was raked by this volley as his right engaged in a static fight with the Thirty-sixth Illinois. Loomis was incapacitated when a tree limb fell on him, and his men were forced to retire. Cheatham tried to make up for his earlier delay by throwing more units at Sheridan. Brig. Gen. Alfred Vaughan led his Tennessee regiments into the fight, but with no support on either the right or left he too was forced to retire.

Despite their successful defense, the men of Woodruff's brigade soon found themselves in retreat. Carlin had fallen back by this time, allowing a lone Rebel regiment, the Ninth Texas, to outflank Woodruff's men. Once again Union regiments took themselves out of line and moved northward, but in a much more orderly fashion than those of Johnson and Davis. Before heading for the Wilkinson Pike, they had forced the Confederates to pay a heavy price. The Twelfth Tennessee, for example, lost over half its strength in this costly attempt to pry Sheridan's men from their first position.

Sheridan scrambled to reposition his regiments now that Woodruff had fallen back. Sill had been shot through the head and died instantly. He was replaced by Col. Nicholas Greusel, who led the brigade as it retired to the Harding farmstead, where Col. Frederick Schaefer's brigade already was in place. There was no terrain advantage for the Union infantry here, but the open nature of the farmstead allowed the Federal artillery a large, clear field of fire. When Col. Arthur M. Manigault's Rebel brigade entered this cleared area, it was stopped by converging fire from two Federal batteries. As he fell back, Manigault encountered Cheatham's last remaining brigade, led by Brig. Gen. George Maney. Determined that a third assault be successful, Manigault spent twenty minutes conferring with Maney about the possibility of coordinating their movements so as to hit both Union batteries at the same time. Meanwhile, their men died as a rain of shells exploded in the air overhead. But coordination was essential; when they finalized their preparations, Manigault moved out to the right and Maney marched off to the left.

Sheridan made good use of this lull once again to readjust to the collapse of units to his right. By this time, about 9 A.M., McCown's and Cleburne's men were off to his right rear, as far north as the Wilkinson Pike. Sheridan had to realign along that same road, his third position of the morning, and anchor his line on Col. George W. Roberts's brigade. Greusel and Schaefer were able to withdraw to the pike and reform along its southern edge. The Federal guns redeployed as well, causing confusion when Manigault and Maney launched their carefully planned attack—they found no cannons where they expected and plenty of artillery where there should have been none. The open nature of the Harding homestead allowed the Union gunners to rain shells onto both brigades as they right wheeled to the north. Sheridan succeeded in organizing a solid line of three brigades along one of the best roads on the battlefield, supported by ample artillery. Manigault and Maney advanced about halfway across the Harding farmstead and were joined by Vaughan's brigade, which came up to Maney's left. The three Rebel units stopped, taking cover as best they could, while officers scrambled to find enough artillery to soften up Sheridan's line for another attack.

The Federals probably could have held out for a long time in this place, but they did not have the opportunity to try. Off to the west, all their comrades south of the Wilkinson Pike had already fled and several Confederate brigades were marching eastward to hit Sheridan in the flank. Sheridan saw this himself when he rode west to find out what was happening to the right wing. Men were streaming away from any contact with the advancing Confederates. The wounded Carlin, the distraught Davis, and the indifferent Woodruff, who simply sat and gazed at his retreating men, could do nothing to protect Sheridan's flank.

Thus the Federal commander was forced to refuse his right, and he did so in a very big way. Rather than simply place a regiment or two at right angles to his front, he ordered two-thirds of the line to bend backward. Greusel and Schaefer moved north of the Wilkinson Pike into a thick expanse of cedars that stretched eastward to McFadden Lane. Only Roberts remained south of the Wilkinson Pike. His brigade now formed a very acute angle in the line in front of Manigault's brigade. It was a strong position, for Greusel and Schaefer had an open field to their front and their men could take shelter behind the limestone outcroppings in the edge of the wood.

McCown's and Cleburne's men came from the west and tested the strength of this new position. In a series of uncoordinated attacks, first Wood, then Johnson, then Polk swept into the open and were punished by a rain of rifle fire that seemed to come out of the trees and rocks rather than from weary, beleaguered soldiers. None of these attacks even dented the Federal line, much less broke it. Manigault tried his hand as well, his Alabama and South Carolina regiments rushing toward their stubborn foe. Manigault aimed at Roberts's brigade, the angle in the new Federal line, which was under the cover of thick brush. He was repulsed, demonstrating that a coordinated assault by all available forces was necessary if Sheridan were to be driven away.

Neither Bragg, Hardee, nor Cheatham was available to organize such coordination so Manigault sought help from the unit to his right. Anderson's brigade had waited in its crude earthworks all morning for the opportunity to go in, and he needed little encouragement. He sent two of his regiments to help Manigault attack Roberts, but the assaulting force was mowed down by artillery fire. Roberts had the enviable position of being supported on both flanks by heavy concentrations of artillery, three batteries on each side. His brigade might have formed a protruding angle, but it was an especially tough object to hit.

Anderson was forced to call up the rest of his brigade, which attacked the artillery by moving through a patch of woods, burrowing through the underbrush that shattered their alignment. Heavy discharges from the guns pounded the men, many of whom were knocked down by falling branches. Then the final two hundred yards of open ground appeared in their front, and rifle fire from the supporting brigade of Col. Timothy R. Stanley began to rip into the Mississippians. Their losses were enormous. Lieut. Col. J. J. Scales of the Thirtieth Mississippi watched in awe as "men fell around on every side like autumn leaves and every foot of soil over which we passed seemed dyed with the life blood of some one or more of the gallant spirits whom I had the honor to command." They marched within seventy-five yards of the guns before they were compelled to drop to earth for protection. There was precious little cover in this cornfield, so the Mississippians lay immobile despite their officers' efforts to get them to retreat. Finally, word was passed along the line and Anderson's brigade withdrew. His short attack had littered the cornfield with bodies, and the Federal fire crashing through the woods had left the timber "torn and crushed."

The decisive blow against Sheridan would come from a fresh brigade, led by Brig. Gen. Alexander P. Stewart, which had taken Anderson's place in line after he launched his first attack. Stewart hit Roberts hard. The Federal right flank held on, but, within a few minutes of contact, Roberts was killed, his successor was shot down, and the brigade became leaderless. Ammunition also began to run short at the height of the assault. Sheridan realized that he would have to pull back, and he ordered Roberts's men to withdraw. Greusel also pulled back, under direct orders from McCook, and Schaefer successfully covered the withdrawal of both units as he retreated fighting. Sheridan's division retired to the northeast, keeping as close to the remaining Federal line as possible until it found safety at the Nashville Pike.

Sheridan's withdrawal, at about 10:45, not only shortened the diminishing Federal line but left exposed and vulnerable the division of Lovell H. Rousseau, of Thomas's wing. Rousseau had been in reserve when he received an order from Rosecrans to respond to the sounds of battle rolling in from the southwest. He found Sheridan's right flank and deployed his three brigades, connecting his left with the end of Sheridan's line and facing southwest. Col. John Beatty's brigade and Lieut. Col. Oliver H. Shephard's brigade held Rousseau's front line while Col. Benjamin F. Scribner's brigade deployed to their rear as a second line. All three units were in the thick woods so skirmishers were sent out to see if the enemy was close.

They certainly were coming on now that Sheridan had retreated and stripped Rousseau's left flank of support. McCown's division advanced directly toward the Federals, and his three brigades outflanked their right.

When Rousseau received word of a large Rebel force moving his way, he realized it was impossible to hold on and decided to withdraw. The thick woods made this difficult, especially as the Rebel skirmishers began to engage his own. First, Rousseau rode to the rear to find a new position at the Nashville Pike, deciding on a rise of ground between it and the railroad only a half mile northwest of McFadden's Lane. By the time he rode back to his division, Shephard's brigade of regulars had begun a sharp fight in the trees with Rains's men, but this ended when Rousseau ordered a withdrawal. Scribner's brigade, which was unengaged, also fell back, but Beatty's men never received the order to retire. They stood their ground and temporarily halted the advance of Polk's brigade, which had come up to join the assault. Polk suffered heavy losses, and his attempt to outflank Beatty's right was stopped. The Federals had fought stubbornly and well, but they now began to realize that they were alone. Beatty suddenly decided that he had to retreat or suffer the consequences. Pressured by Polk's renewed advance, the Federals scrambled hastily out of the thicket and ran for their lives across the large open cotton field that bordered the western side of the Nashville Pike.

The new line taking shape along the pike would be the last one, and it would not be moved. Rains's men pushed on in pursuit of the Federals and suddenly stumbled into the southern edge of the cotton field. A mass of blue-clad infantrymen were assembling along the road, five hundred yards away, and off to the left was a cluster of Federal guns on the high ground that Rousseau had occupied. A Federal lieutenant named Alfred Pirtle saw Rains's brigade emerge from the woods and later recalled that "in an instant the edge of the timber was alive with a mass of arms, heads, legs, guns, swords, gray coats, brown hats, shirt sleeves, and the enemy were upon us, yelling, leaping, running." The guns opened fire and the infantry began to volley, dropping Rains and killing him instantly. His men halted their impetuous charge and took cover in the woods.

Soon afterward, at about noon, Ector's brigade attempted the same thing to Rains's left. His Texans ran into a heavy concentration of fresh troops positioned farther up the pike than Rousseau's artillery, and it was supported by two batteries. They drove deeply into the cotton field and engaged Morton's Pioneer brigade and Col. Samuel Beatty's brigade in the open. After a fierce, close-range encounter, Ector withdrew for lack of support on either flank. Beatty's men and another brigade under Col. James P. Fyffe pursued the Rebels into the woods. They advanced a few hundred yards west of the Nashville Pike and unwisely halted in an isolated position. Yet these first two Confederate attacks on the last stand of the Union right wing were bloodily repulsed and offered proof that Bragg's plan was running into serious trouble.

If the Yankees were to be driven from the pike, the Confederates would have to consolidate their scattered forces and launch coordinated attacks, supported by ample artillery. But that would take a great deal of time and effort, and it could not be done until the Rebels consolidated the gains they had made up to this point. There were still sizable numbers of Federal troops, well organized and ready for a fight, west of the Nashville Pike. They were positioned on the southern and northern edges of the battlefield, and much time and blood was expended in dealing with them.

On the southern side of the battlefield, the original Union line still held from Wilkinson Pike along the west side of McFadden Lane all the way to the Nashville Pike. Cleburne had refused to advance too far north behind it when Sheridan retired, fearing these Unionists might attack his right flank as he chased Greusel, Schaefer, and Roberts. He kept his exhausted men in the open field north of the Wilkinson Pike, sent Wood's brigade back to the rear to guard trains (it had only five hundred men left), and ordered Johnson's brigade to march north and find Liddell. Vaughan's brigade and Polk's men followed to Johnson's right. Cleburne realized the need to find the Union right flank, wherever it now lay, and bypass it to gain the Nashville Pike. His men would eventually discover Beatty's and Fyffe's commands on the northern edge of the battlefield and send them retreating.

But the other Federal concentration west of the pike, to the south along McFadden Lane, would have to be dealt with by other units. Anderson's and Stewart's brigades of Withers's division renewed their attacks by coordinating the fire of several batteries posted on high ground well to the east of the lane. The barrage against Stanley's brigade of Negley's division was very effective, killing and wounding many blue-clad soldiers. Manigault and Maney followed up this punishment by outflanking Stanley's men, and the Federals retreated.

Negley's next brigade, under Col. John Miller, held out longer under the hail of artillery fire and the Rebel flankers who were working their way through the trees. When individual regiments took it upon themselves to flee, Miller personally led them back into line until he too realized that all the bravery in the world could not win this unequal fight. The Twenty-first Ohio, armed with Colt's revolving rifles, held the Rebels at bay in the cornfield to Miller's front, giving them "hell by the acre" as its commander put it, while other units retired. Finally, a bayonet attack by the Twenty-first

Ohio and the Nineteenth Illinois gave Miller's brigade the time it needed to find a safe path to the rear. The Ohio regiment paid dearly for its heroic stand, losing an entire company when the Twenty-seventh Mississippi overran its position.

The last Federal unit holding the line along McFadden Lane was Brig. Gen. Charles Cruft's brigade of Brig. Gen. John M. Palmer's division. It was the rightmost unit of Crittenden's Wing, already bloodied in failed Confederate attempts to charge across the open fields from the east. A bit after 8 A.M., Chalmers's Mississippi brigade had attacked over an open space of eight hundred yards into the teeth of infantry and artillery fire from Cruft's men. His unit was split by the Cowan house, whose burned ruins stood on a rise of ground directly in front of the brigade. While the right regiments veered off toward the Round Forest at the junction of Nashville Pike and McFadden Lane, the left wing closed with Cruft's men and stood its ground for thirty minutes. Chalmers was hit and so many of his men fell that the ground came to be called the "Mississippi Half-Acre." His survivors fell back. Then came Brig. Gen. Daniel Donelson's Tennessee brigade, which also split into two wings at the Cowan house. Just like Chalmers before him, Donelson watched as his right wing veered off toward the Round Forest while the left wing went straight for Cruft. But Donelson's attack was successful because Stewart's brigade just then began to roll up Cruft's right flank after it had forced Miller's stubborn regiments to leave their place in line. Cruft disengaged much as Miller had done before him. Precious time was dearly bought by the Federals when Shephard's regular brigade advanced into the woods and fought the attacking Confederates so well that it mauled Stewart's brigade, and then it too retired. While they bled the Rebels, other Union commanders were able to reposition their retreating units along the pike into a more cohesive and orderly line.

The battle was fast reaching its decisive moment at this crucial road junction, covered as it was by a small wood known as the Round Forest. Col. William B. Hazen's brigade of Palmer's division held the forest against the two attacks already launched by a portion of first Chalmers's and then Donelson's brigades. These were the wings that had veered off from their comrades because of the obstruction caused by the Cowan house. But the Federal line would peel no more; its long dismantling had reached its limit. Hazen held firm in the forest against the worst that Chalmers's and Donelson's fragmented commands could offer. On this little rise of ground that the forest occupied, no more than three feet above the surrounding terrain, the Confederate right wheel ground to a halt even as all remaining troops were driven from the southern part of the battlefield.

About a mile to the north, Cleburne's division successfully cleared the remaining Federal units from the northern edge of the battlefield to complete the Confederate conquest of the woods west of the Nashville Pike. He was opposed by three brigades of Federal troops. Samuel Beatty's and Fyffe's brigades of Van Cleve's division had chased Ector's men and taken position in the southern part of a cleared, open field that stretched westward from the Nashville Pike. The woods began sixty yards to their front and stretched southward for hundreds of yards. Col. Charles G. Harker's brigade of Wood's division later came forward and was posted to Fyffe's right.

Some time after 1 P.M., not long after Ector's retreating Texans escaped from Beatty and Fyffe, the Federals were hit by four brigades under Cleburne's command. Victory fell into Cleburne's lap when Harker pulled his men out of line and retired a couple of hundred yards to the rear where a rise of ground offered a more defensible position. This move exposed Fyffe's right flank, and the Rebels easily turned it. Both his and Beatty's regiments were forced to retreat, and Harker, who found himself alone and isolated against four times his number, followed after them.

Cleburne easily dispersed this last resistance west of the Nashville Pike, but he did not have the strength to follow it up. Rosecrans was busy extending his line farther northwest along the pike to match any Confederate move on it. As a result, there were just enough bloodied but intact units—Morton's Pioneers, most of Beatty's and Fyffe's brigades, and two regiments of Roberts's brigade of Sheridan's division—to stand in Cleburne's way. Surprisingly, only a few volleys from these men, posted at and near the pike, sent the Confederates into headlong retreat. Vaughan's people apparently broke and fled when Roberts's two regiments counterattacked, even though the Federals were entirely out of ammunition. All of Cleburne's other brigades were infected by Vaughan's nearly panicked withdrawal and retreated into the woods. These men had fought magnificently all day, but their stamina and nerve had limits. It was now past 3 P.M., eight hours since their first attack. Cleburne explained it when he noted that his "men had had little or no rest the night before; they had been fighting since dawn, without relief, food, or water; they were comparatively without the support of artillery, . . . their ammunition was again nearly exhausted and our ordnance trains could not follow." They had used up all the spunk they had, and there were no replacements to take up the attack and drive it home to the pike.

The battle of Stones River had reached its turning point. After an initial shattering of the far right, the Union army had successfully withdrawn to a strong defensive position along the Nashville Pike and the Nashville and Chattanooga Railroad, reinforced by detached units from the left wing. Initial Confederate attacks on the anchor of this line, held by Hazen in the Round Forest, were unsuccessful. Like Cleburne's men, those Confederate brigades that had accomplished the impressive feat of driving the Federal right over three miles through difficult terrain were bloodied and exhausted, and there were precious few reinforcements.

Generalship played only a limited role in this great battle. The performance of Rosecrans's subordinates was mixed, even dismal. McCook was nearly invisible all day, offering no direction in the confused withdrawal of his wing. Now and then he gave an order to a brigade, but he mostly drifted with events rather than trying to control them. Sheridan stood out as the only division leader on the right who maintained control of his command. His impressive fighting retreat was a key factor in slowing the Rebel right wheel, gaining precious time for Rosecrans to organize a defensive line along the pike. The fact that Sheridan did not allow his men to scatter, as Johnson and Davis had done before him, meant that there would be large numbers of organized troops along the pike to act as a reserve in defense of the last Federal stand. Several Union brigade leaders, such as Miller, Greusel, Schaefer, and Cruft, acted very well indeed. But others lost control of their men just as readily as did their division and wing leaders.

Rosecrans's performance on December 31 was the best of his career. He had been superintending the deployment of his left wing early that morning, preparing for the attack he hoped to spring on Bragg, when disturbing signs of trouble on the right began to filter in. The initial phase of his attack had already begun. Samuel Beatty's brigade forded Stones River at 7 A.M., to be followed by many more men. Then the sound of firing grew louder and, more ominously, was moving quickly to the north. The right wing obviously was breaking apart and scattering. When a staff officer arrived from McCook with detailed information about the crisis on the right, Rosecrans called off the attack and sprang into action. For the rest of that day he was in a nervous fever of activity, desperately trying to regain control of the army and prevent a catastrophic defeat. Many of his actions were counterproductive—shouting impromptu instructions to regimental and brigade commanders without taking into account their prior instructions from other officers, interfering with the efforts of subordinates to bring order out of chaos, even rashly exposing himself in the line of fire of his own men.

Yet Rosecrans received widespread praise from all ranks for the moral effect of his presence on the battlefield. Soldier after soldier marveled at his ubiquitous presence; he seemed to visit every part of the field and talk to every unit at one time or another during the course of the day. Many were impressed with his energy, his self-confidence, and his passionate drive to save the army. His most important work was to divert several units from Crittenden's Wing to shore up the right. The dispatch of Rousseau to aid Sheridan and of Samuel Beatty, Fyffe, and Harker to hold the northern sector of the field helped to slow the Confederate advance. Most important, Rosecrans was responsible for placing units along the Nashville Pike, believing that it was the key to his army's survival. The army commander posted much of the artillery, as well as Morton's Pioneers, where they played key roles in stopping Ector's and Cleburne's attempts to seize the pike.

On the Confederate side, the performance of division leaders was also mixed. Cleburne and McCown stood out as exceptionally able directors on the far left. Cleburne performed extremely well on every battlefield of his career, and no other division leader on the Rebel side kept as tight control over his brigades. McCown's performance was surprisingly good, considering the low esteem with which everyone in the army regarded him. Hardee had little impact on the course of the fighting, and Cheatham wasted his men in uncoordinated attacks. Many Confederates were convinced that Cheatham was drunk that day, and there was evidence to support the charge that he imbibed a little too freely of the whiskey that had been carefully ladled out to the rank and file early that morning. The Confederate brigade leaders did a superb job. They made the right wheel work under terrible conditions, sustaining losses that drained their ranks of manpower and keeping the attacks pounding on despite the exhaustion of their men. The success of the Rebel effort that day rested on the shoulders of the brigade commanders and on the stamina and courage of the rank and file. It was a truly impressive performance by the hard-bitten veterans of the Army of Tennessee.

Unfortunately for the Southern cause, the same cannot be said of Bragg. He was flustered all day because he had so few troops available to press home the attack. Hardee's and Polk's men were doing better than could be expected, but Bragg needed more troops. His only reserve was Breckinridge's division east of Stones River. Bragg toyed with the idea of using these men in some way all morning. Rumors of Federal troops hovering around Lebanon Pike froze Breckinridge in his place and infuriated Bragg, who could not believe them to be true. Finally, after reviewing the results of a cavalry reconnaissance in that area, the army leader ordered Breckinridge into action at 1 P.M. He was to leave one brigade east of the river and send the remaining four brigades to Polk's corps. While Brig. Gen. Roger Hanson's Kentucky regiments remained in place, the brigades of Brig. Gen. Daniel W. Adams, Col. Joseph B. Palmer, Brig. Gen. William Preston, and Brig. Gen. John K. Jackson forded Stones River and marched toward the fighting.

Polk decided to feed these units into a series of assaults against the Round Forest beginning in midafternoon. The stage was set for the final phase of the battle. Hazen still held the forest, where the Union line formed a ninety-degree angle. Col. George D. Wagner's brigade of Wood's division held the line to his left. Wagner's own left flank rested on Stones River nearly opposite Wayne's Hill, which was occupied by Hanson's Confederates and three Rebel batteries.

Adams's Louisiana brigade attacked along the Nashville Pike toward the Round Forest. His alignment was cut up by the Cowan house and its fences, forcing him to reform the brigade after it cleared the farmstead, but his men were met with a hail of musketry and the concentrated fire of four Union batteries. They pushed back the Federal skirmishers but were in turn outflanked when Wagner sent two regiments out to conduct a spoiling attack. Adams withdrew, leaving over four hundred casualties behind after only thirty minutes of fighting. Jackson's Georgia and Mississippi regiments went in right after Adams, but they moved into a slaughter pen. Observant Federals could clearly see the solid ranks, "in steady column, notwithstanding the murderous fire," but their losses were too heavy. Jackson's men were "falling like leaves," in the words of Gilbert Stormont of the Fifty-eighth Indiana. This, the fourth Confederate attack on the Round Forest, cost nearly three hundred casualties and failed to hurt the Federals at all.

By this time, Breckinridge had arrived on the scene with his last two brigades. He was appalled at the dreadful waste of life, attributable to Polk's decision to attack piecemeal, and decided to send Palmer and Preston in tandem. Preston would advance along the same line as that taken by Adams and Jackson, a daunting task by now, because the ground was littered with over a thousand casualties from the day's futile efforts. Palmer would march off to the west, enter the woods on the other side of McFadden Lane, and attack the Round Forest from the south. It was a reasonable plan, but it went awry almost from the beginning. Preston's formation was broken by the Cowan house and its fences, and it was hit by such a heavy fire when it cleared that fatal spot that the attack came to a halt before it even got started. Preston led the survivors directly toward the cedars west of McFadden Lane, where they found cover in the woods. The remaining brigade, led by Palmer, did essentially the same thing. It dutifully marched into the cedars and up to the cotton field west of the Nashville Pike but failed to attack because to do so was obviously futile. Breckinridge's division, the army's only reserve, could do no more.

The Confederates failed to make much use of their artillery to support Breckinridge's attack. Rebel guns on Wayne's Hill managed to hit some of Hazen's and Wagner's men but not nearly enough to make a difference. A round from one of these guns came close to killing Rosecrans. While Breckinridge's attack on the Round Forest heated up, Rosecrans rode at full tilt along the Nashville Pike to the scene of action, trailed by his aides. Suddenly an unexploded shell decapitated Col. Julius Garesche, his chief of staff. The darling of Rosecrans's military family died instantly. His body remained seated for several moments even while his horse continued to pound on, then the headless trunk slid off and fell to the ground. Blood and bits of brain splattered over several men nearby, but Rosecrans was so intent on what lay before him that he did not realize Garesche was dead until much later. Many men remembered that, earlier in the morning, Garesche had taken a book out of his pocket and prayed silently during a mass at Rosecrans's headquarters tent. His devout life endeared him to his colleagues as much as his very public and shocking death stunned and awed them.

Now, as the early winter day began to end, the fighting on December 31 sputtered to a halt. The Army of Tennessee had fought itself out, just short of its goal. Along the Nashville Pike, and especially at the angle held by Hazen, a solid line of blue refused to be moved from its precious supply line. If Breckinridge's fresh brigades had been brought up to help Cleburne and McCown as their men approached the pike farther north, the tide might have turned. But Rosecrans now held the upper hand with his numerical superiority, even though many of his brigades had been mauled. There was little chance of a major Federal attack, but at least Rosecrans did not have to worry about an immediate defeat.

The sky had never completely cleared all day, and now and then the sun peeped out through breaks in the heavy cloud cover. The temperature rose high enough by midafternoon to thaw the frosty ground, making it wet and slippery. But that would change with dusk. A cold night lay ahead and thousands of dying men lay scattered over the fields and through the woods outside Murfreesboro.

CHAPTER TWELVE

Fight or Die

It had been a day of terrible fighting for the men of both armies, and the night of December 31 would be remembered forever by the survivors. The temperature plummeted as soon as the sun went down. Everyone in the two opposing armies was tired. Thousands of Federals had just experienced their first battle, and commanders had to deal with the chaotic conditions that always resulted from a major engagement. On the Union side, many units were still jumbled and disorganized, haversacks and cartridge boxes were empty, and everyone wondered if the army's supply line to Nashville would be cut. On the Confederate side, losses had been so heavy that all survivors had to deal with the death of friends, comrades, and respected officers. Despite their exhaustion, the Rebels spent part of the night fortifying their line. Across the vast track of cedars west of the Nashville Pike, each brigade gathered fallen logs, brush, and rocks to build a breastwork. They wanted to keep the ground they had spent so many lives taking from the enemy.

The most poignant episodes of that night were the many attempts to help the wounded. Roughly fourteen thousand dead and wounded men of both armies were scattered over an area of six square miles. The walking wounded were already mostly gone, and those who still lived were too badly injured to help themselves. They feared for their lives, not only endangered by wounds but threatened by the dropping temperature and the wet atmosphere. Rescuers scoured the woods and fields well into the night, sometimes finding men frozen to the ground in their own blood. No one fully controlled most of this area, and there were many instances of kindness between enemies as roaming Rebels left food, water, or blankets behind for wounded Yankees they happened to see. Even when burial squads or groups of stretcher bearers happened to meet each other, Federals and Confederates often were able to set aside the bitterness of battle and cooperate in their merciful errands. As Col. William Blake of the Ninth Indiana put it, "The fierce acerbity of the deadly strife had given place to the mutual expression of kindness and regard."

Other rescuers found plenty of evidence to remind them of the "fierce acerbity" of battle. Ohioan William Erb and a friend went back to the place where his regiment had fought and "found no one alive," but he could easily place his regimental battle line by the corpses that were stretched out in the woods. Erb paid respect to his comrades by straightening their bodies and noting their names when possible. A group of Rebels happened on this quiet, sad scene, but there was no tension. Erb and his friend talked familiarly with their enemy, then went back to the regiment.

Only a few such encounters resulted in hostile action. Some members of the Thirty-eighth Indiana and the Fifteenth United States Infantry were taken prisoner by roving Confederate patrols while trying to help the wounded. Mostly the sense of pity overwhelmed everyone who wandered over the battlefield that night. Mississippi gunner John Euclid Magee rode around in the night looking for abandoned sets of harnesses for his battery horses and was so moved by the sight of the wounded that he often stopped to build fires for them. "Many, many were chilled to death already that might have been saved could they but have had attendance." Brigade leader William Preston spent the night in the dense woods near the Round Forest. He later wrote, "The frost, the dead and dying and the dark cedars among which we bivouacked were wild enough for a banquet of ghouls."

The commanders of both armies had to contend with many problems that night. Rosecrans's men suffered food shortages because Joseph Wheeler had taken his cavalry brigade on a raid against the supply line. He started out on the night of December 29 and on the next day hit wagon trains at Jefferson, Lavergne, Rock Springs, Nolensville, and Franklin. His hard-riding horsemen burned nearly a thousand wagons and captured and paroled at least six hundred soldiers. They also prevented two infantry brigades from joining Rosecrans's army in time to participate in the fighting on December 31.

Rosecrans called his subordinates together on the chilly night of the thirty-first to discuss the army's future. Some, especially McCook, talked of retreating, fearful of a resumption of the stunning Confederate attacks. There was no consensus of opinion, though, as Crittenden and Thomas advised fighting it out. Rosecrans felt the need to see the condition of affairs firsthand. While his lieutenants waited, the army leader and McCook rode into the night. They came to Overall Creek and saw numerous fires scattered around the area. Rosecrans was stunned. He jumped to the conclusion that the Rebels had gotten into his rear and cut off his army. It was a mistake, for the lights actually were held by Federal cavalrymen who were building fires for the walking wounded in the rear. But the error firmed up Rosecrans's thinking. He and McCook rode back to headquarters and informed the tired commanders that the army was "to fight or die."

Bragg did not call a council of his officers because he felt jubilant over the day's work. Assuming he had won a great victory, he sent a glowing message to the authorities in Richmond: "We assailed the enemy at seven o'clock this morning, and after ten hours' hard fighting have driven him from every position except the extreme left." He returned Palmer's brigade to the east side of Stones River that night but expected that Rosecrans would probably be gone at dawn.

Thursday, January 1, was the day that Lincoln's Emancipation Proclamation went into effect, freeing all slaves who were still in areas controlled by the Confederacy. As the sun came up, the frontier between free and slave territory suddenly shifted outside Murfreesboro and was redrawn along the no-man's land between the opposing armies. Bragg and Rosecrans still glared at each other from exactly the same spot where their life-and-death struggle of the day before had ended. Neither army felt able or willing to make a serious move against the other as the mists cleared away to reveal a bright, sunny day.

Bragg received good news. Wheeler and Wharton both sent back word that wagons were moving from Rosecrans's army along the Nashville Pike toward the state capital. Bragg believed this was a prelude to a general withdrawal, but he was wrong. The wagons were empty and had been sent out to search for food.

Rosecrans began to shuffle units on his left flank very early in the morning so as to secure McFadden Ford. He had been forced to relinquish this key crossing twenty-four hours before and now meant to retain the option of using it to resume his original plan of attack. Van Cleve's division, now under the charge of Samuel Beatty because a foot wound had taken Van Cleve out of action, began to cross Stones River at dawn. Col. Samuel Price's brigade and Fyffe's brigade waded across and took post atop a bit of high ground that covered the eastern approach to the ford, while Col. Benjamin Grider, now in charge of Beatty's brigade, placed two regiments on either side of the river.

Except for this potentially significant move, the armies waited and watched all day. When the sun went down, nothing had changed. The Federals still had scant rations and the Confederates still did not have a victory. Bragg's confidence, however, began to turn into doubt. Even his soldiers began to sense that they could not beat Rosecrans in a waiting game, and throughout the Army of Tennessee an old familiar feeling began to creep into everyone's heart. It was a feeling of déjà vu for anyone who remembered the retreat from Kentucky, a helpless fear that, after all their suffering, Bragg was going to withdraw.

Friday, January 2, began with an increasingly desperate Bragg searching for a solution to the tactical stalemate that had deadened his optimism the previous day. He realized that the extreme Union left, which had not been tested on December 31, might now be weak. If he could catch Rosecrans unprepared, he might be able to convince the Federal commander to withdraw after all. Thus as the day dawned with a gray overcast, he sent his aide, Col. George Brent, and artillery Capt. Felix Robertson to reconnoiter the ground near McFadden Ford.

Brent and Robertson found Beatty's and Price's men already on the east side of Stones River and firmly planted on the high ground they thought they needed as an artillery post to attack the Federals. When they informed Bragg of this he immediately concluded that the first attack had to be against this force. The high ground could be used to enfilade the Federal line across the river. Breckinridge's division was the only relatively rested force he had; at least two of its brigades had suffered limited losses on December 31. Wharton would provide cavalry regiments to cover Breckinridge's right flank, and Robertson was to employ ten guns to support the infantry.

When Bragg related his instructions to Breckinridge at noon, the division leader raised a passionate protest. He had been busy most of the morning personally scouting the terrain near McFadden Ford. Even if he drove Price and Fyffe away, other Federal units posted on slightly higher ground to the northwest on both sides of Stones River could command his position. But Bragg refused to be deterred, probably because he increasingly came to view this assault as his last chance to salvage a victory from the heavy fighting of December 31. The attack was scheduled for 4 P.M. in hopes that darkness, one hour later, would prevent a Federal counterstroke. Breckinridge had no choice, but he made certain that everyone knew the assault ran counter to his better judgment.

Because the Confederates prepared for an hour and a half, and because the ground east of McFadden Ford was open, it was not difficult for alert observers to see that something was up. Samuel Beatty requested help, and Col. William Grose's brigade was shifted across the river to build breastworks behind Fyffe. A Wisconsin battery also was brought over the river to add weight to the Federal position. The popping of skirmish fire and an intermittent Confederate artillery bombardment reinforced the sense that a battle was imminent. More Federal help arrived when Rosecrans was apprised of the Rebel buildup. Four brigades under Miller, Stanley, Cruft, and Morton and eighteen cannon gathered on the high ground west of McFadden Ford.

On the Confederate side preparations continued for an attack that no one wanted to make. Col. Roger Hanson, leader of the famed Orphan Brigade from Kentucky, had taken his men off Wayne's Hill to the south and assembled them 1,000 yards from the Federals. He would be the left flank of Breckinridge's formation. Hanson, like his division leader, believed this assault amounted to murder, but he tried to whip up enthusiasm among the men as they formed line and looked north along the undulating ground, open save for a scattering of brush and trees. To his right was Palmer's brigade, now led by Brig. Gen. Gideon J. Pillow. A second line assembled 150 yards to the rear consisting of Adams's brigade on the left, now led by Col. Randall Gibson, and Preston's brigade on the right. Robertson's guns would trail behind the division and take post on the high ground occupied by Price and Fyffe as soon as the infantry drove them off. Breckinridge hoped, however, that the artillery normally assigned to his division, which was not under Robertson's direction, would keep pace with the infantry and offer effective fire support as it advanced.

Just when everything was ready, the weather turned nasty. Rain and sleet began to fall on the battlefield and slowly turned the ground into a slippery muck. With all the expectations of a Greek tragedy, a signal gun fired one round at exactly 4 P.M. and Breckinridge's veterans set off. Federal artillery opened on them before they had taken more than five steps. One shell exploded in the middle of the battle line, killing or wounding twenty men, and other rounds did severe damage to flesh and bones as well. The Union infantry waited and watched. When the Rebels were one hundred yards away, great volumes of rifle fire poured from the Union formations. Hanson's brigade, which was the first to receive this fire, shuddered momentarily but kept going. It had orders to close with the bayonet, not to stop and trade volleys, and this tactic worked. Price's men lost their nerve and began to fall back, wreaking havoc with the formations in Beatty's brigade to their rear. Just as his orphans were taking charge of the hill, Hanson was hit by a shell

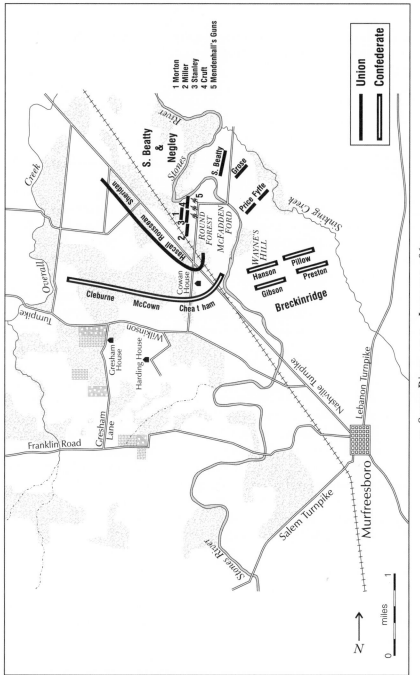

11. Stones River, 4 P.M., January 2, 1863

Union
Confederate

1 Morton
2 Miller
3 Stanley
4 Cruft
5 Mendenhall's Guns

S. Beatty & Negley

Stones River

S. Beatty

Grose

Price Fyffe

ROUND FOREST

McFADDEN FORD

Sheridan

Hascall Rousseau

WAYNE'S HILL

Cowan House

Hanson
Gibson

Pillow
Preston

Breckinridge

Cleburne McCown Cheatham

Overall Creek

Turnpike

Wilkinson

Gresham House

Harding House

Gresham Lane

Franklin Road

Sinking Creek

Nashville Turnpike

Lebanon Turnpike

Murfreesboro

Salem Turnpike

Stones River

N

miles
0   1

fragment that ripped open an artery in his leg. He bled so freely that Breckinridge, who had ridden right behind his beloved brigade, had difficulty
keeping back the tears as his favorite subordinate was lifted into an ambulance and driven to the rear, where he later died.

Pillow's men helped to push back Fyffe's Federals, but Pillow himself deserved no credit for this feat. He was a tainted commander whose reputation
had been nearly wrecked by the cowardly way he escaped responsibility for
surrendering Fort Donelson the previous February. He was leading the brigade, forcing poor Palmer to revert to command of the Eighteenth Tennessee, because he manipulated his friendship with Bragg to get the command
and showed up at Murfreesboro just in time to play a sorry part in this tragic
drama. Breckinridge rode on from the scene of Hanson's mortal wounding
to find Pillow shuddering with fear behind a tree while his brigade went on
without him.

As Pillow's men came up to the Federal line they found their right outflanked by Fyffe. This allowed two Federal regiments to fire obliquely into
them. Their advance came to a halt, and for three-quarters of an hour the
two combatants traded volleys with each other. When Preston came up, his
regiments intermingled with Pillow's, causing much confusion but increasing the volume of fire pouring into Fyffe's outnumbered brigade. The
Unionists also realized that, with Price's withdrawal, their own right was
unsupported as well. As dusk began to descend, all of Fyffe's regiments retreated from Pillow's and Preston's front.

As this sharp little battle neared its climax the Confederates became more
and more disorganized. The snaking course of Stones River tended to funnel
most of Hanson's brigade toward the right, where it became intermingled with
both Pillow's and Preston's men. A few companies of the Second and Sixth
Kentucky, on Hanson's left, actually crossed the river opposite the high
ground that had just been captured, but they were too few in numbers to
threaten the growing concentration of Federal units west of McFadden
Ford. Gibson's brigade also got mixed up with Hanson's line, and two of his
Louisiana regiments crossed the river to join the Kentuckians.

The Federal second line now sprang into action. Beatty's brigade moved
forward on the double-quick to challenge Confederate control of the rise of
ground. At a distance of one hundred yards, the Nineteenth Ohio and
Ninth Kentucky stopped and began to fire into the Orphan Brigade while
the sleet continued to pelt everyone. As Marcus Woodcock, a Tennessee
Unionist in the Kentucky regiment, put it, "there we stood, two solid columns within pistol shot of each other using their weapons of death with all

the rapidity and precision their capacities would allow." Woodcock himself fired four rounds before Rebel bullets dented his rifle so badly that he could not reload it. The Nineteenth Ohio retreated when some of Hanson's men advanced beyond its right flank, but the Kentucky Unionists did not realize for some time that they were alone. When the awful truth sank in, Woodcock's comrades began to peel out of line from right to left and ran for the ford. Right behind them were Hanson's screaming men, "yelling like the very furies and pouring showers of balls after us at every step." Beatty's and Price's brigades splashed across the ford and tried to reassemble on the west bank of Stones River. On the left, Fyffe's brigade fell back to Grose's position on the high ground that lay due north of McFadden Ford, still on the east bank of Stones River but in a general alignment with the heavy concentration of blue-clad infantry and the growing accumulation of artillery west of the ford.

The crisis point of Breckinridge's attack had arrived. It brought the crucial tactical problem that he had foreseen. Union control of the high ground could doom his men, whose successful attack had taken them into point-blank range of their more numerous adversary. By this time, forty-five cannon had been gathered on the west side of Stones River by Capt. John Mendenhall, the chief of artillery in Crittenden's Wing. Acting on the instructions of his wing leader, Mendenhall had quickly ordered all batteries within hailing distance to rush their guns to the ford.

These guns began to fire even as Beatty's men retreated across the river. Woodcock looked up and saw "a continual flash of lightening" and heard "peal upon peal in such quick succession as to form almost an unbroken continual roar." The Confederates had been under artillery fire ever since they began their attack, but now the full load of Mendenhall's concentration crashed upon their heads. The guns were positioned hub to hub on a rise of ground that was several feet higher than that occupied by Breckinridge's men, about three hundred yards away, and the few trees that stood in the stream bed separating the gunners from their targets offered no cover.

The Confederates were blasted with a torrent of shell and canister. "The very earth trembled as with an exploding mine," wrote Edward Porter Thompson of the Orphan Brigade. "The artillery bellowed forth such thunder that the men were stunned and could not distinguish sounds. There were falling timbers, crashing arms, the whirring of missiles in every direction, the bursting of the dreadful shell, the groans of the wounded, the shouts of the officers, mingled in one horrid din that beggars description." With the noisy confusion disorienting them, straining their nerves to the breaking point, and the exploding ordnance tearing up men by the dozens, Breckinridge's veterans gave up. First by ones, then in whole groups, the rank and file took it upon themselves to retire from their exposed position. "Some rushed back precipitately", Thompson continued, "while others walked away with deliberation, and some even slowly and doggedly, as though they scorned the danger or had become indifferent to life."

The sight of retiring Rebels inspired many Federals to pursue. The Seventy-eighth Pennsylvania of Miller's brigade crossed Stones River without orders, followed by the Nineteenth Illinois. Soon the rest of the brigade splashed across in the deepening darkness. At the same time, two regiments of Cruft's brigade cleared the Kentucky and Louisiana troops from the west bank of the river. All along Breckinridge's line of advance the Confederates ran for safety. Many of them were in a panic and threw down their weapons and equipment. Some conscripts deliberately surrendered rather than retreat, begging their Union captors for mercy. It was a sad ending for such a heroic charge. Staff officers drew pistols on the retreating men to get them to slow down while Preston grabbed a flag and beat running soldiers with the flat of his sword. The blows, he reported, were more effective than the symbolic waving of the colors in restoring a degree of order to his crumbled ranks.

The Confederate artillerists had no chance to neutralize Mendenhall's guns. They were greatly outnumbered and had scant time to take position before the infantry retreated. The heavy Federal bombardment overwhelmed them, and most batteries had difficulty withdrawing when their infantry support suddenly collapsed.

More Union troops plowed across Stones River to join the pursuit. Eventually four brigades—Miller's, Stanley's, Beatty's, and Hazen's—took part in this impromptu sortie into Confederate territory. They were easily stopped by a line patched together by the Rebels near the starting point of Breckinridge's attack, composed of Wharton's cavalry and some artillery. Bragg initially sent Patton Anderson's brigade to support Breckinridge, then later dispatched McCown and Cleburne to the east side of Stones River to shore up his now shattered right flank. Rosecrans also sent fresh troops to relieve several brigades that had seen hard service in this short but deadly affair.

Breckinridge would never forget the agony of this evening. He was seen roaming among his regiments raging "like a wounded lion" and saying over and over, "My poor Orphans! My poor Orphans!" His division lost seventeen hundred of the five thousand men who took part in the charge. The

Orphan Brigade suffered the most because of its prominent position in the formation.

The bloody failure of Breckinridge's attack killed any chance that Bragg could stay at Murfreesboro and continue to play the waiting game with Rosecrans. In hindsight it was difficult to see how the assault could have tipped the scales in his favor anyway. The plan could have worked only if the assault had been a surprise and if Bragg had one or two divisions waiting in reserve to exploit any success Breckinridge achieved. But Bragg had neither of those advantages. The result was an attack that eerily foreshadowed Pickett's charge at Gettysburg six months later, albeit on a smaller scale. Breckinridge's attack led to one of the more spectacular examples of artillery practice during the war. Along with the Confederate concentration of 62 guns against the Hornet's Nest at Shiloh and Lee's concentration of 142 guns to prepare the way for Pickett's attack, Mendenhall's concentration of 45 guns at McFadden Ford was one of the greatest assemblies of field artillery in any battle fought in the Western Hemisphere. It also was much more effective than either of the other actions in achieving its tactical goals, pointing to the fact that Federal artillery tended to be more efficiently manned than Confederate guns.

Although the sleet stopped soon after dark, replaced by a cold rain, the mood in the Confederate army was miserable. Bragg still had not decided to withdraw but many of his subordinates sought to change his mind. Cheatham and Withers, who now commanded the only Rebels west of Stones River against the bulk of Rosecrans's army, believed that retreat was the only option left to them. Both generals sent a letter to Bragg at 2 A.M. advising retreat, citing a general lack of confidence among the generals and men of the army. Bragg would have none of it, even though Polk had endorsed the message.

Saturday, January 3, was another cold, rainy, and muddy day. At midmorning, Bragg called a conference of corps leaders at his headquarters, the Murphy house, and surprised them with the announcement that the army would retreat that night. He had made that decision because of alarming news from Wheeler that the Federals were being heavily reinforced so that Bragg feared he would soon be outnumbered two to one. Also, the pouring rain undoubtedly would swell Stones River and threaten to separate the Confederate left and right wings. Polk and Hardee offered no objections, and plans were laid to begin the retrograde movement that night.

Bragg further reiterated his reasons for retreating to Liddell. The brigade commander happened onto Bragg at the Murphy house and did not hesitate to drop in unannounced and ask him what the army could expect. He was stunned at the reply. Bragg told him the men were "exhausted with such continued fighting," and Rosecrans was receiving fresh troops. Liddell could not believe it. If more Federals were arriving, surely his own or someone else's brigade would have noticed it. Liddell advised Bragg to stay put because, "everything depends upon your success here." He suggested a move forward to place troops between Rosecrans and Nashville to cut his line of communications. "Then I would fight Rosecrans to the last. I would rather bury my bones here than give up this field and our previous success. Great results will follow complete victory. You have Rosecrans in a close place. You have only to push him to extremities."

The pugnacious Liddell was wrong. Bragg had lost whatever advantages he had in contesting Rosecrans on this particular field of battle. Liddell went back to his men, disgusted with the turn of events. "What's up now, General?" his men wanted to know. "Ask General Bragg" was the answer. The men knew what Liddell meant by this oblique criticism of their superior. "Well, boys, retreat again," they told themselves. "All our hard fighting thrown away, as usual."

The army began a long and sullen retreat at 10 P.M. when Breckinridge moved out. The rain of the preceding day continued into the night, making the road to Shelbyville a perfect slop. Bragg left Murfreesboro near midnight, and Cleburne and McCown brought up the rear at dawn. All day of January 4, which turned out to be clear and sunny, the Rebels plodded on. Food was in short supply, the roads were still awful, and Bragg's soldiers were exhausted after several days of fighting. When they reached Shelbyville on January 5, Bragg suddenly became irresolute, deciding to place the army along the Elk River, which was much farther south. After two days of reconnoitering and assessing the fords on the Elk he decided to split the army. Polk would defend Shelbyville and the line of the Duck River while Hardee would occupy Tullahoma and the line of the Elk. The two sections of the Army of Tennessee rested twenty-two and thirty-five miles due south of Murfreesboro. It was the best position Bragg could take so that his men were firmly planted on the Nashville and Chattanooga Railroad and were still on the Plateau of the Barrens. Bragg needed about thirty miles distance from his enemy, and this was as far as he could go without ascending the Cumberland Plateau and dealing with the rugged terrain of the mountains.

The reports of Federal reinforcements, so influential in prompting Bragg to withdraw, were false. Rosecrans never received significant additions save for Col. Moses Walker's and Col. John C. Starkweather's brigades, which were too busy dealing with Wheeler's raid to join the army until the evening of December 31. Rosecrans had no intention of pursuing Bragg, and he followed up the Confederate retreat with excessive caution. It was not until the afternoon of January 4, some eight hours after the last Rebel infantryman had left, that Rosecrans tested the waters. A brigade of infantry cautiously advanced along the Nashville Pike to its crossing of Stones River and found only Wheeler's cavalry pickets. Rosecrans waited until the next day to send Negley's division into Murfreesboro. Some Federal cavalry patrols started on the roads south to find the Confederate army, but no infantry units moved beyond the town. They found Murfreesboro filled with the leftover wounded of Bragg's army. The Stones River campaign, or the Murfreesboro campaign as the Confederates called it, was over.

The losses in both armies were terrible. More than a third of Bragg's force and nearly the same proportion of Rosecrans's men were killed, wounded, or captured. Both armies lost about thirteen thousand men from a total of thirty-four thousand Confederates and forty-four thousand Federals. Most of the dead were still unburied, having lain under the sleet, rain, and bright sun for four days. Marcus Woodcock was assigned to a burial detail on the battlefield of December 31. He found Rebels "laying almost in heaps . . . shot or mangled in every conceivable manner, and the various features that were presented to me by this evening's ramble would be food for many a writers pen that would go on from page to page to detail the horrors of a battlefield." Woodcock finally was relieved of this duty at dusk when his regiment left the field and "had the opportunity to breathe tolerably pure air."

Reaction to the campaign among Southerners was predictably harsh. Bragg would have to fight for his job, as he had done after the Kentucky campaign and as he would have to do after each future campaign. The criticism coming from all parts of the Confederacy depressed him. "With so little support, my aching head rebells against the heart, and cries for relief," he wrote to a friend, "still I shall die in the traces." Bragg obviously felt like a martyr to the cause he still believed in. He sent a letter to all corps and division leaders noting the public displeasure toward him and accusing various staff members of spreading the idea that he had retreated from Murfreesboro without his generals' approval. Bragg asked them to set the record straight and also implied that he would resign if his subordinates had no confidence in his leadership.

It was a golden opportunity for his most severe critics in the army. Most commanders responded truthfully, that they had concurred with the decision to withdraw and that it would be best for all concerned if Bragg left. Several of his supporters happened to be on leave and thus failed to weigh in on Bragg's behalf. The army leader also had the continued support of Jefferson Davis, who considered the battle a success of sorts and who also believed the withdrawal had been justified under the circumstances. But the reaction to Bragg's letter deeply disturbed the president, who decided to send Gen. Joseph E. Johnston to investigate. Johnston was not satisfied with his newly assigned role as commander of Confederate forces in the West, much preferring to lead a field army, and he also was unwilling to become entangled in this messy squabble. Davis gave him authority to decide whether Bragg should go. Johnston reached Tullahoma near the end of January and found several severely disgruntled generals, including Hardee, Polk, McCown, Breckinridge, and Cheatham. The men, however, seemed to be in good spirits and enjoying reasonably abundant supplies of food and equipment. Furthermore, Johnston found no fault with Bragg's handling of the campaign and recommended that he retain his command.

Davis, ever the meddler but reluctant to intervene decisively, believed that Bragg's career was doomed if there was so much dissatisfaction among his most important subordinates. He searched for a way to ease Bragg out and replace him with Johnston, suggesting that the theater commander could move his headquarters to Tullahoma and appoint Bragg his chief of staff. Johnston would have none of this, telling Davis that if anyone replaced Bragg it should be a general who was not a player in the army's past campaigns or in the move to oust him from command. Davis tried again in March by ordering Bragg to come to Richmond for consultation, intending to assign him to an inspector's post for the army as a whole and asking Johnston to assume command at Tullahoma on a "temporary" basis. Johnston sabotaged this scheme by informing the president that Bragg's wife, who was staying at nearby Winchester, was too ill to be left alone. He also noted that a Federal advance was expected any day and that Bragg could not possibly be spared. When Johnston fell ill in April, Davis was forced to give up and allow Bragg to remain in charge of the Army of Tennessee. He would have to put up with this strangely sullied general for the rest of the year.

Public morale in the South was taken on a roller-coaster ride of emotions during the days following the battle. Bragg's initial dispatch inspired everyone. It "put us almost 'beside' ourselves with joy, and caused even enemies to pause and shake hands in the street," according to clerk Jones in Richmond. Catherine Ann Edmonston in North Carolina exulted over the apparent victory: "That is the New Year's Gift presented by our brave soldiers to the country. We thank you, gallant men, thank you from the bottom of our hearts."

Then later dispatches began to arrive from Murfreesboro and it became clear that yet another reverse had taken place. Rumors circulated throughout Richmond on January 5, the day after Davis returned to the capital from his western trip, that Bragg had been defeated. Those rumors were confirmed the next day, and Jones reported, "We are all *down* again." Newspaper commentary reflected the same ups and downs, rejoicing in the early positive reports and displaying confusion and regret at the later dispatches. "It must be confessed that a good deal of fortitude is required to support so painful a disappointment with equanimity," admitted the *Richmond Examiner*. Other newspaper editors tried to put the best face on the setback, arguing that it was "not as encouraging as we had hoped" but was "nevertheless, by no means discouraging." Patriotic Southerners contented themselves with the knowledge that, despite the heavy losses, Bragg had retreated only a short distance and was still firmly planted on the railroad that penetrated the heart of the Confederacy.

Northerners had a great deal more to feel good about in those early days of January. The first day of the new year was bright and sunny in Washington. With the advent of emancipation there was an air of revolutionary vigor in the capital. "The character of the country is in many respects undergoing a transformation," wrote Gideon Welles in his diary. "The great upheaval which is shaking our civil fabric was perhaps necessary to overthrow and subdue the mass of wrong and error which no trivial measure could eradicate." Initial reports from Murfreesboro were scattered and inconclusive, but by January 9 there was no doubt that Bragg had been defeated and driven south. "Rosecrans has done himself honor and the country service," opined Welles. Everyone realized it was a qualified success bought at great cost. New Yorker George Templeton Strong termed it "a very earnest struggle while it lasted and involved great consumption of men and of material. It may have been indecisive, but our resources will stand the wear and tear of indecisive conflict longer than those of slavedom, and can be sooner repaired."

Exactly what had Rosecrans accomplished with his bloody victory? He had advanced thirty miles along the vital rail line that penetrated the southeastern portion of the Confederacy. For that he had lost 433 men for each mile he advanced. The North could hardly afford to pay that price indefinitely. At that rate it would cost an additional 38,104 men to get from Murfreesboro to Chattanooga and another 43,399 men to capture Atlanta. If this slaughter continued, the Confederate army could force the Federals into a war of exhaustion, assuming it had enough men to hold out longer than its opponent.

The campaign was a Union victory, but it had little appreciable effect on foreign relations. Napoleon III of France made an informal and unilateral offer of mediation in January following the battle of Fredericksburg. The British refused to cooperate with him in this endeavor because they did not believe this horrible defeat would convince the North that it was impossible to destroy the Confederacy. Lincoln's government rejected Napoleon's offer. From that point the prospects of foreign intervention rapidly declined. The cotton famine ended in English textile miles later in 1863 as India began to replace the South as a major supplier of the fiber. The twin Rebel defeats at Vicksburg and Gettysburg in July helped to forestall further efforts at mediation, and England and France increasingly became more concerned with European affairs.

Yet the news of Stones River could not be received with unalloyed happiness in the North. The defeats at Fredericksburg and Vicksburg in December depressed morale, and Rosecrans's battle was not an unqualified success. Copperhead sentiment was riding high in the wake of the fall congressional elections and antiadministration newspapers refused to let Lincoln off easy. The *Cincinnati Daily Enquirer* questioned the results of the recent campaigns: "Thousands of lives have been sacrificed, and for what? Are we any nearer the subjugation of the South than before those battles and terrible loss of life?" Administration papers would proclaim a great victory, many Northerners would believe it, and the war would go on; "thousands of lives more will be offered up in this fruitless contest. And after all the loss of blood and treasure, and the piling up of a huge national debt that the youngest among us will not live to see liquidated, it will have to be settled by compromise. How the abolitionists hate that word."

For staunch supporters of the war effort the Stones River campaign offered limited but important gains. Not only was territory captured, but just as many Rebel soldiers were put out of action as Rosecrans had lost. More than a year later Grant would trade huge casualties for short territorial gain in his overland campaign in Virginia, but he could afford those costs because the losses in Lee's army were proportionately the same and the South could not replace them. More important, the significance of victory at Stones River was greatly enhanced because nearly all other Federal offensives had failed that winter. Grant's invasion of north central Mississippi was turned back by Earl Van Dorn's cavalry raid on Holly Springs, which cut his rail supply line, and Ambrose Burnside's attack on Lee at Fredericksburg was stopped with stunning losses. In the middle of all this gloom, any victory was as good as gold. Several months after he took Murfreesboro, Rosecrans received a letter from Lincoln reminding him how everyone in the North felt in those dark days of winter. "I can never forget, whilst I remember anything, that about the end of last year and the beginning of this, you gave us a hard-earned victory, which, had there been a defeat instead, the nation could scarcely have lived over."

Even though his victory was clear, the battle of Stones River had a traumatic effect on Rosecrans. Always of an impressionable, excitable nature, he never regained the innate optimism and self-confidence that had characterized his earlier war career. Those awful hours spent trying to save his army from a real and imminent disaster on December 31 produced a more cautious and carping commander. For six months following the battle, Rosecrans dallied at Murfreesboro, preparing for a continuation of the drive along the rail line into the heart of the Confederacy. He filled dispatch bags with pleas for more men, more equipment, more cavalry, and complained strongly when it seemed his army was bypassed in favor of the other Union armies in Mississippi and Virginia. He also busied his men with building huge complexes of earthen fortifications. Fortress Rosecrans, constructed just outside of Murfreesboro, was the largest enclosed earthwork of the entire war, encompassing two hundred acres with three miles of earthen parapet and fifty artillery pieces. It would have taken an entire field army to man it properly. But that was not all. When Van Dorn threatened to advance on Nashville from the south in March 1863, Rosecrans ordered the construction of slightly smaller fortifications at Triune and Franklin.

Rosecrans was justified in taking the time to rebuild his shattered army following Stones River. He also was justified in fortifying Murfreesboro and posts to the west, although it should have been done on a smaller and less expensive scale. He also was correct in delaying the start of a new campaign until the spring weather made military movements feasible. But May came and went with no forward move. When Grant was operating against Vicksburg and Maj. Gen. Joseph Hooker was attacking Lee at Chancellorsville, Rosecrans remained in Murfreesboro. He continued to delay in the face of strong words from Washington until late June. His success in maneuvering Bragg out of Shelbyville, Tullahoma, and then Chattanooga, with the loss of only a few hundred men, was overshadowed by the great beating the Army of the Cumberland received at Chickamauga on September 20 and its subsequent stand in besieged Chattanooga. Rosecrans was relieved of his command by Thomas. Grant came in to coordinate the spectacularly successful victory at Chattanooga in late November that finally caused Davis to relieve Bragg of his command as well. Stones River was one bloody step in the long story that began at Fort Donelson and ended when the Army of Tennessee was nearly destroyed at the battle of Nashville in December 1864.

The last half of 1862 offered a stark contrast to the first six months of that year. The Confederate cause in the West suffered a series of severe blows from February through May as Rebel holdings in Kentucky, Missouri, parts of Arkansas, most of Tennessee, and even much of northern Mississippi were taken by the invading army of the North. Tens of thousands of soldiers were lost, several major cities and towns, all of the upper Mississippi valley, and many acres of productive farmland were lost to the Southern war effort. It seemed to many overconfident Northerners that the war would indeed be short and easily won.

But out of the ashes grew a raging Southern desire to recoup the crippling losses of the winter and spring. Braxton Bragg brought much needed energy and discipline to the Army of the Mississippi and transformed it into the famous Army of Tennessee. He took it on the first major Rebel offensive of the war deep into territory the Confederacy had never controlled. He delineated the high-water mark of the Rebel war effort in the West and then retreated home. This began a long and controversial habit with the Army of Tennessee and its commanders. Bragg never overcame the mistrust his subordinates and his men felt toward him for giving up Kentucky. This mistrust simply deepened with the outcome of the Stones River campaign.

But was Bragg dealt an unfair hand? One could make a strong argument either way. If the Army of Tennessee had not suffered chronic shortages of men and supplies, if it had not begun the war as a ragtag field force with poor staff and administrative training, if its corps and division leaders had been more cooperative with their commander, maybe Bragg would have had the opportunity to do great things. The only thing that could save the fortunes of this unique army was the tough fighting ability of the rank and file, who had a skill and a heart for war that was the equal of any other army. In the end, as Bragg's men took up their posts at Shelbyville and Tullahoma, he could find solace in knowing that his efforts had at least saved much of Middle Tennessee. In losing Kentucky Bragg had given up nothing that the Confederacy had possessed at the start of the war, only an opportunity to alter the strategic picture in the West dramatically. He had forced the Federals to spend large numbers of casualties in an effort to reassert their control of Kentucky and to consolidate their hold on Middle Tennessee. He had also set the Union invasion of the Deep South back by at least six months. When it did come, in September 1863, he would be ready with a rested force to meet Rosecrans in the battle of Chickamauga and win his only clear tactical victory of the war.

It had also been a troubling six months for the Federals. Their nearly bloodless capture of Corinth in May had given way to a much needed dispersal of forces to secure the Upper South and prepare for further operations in the Lower South. Bragg's invasion of Kentucky upset all such plans. Buell was forced to suffer the humiliation of retreating northward to fight for its possession. His career was derailed by this Confederate thrust even though he handled it reasonably well. Buell's performance at the critical meeting of the two armies at Perryville was terrible, but he did save the state. He became the victim of his own uneven performance and of his superiors' inability to understand the limitations of campaigning in the rugged mountains of the Southern Appalachians, which blocked his approach to Chattanooga both before and after the Kentucky campaign.

Rosecrans would have to deal with Bragg when Buell faded into retirement. Displaying the energy that his predecessor lacked, he aggressively set out on a winter campaign to fight one of the most costly and bitter battles of the war, losing an unacceptably high percentage of his men for relatively little gain. Yet the war would have to be fought this way, as Grant and the nation would come to realize in 1864.

Operations in northern Mississippi were meant to be a significant part of all this, at least in the summer of 1862, but they turned into a side drama, a separate theater of their own. The campaign of Price and Van Dorn against Grant's forces demonstrated typical problems that plagued Confederate operations, a lack of unified command, a shortage of men, and poor logistical preparations. Like Perryville and Stones River, the battles at Iuka and Corinth became sterling examples of the battle spirit of the Confederate armies with hard-hitting tactical offensives that yielded no strategic value for the cause. Valiant efforts and sacrifices by the common soldier were not enough to bring victory.

The period from June 1862 through January 1863 was an interim phase of the war in the West. It connected the Confederate disasters of February through May with the more mature, comparatively better organized defensive efforts of 1863. In early 1862 Rebel forces in the West were spread out in a single theater of operations, along a line that stretched across southern Kentucky. By early 1863, those forces had dispersed into two major concentrations in Mississippi and in Middle Tennessee. The course of the Confederate war in that year would be guided by this dispersion and result in disaster, for the South did not have enough resources to defend all important parts of its territory.

The last half of 1862 would be a time of interruption for the Union war effort as commanders strove to restore the strategic momentum that had resulted in such inspiring victories. Ultimately the Confederate failure to take the strategic initiative from their enemy and control the course of the war in the West doomed the entire Confederacy. Never again would the Rebels have such an opportunity to do this as they had in the summer of 1862. Their failure may have been the decisive turning point of the western campaigns.

Notes

1. BANNERS TO THE BREEZE

For general information about the strategic background of the war in the West during the summer of 1862, see James L. McDonough, *War in Kentucky: From Shiloh to Perryville* (Knoxville: University of Tennessee Press, 1994), 43–102; Steven E. Woodworth, *Jefferson Davis and His Generals: The Failure of Confederate Command in the West* (Lawrence: University Press of Kansas, 1990), 90–136; Charles Champion Gilbert, "Bragg's Invasion of Kentucky," *Southern Bivouac* n.s., 1 (June 1885–May 1886): 217–18; and Herman Hattaway and Archer Jones, *How the North Won: A Military History of the Civil War* (Urbana: University of Illinois Press, 1983), 208. Ezra J. Warner, *Generals in Blue: Lives of the Union Commanders* (Baton Rouge: Louisiana State University Press, 1964), 51–52, provided useful biographical material on Don Carlos Buell. For the same subject, see Stephen D. Engle, "Don Carlos Buell: Military Philosophy and Command Problems in the West," *Civil War History* 41 (June 1995): 89–115.

For information on the political context in which these campaigns began, see Leroy P. Graf and Ralph W. Haskins, eds., *The Papers of Andrew Johnson*, vol. 5, *1861–1862* (Knoxville: University of Tennessee Press, 1979), 442; Roy P. Basler, ed., *The Collected Works of Abraham Lincoln*, vol. 5 (New Brunswick NJ: Rutgers University Press, 1953), 255–87, 291–97, 300–313, 317–19, 328–38, 436–37; Howard K. Beale, ed., *Diary of Gideon Welles*, vol. 1 (New York: Norton, 1960), 70–71, 89–90; and John Niven, ed., *The Salmon P. Chase Papers*, vol. 3, *Correspondence, 1858–March 1863* (Kent OH: Kent State University Press, 1996), 244. For the diplomatic context in which the war was taking place that summer, see Howard Jones, *Union in Peril* (Chapel Hill: University of North Carolina Press, 1992), 126–31.

The quote from staff officer Samuel H. Lockett is in an undated fragment of letter to his wife, written ca. June 1862, Samuel H. Lockett Papers, #432, Southern Historical Collection, Wilson Library, University of North Carolina at Chapel Hill. For information on the amount of supplies the Confederates left behind when they evacuated Corinth, see Day Elmore to father and mother, June 10, 1862, Day Elmore Papers, Chicago Historical Society. The quotes from Bragg ("banners to the breeze"), Roger, and Morgan are in McDonough, *War in Kentucky*, 43–102.

For insight into the political context in which the Confederates operated during the summer of 1862, see Lynda Lasswell Crist, ed., *The Papers of Jefferson Davis*, vol. 8, 1862 (Baton Rouge: Louisiana State University Press, 1995), 257–58, 292–94, 303, 322, 328, 347, 372. The tortured political history of Kentucky is explained in Lowell H. Harrison, ed., *Kentucky's Governers, 1792–1985* (Lexington: University Press of Kentucky, 1985), 65–77, and Lowell H. Harrison, "George W. Johnson and Richard Hawes: The Governors of Confederate Kentucky," *Register of the Kentucky Historical Society* 79 (winter 1981): 3–39.

Commentary on events by Southern civilians came from Frank E. Vandiver, ed., *The Civil War Diary of General Josiah Gorgas* (University: University of Alabama Press, 1947), 11; Beth G. Crabtree and James W. Patton, eds., *"Journal of a Secesh Lady": The Diary of Catherine Ann Devereux Edmondston, 1860–1866* (Raleigh: North Carolina Division of Archives and History, 1979), 222, 225, 236; and J. B. Jones, *A Rebel War Clerk's Diary at the Confederate States Capital*, 2 vols. (Philadelphia: J. B. Lippincott, 1866), 1:141–42.

2. BOLD STRIKE INTO THE BLUEGRASS

Smith's campaign from East Tennessee to Big Hill is well covered in several secondary and primary sources. See chiefly McDonough, *War in Kentucky*, 114–24, which also contains the Mims quote. Several primary sources provide insight into the military movements and the region. See Paul F. Hammond, "General Kirby Smith's Campaign in Kentucky in 1862," *Southern Historical Society Papers* 9 (1873):247–49; J. G. Law, "Diary of Rev. J. G. Law," *Southern Historical Society Papers* 12 (1875):391–92; William Kennedy Estes Diary, August 19–27, 1862, Eleanor Brockenbrough Library, Museum of the Confederacy. Dispatches in U.S. War Department, *The War of the Rebellion: A Compilation of the Official Records of the Union and Confederate Armies*, 70 vols. (Washington DC: U.S. Government Printing Office, 1880–1901), Ser. 1, vol. 16, pt. 2, 755, 766–67, 777, 782, are useful as well. For Federal activities in Kentucky during this phase of the campaign, see Gilbert, "Bragg's Invasion of Kentucky," 219–20.

For the battle of Richmond, see McDonough, *War in Kentucky*, 127–45; Manson's and Cruft's reports in *Official Records*, vol. 16, pt. 1, 913, 921; and Edward B. Allen to W. H. Fairbanks, September 8, 1862, Edward B. Allen Papers, Indiana Historical Society. The Allen document is the only official report of the Seventy-first Indiana for the battle of Richmond. It was not published in *Official Records* or any other collection.

The completion of Smith's campaign following the battle of Richmond can be seen in McDonough, *War in Kentucky*, 145–54; Gilbert, "Bragg's Invasion of Kentucky," 220–21; and Hammond, "General Kirby Smith's Campaign," 289–97. For information on the Federal defense of Cincinnati, see the articles in *Blue & Gray* 3 (April-May 1986): 16–18.

Morgan's retreat from Cumberland Gap is well documented. Begin with Morgan's report in *Official Records*, vol. 16, pt. 1, 992–97, and also read George W. Morgan, "Cumberland Gap," in Robert U. Johnson and Clarence C. Buel, eds., *Battles and Leaders of the Civil War*, 4 vols. (1887–88; rpr. New York: Thomas Yoseloff, 1956), 3:62–69. For good descriptions of the retreat by Morgan's men, see the commentary by Owen Johnston Hopkins in Otto F. Bond, ed., *Under the Flag of the Union: Diaries and Letters of a Yankee Volunteer in the Civil War* (Columbus: Ohio State University Press, 1961), 41–42, and Frank H. Mason, *The Forty-Second Ohio Infantry* (Cleveland: Cobb, Andrews, 1876), 129–34. For information on the scalpings at Baptist Gap, see Vernon H. Crow, *Storm in the Mountains: Thomas' Confederate Legion of Cherokee Indians and Mountaineers* (Cherokee NC: Museum of the Cherokee Indians, 1982), 15–16.

For public reaction to Smith's campaign, see *Indianapolis Daily Journal*, September 5, 1862; Vandiver, ed., *Civil War Diary of General Josiah Gorgas*, 14–15; Crabtree and Patton, eds., *"Journal of a Secesh Lady,"* 256–57; and Jones, *Rebel War Clerk's Diary*, 152–54. Insights into the diplomatic scene are found in Jones, *Union in Peril*, 138–40, 164–65.

3. BRAGG, BUELL, AND KENTUCKY

For the early phase of Bragg's campaign into Kentucky, before the confrontation at Munfordville, see McDonough, *War in Kentucky*, 99, 105–13, 154–55. The Winchester quote is also in McDonough, *War in Kentucky*. Several primary sources were very helpful in providing detailed information and interesting perspectives. E. T. Sykes, "A Cursory Sketch of General Bragg's Campaigns," *Southern Historical Society Papers* 11 (1883): 466, and Joseph Wheeler, "Bragg's Invasion of Kentucky," in Johnson and Buel, eds., *Battles and Leaders of the Civil War*, 3:7, are two easily accessible accounts written by Confederate participants. Two less accessible primary sources are Henry C. Semple to wife, August 19 and 22, 1862, Henry C. Semple Papers, Southern Historical Collection, Wilson Library, University of North Carolina at Chapel Hill; and Edward B. Taylor to Jeremy Gilmer, August 20, 1862, Jeremy Francis Gilmer Papers, #276, Southern Historical Collection, Wilson Library, University of North Carolina at Chapel Hill.

The Munfordville incident has been covered by several accounts written by participants and modern historians. See McDonough, *War in Kentucky*, 158–89, and Kenneth A. Hafendorfer, *Perryville, Battle for Kentucky* (Louisville KY: KH Press, 1991), 41–55. Primary sources from the Confederate perspective include Sykes, "Cursory Sketch of General Bragg's Campaigns," 466–68; Wheeler, "Bragg's Invasion of Kentucky," 9–11; Henry C. McNeill diary, September 23, 1862, Civil War Collection, Tennessee State Library and Archives; Henry C. Semple to William J. Hardee, November 28, 1862, Semple Papers; Henry Delamar Clayton to wife, September 14, 1862, Henry Delamar Clayton Papers, William Stanley Hoole Special Collections Library, University of Alabama; Sterling A. M. Wood to wife, September 26, 1862, Sterling A. M. Wood Papers, Alabama Department of Archives and History. Two useful Northern accounts are Gilbert, "Bragg's Invasion of Kentucky," 298, and John T. Wilder, "The Siege of Munfordville," *Sketches of War History, 1861–1865: Papers Prepared for the Commandery of the State of Ohio, Military Order of the Loyal Legion of the United States, 1903–1908*, vol. 6 (Cincinnati: Monfort, 1908), 296–304.

For information on activity in Louisville during September 1862, see Gilbert, "Bragg's Invasion of Kentucky," 298–99; McDonough, *War in Kentucky*, 191–93; and Hafendorfer, *Perryville*, 58–66. The quote from Colonel Gilmer is from Jeremy Francis Gilmer to wife, September 27, 1862, Gilmer Papers.

Information on Northern responses to the campaign came from Allan Nevins and Milton Halsey Thomas, eds., *The Diary of George Templeton Strong: The Civil War, 1860–1865* (New York: Macmillan, 1952), 253; Virginia Jeans Laas, ed., *Wartime Washington: The Civil War Letters of Elizabeth Blair Lee* (Urbana: University of Illinois Press, 1991), 186; *Indianapolis Daily Journal*, September 19, 30, 1862; and Rachel Sherman Thorndike, ed., *The Sherman Letters: Correspondence Between General Sherman and Senator Sherman from 1837 to 1891* (New York: Da Capo, 1969), 163. Andrew Johnson's reaction to Buell's campaign is expressed in Graf and Haskins, eds., *Papers of Andrew Johnson*, 5:559–62, and 6:4–5.

The Confederate president's views on the proclamation Bragg issued to Kentucky residents is in Crist, ed., *Papers of Jefferson Davis*, 8:386. For the perspective on foreign affairs, see Jones, *Union in Peril*, 166–78.

4. GIVE HIM BATTLE

Buell's advance from Louisville to Perryville and Bragg's confused maneuvers to meet it are amply detailed in McDonough, *War in Kentucky*, 92–213, and in Hafendorfer, *Perryville*, 66–214. The quotes from Thomas, Halleck, Connally, Telford, and Winchester are in McDonough, *War in Kentucky*.

For Senator Sherman's comment on the need for action in Kentucky, see Niven, ed., *Salmon P. Chase Papers*, 3:263. For Confederate optimism about the outcome of the campaign, see Crist, ed., *Papers of Jefferson Davis*, 8:417; *Augusta Daily Constitutionalist*, September 18, 1862; and Jones, *Rebel War Clerk's Diary*, 1:157–58. For information on the installation of Governor Hawes, see Harrison, "George W. Johnson and Richard Hawes," 33–35.

5. PERRYVILLE

My major source for the battle of Perryville was the richly detailed and thoroughly analyzed study by Hafendorfer, *Perryville*, 215–376, which also provided the source of all quotes not otherwise attributed in this chapter. I also used primary material from two sources. See Junius Gates to David Gates, October 29, 1862, Gates Family Papers, Mansfield Library, University of Montana, Missoula; and John Euclid Magee diary, October 8, 1862, *Supplement to the Official Records of the Union and Confederate Armies* (Wilmington NC: Broadfoot, 1994), vol. 3, pt. 1, 218.

6. GOOD-BYE, KENTUCKY

The major source consulted for this chapter was Hafendorfer, *Perryville*, 346, 377–443, which also is the source of all quotes not otherwise attributed. Other secondary sources that proved to be useful were McDonough, *War in Kentucky*, 310–14; Woodworth, *Jefferson Davis and His Generals*, 166–69, and Peter Cozzens, *No Better Place to Die: The Battle of Stones River* (Urbana: University of Illinois Press, 1991), 7–30.

Good primary material can be found in Magee diary, October 16, 1862, *Supplement to the Official Records*, vol. 3, pt. 1, 221; Henry C. Semple letter, November 28, 1862, Semple Papers; Jeremy Francis Gilmer to wife, October 19 and 22, 1862, Gilmer Papers.

Material on the Southern reaction to the end of Bragg's campaign can be found in Crabtree and Patton, eds., "*Journal of a Secesh Lady*," 276; *Augusta Daily Constitutionalist*, October 22, 1862; Crist, ed., *Papers of Jefferson Davis*, 8:448, 455, 469. For reaction among Northerners, see James G. Smart, ed., *A Radical View: The "Agate" Dispatches of Whitelaw Reid, 1861–1865*, 2 vols. (Memphis: Memphis State University Press, 1976), 1:91–92, 102; *Indianapolis Daily Journal*, October 22, 27, 1862; Niven, ed., *Salmon P. Chase Papers*, 3:304–6.

7. THE ROAD TO IUKA

Several sources were instrumental in understanding the events explained in this chapter. The best is Peter Cozzens, *The Darkest Days of the War: The Battles of Iuka and Corinth* (Chapel Hill: University of North Carolina Press, 1997), 1–134.

For primary material on the Confederate side, see Thomas L. Snead, "With

Price East of the Mississippi," in Johnson and Buel, eds., *Battles and Leaders of the Civil War*, 2:717–34; Ephraim McDowell Anderson, *Memoirs: Historical and Personal* (Dayton OH: Morningside, 1972), 218–25; W. H. Tunnard, *A Southern Record: The History of the Third Regiment Louisiana Infantry* (Dayton OH: Morningside, 1970), 182–85; and Frank Von Phul, "General Little's Burial," *Southern Historical Society Papers*, 29 (1901): 212–15.

For the Federal side, see William S. Rosecrans, "The Battle of Corinth," in Johnson and Buel, eds., *Battles and Leaders of the Civil War*, 2:735–57; John Y. Simon, ed., *The Papers of Ulysses S. Grant*, vol. 6 (Carbondale: Southern Illinois University Press, 1977), 23–24, 39, 43–44, 46, 168–73; Charles S. Hamilton, "The Battle of Iuka," in Johnson and Buel, eds., *Battles and Leaders of the Civil War*, 2:734–36; and Henry M. Neil, *A Battery at Close Quarters; Paper Read Before the Ohio Commandery of the Loyal Legion* (Columbus OH: Champlin, 1909), 3–20.

Two secondary works were helpful as well: Jack W. Gunn, "The Battle of Iuka," *Journal of Mississippi History* 24 (July 1962): 142–57, and Ben Earl Kitchens, *Rosecrans Meets Price: The Battle of Iuka, Mississippi* (Florence AL: Thornwood, 1987), 192.

8. CORINTH

The best source for the fighting of October 3 is Cozzens, *Darkest Days of the War*, 135–231, which also provided the source of all quotes not otherwise attributed in this chapter. Other useful accounts include *Official Records*, vol. 17, pt. 1, 335–406, and pt. 2, 233–50, and Gunn, "Battle of Iuka," 142–57.

For the Union side, see Charles S. Hamilton, "Hamilton's Division at Corinth," in Johnson and Buel, eds., *Battles and Leaders of the Civil War*, 2:757–58; Mildred Throne, ed., *The Civil War Diary of Cyrus F. Boyd, Fifteenth Iowa Infantry, 1861–1863* (Baton Rouge: Louisiana State University Press, 1998), 72–73; Rosecrans, "Battle of Corinth," 737–57; John S. Wilcox to wife, October 9, 1862, John S. Wilcox Papers, Illinois State Historical Library, Springfield, Illinois.

For the Confederate side, see Snead, "With Price East of the Mississippi," 717–34; Anderson, *Memoirs*; 232–33; John Tyler Jr. to William Lowndes Yancey, October 15, 1862, John Tyler Jr. Papers, Western Historical Manuscripts Collection, University of Missouri-Columbia; George R. Elliott Diary, October 3, 1862, Tennessee State Library and Archives.

9. BLOODY OCTOBER

Several sources were important in providing information for this chapter. See Cozzens, *Darkest Days of the War*, 232–324, and *Official Records*, vol. 17, pt. 1, 154–461, and pt. 2, 728.

For Union accounts of the fighting on October 4 and the pursuit, see Rosecrans, "Battle of Corinth," 737–58; Neil, *Battery at Close Quarters*, 19; Wilcox to wife, October 9, 1862, Wilcox Papers; Throne, ed., *Civil War Diary of Cyrus F. Boyd*, 74–77; and Oscar L. Jackson, *The Colonel's Diary* (N.p., ca. 1922), 69–88.

For Confederate accounts, see Anderson, *Memoirs*, 233–38, 240–45; Tyler to Yancey, October 15, 1862; *In Fine Spirits: The Civil War Letters of Ras Stirman* (Fayetteville AR: Washington County Historical Society, 1986), 52; J. A. McKinstry, "With Col. Rogers When He Fell," *Confederate Veteran* 4 (July 1896): 220–22; Tunnard, *Southern Record*, 193; Elliott Diary, October 5, 1862; and Crist, ed., *Papers of Jefferson Davis*, 8:537–38.

For the battle at Davis's Bridge, see *Official Records*, vol. 17, pt. 1, 154–461, and Robert W. McDaniel, "Forgotten Heritage: The Battle of Hatchie Bridge, Tennessee," *West Tennessee Historical Society Papers*, no. 31 (October 1977), 109–16; W. R. Stites, "Fighting About the Hatchie Bridge," *Confederate Veteran*, 18 (October 1910): 468; and Albert Martin Forbes to brother, October 8, 1862, Albert Martin Forbes Papers, Chicago Historical Society.

For the impact of Corinth on Southern public opinion, see Vandiver, ed., *Civil War Diary of General Josiah Gorgas*, 22; Crabtree and Patton, eds., *"Journal of a Secesh Lady,"* 274; Jones, *Rebel War Clerk's Diary*, 1:164–65; *Augusta Daily Constitutionalist*, October 8, 1862; and *Savannah Daily News*, October 13, 1862.

10. ON TO MURFREESBORO

The major source for this chapter was Cozzens, *No Better Place to Die*, 19–80. Other material was taken from James Lee McDonough, *Stones River: Bloody Winter in Tennessee* (Knoxville: University of Tennessee Press, 1980), 78; R. Lockwood Tower, ed., A Carolinian Goes to War (Columbia: University of South Carolina Press, 1983), 52–54; and Nathaniel C. Hughes, ed., *Liddell's Record* (Dayton OH: Morningside, 1985), 106.

For information on home-front conditions in the late fall of 1862, see Thorndike, ed., *Sherman Letters*, 167–68; Basler, ed., *Collected Works of Abraham Lincoln*, 5:518–37, 550–52; 6:6–7, 17; Crist, ed., *Papers of Jefferson Davis*, 8:565–84; and Jones, *Union in Peril*, 210–11.

11. STONES RIVER

The main source of material for this chapter was Cozzens, *No Better Place to Die*, 81–166, which also provided the source for all quotes not otherwise attributed. Additional material can be found in Nathaniel C. Hughes, ed., *Liddell's Record* (Dayton OH: Morningside, 1985), 108–11; Kenneth W. Noe, ed., *A Southern Boy in Blue: The Memoir of Marcus Woodcock* (Knoxville: University of Tennessee Press, 1996), 127;

Louis Garesche, *Biography of Lieut. Col. Julius P. Garesche* (Philadelphia: J. B. Lippincott, 1887), 438, 445, 450.

12. FIGHT OR DIE

The primary source used for developments in the campaign following December 31 was Cozzens, *No Better Place to Die*, 167–218, which is also the source of quotes not otherwise attributed. Useful material was found in McDonough, *Stones River*, 202, and Woodworth, *Jefferson Davis and His Generals*, 194–98. Primary material came from Noe, ed., *Southern Boy in Blue*, 130–40, and Hughes, ed., *Liddell's Record*, 114–16.

Material on Southern reaction to Stones River can be found in Jones, *Rebel War Clerk's Diary*, 1:228–32; Crabtree and Patton, eds., *"Journal of a Secesh Lady,"* 332; *Richmond Examiner* quoted in *Indianapolis Daily Journal*, January 13, 1863; *Savannah Daily News*, January 6–7, 1863; and *Augusta Daily Constitutionalist*, January 7, 1863.

For Northern response to the campaign, see Beale, ed., *Diary of Gideon Welles*, 1:212–18; Nevins and Thomas, eds., *Diary of George Templeton Strong*, 287; Jones, *Union in Peril*, 226–27; and *Cincinnati Daily Enquirer*, January 9, 1863.

Bibliographical Essay

The Kentucky campaign, Corinth, and Stones River were events that participants would never forget, but modern-day historians have not been quite so devoted in their attention to them. Scholarly coverage has been uneven, at best, although more studies have been published in recent years, and still more new ones are likely to appear in the near future.

Bragg's invasion of Kentucky has remained obscure until very recently. James L. McDonough, *War in Kentucky: From Shiloh to Perryville* (Knoxville: University of Tennessee Press, 1994), is the only account of the campaign as a whole. McDonough illustrates the logistical problems Buell faced as he tried to capture Chattanooga early in the campaign, and he also provides much insight into the experience of ordinary soldiers. But his discussion of military engagements in the campaign is not detailed or analytical, and there are aspects of the campaign, such as Buell's advance from Louisville to Perryville, that are glossed over. The only other book of substance on the campaign is Kenneth A. Hafendorfer, *Perryville: Battle for Kentucky* (Louisville KY: KH Press, 1991). It is a detailed tactical study of the battle with a short discussion of the campaign that led to it. No other author has given Perryville its due as Hafendorfer has done, with extensive research, an abundance of good maps, and much attention paid to terrain.

The campaign in northern Mississippi by Price, leading to the battle of Iuka, and by Van Dorn, leading to the battle of Corinth, has also been ignored by historians until very recently. Only a handful of short articles had been written before Peter Cozzens, *The Darkest Days of the War: The Battles of Iuka and Corinth* (Chapel Hill: University of North Carolina Press, 1997), was published. Cozzens has written the only thoroughly researched, detailed, and soundly considered study of this fascinating campaign.

Stones River has gotten the lion's share of attention among historians, compared to the other two campaigns, with two major studies in print. James L. McDonough, *Stones River: Bloody Winter in Tennessee* (Knoxville: University of Tennessee Press, 1980), is the first book on the battle that was not written by a contemporary of the war. Like his book on the Kentucky campaign, it is a good introduction but not a definitive study. Peter Cozzens, *No Better Place to Die: The Battle of Stones River* (Urbana: University of Illinois Press, 1990), goes much farther than McDonough's book toward that desirable goal, providing greater research, more detailed narrative and analysis, and better maps. McDonough provides excellent information on the social and economic significance of Middle Tennessee, but Cozzens wrote a more thorough military study of the campaign.

The Confederate offensives of 1862 have long been seen as an interim period of military operations in the West, bracketed by Fort Donelson and Shiloh on the one end and the Vicksburg campaign on the other. Their potential for redirecting the course of the war should not be overlooked, and the aspirations of thousands of soldiers to do or die in their attempt to win dramatic turning points in the war deserve our attention. Stones River has always received more attention because of its size and furious drama. It was the first major engagement in a long Union drive along the railroad from Nashville to Savannah, a series of campaigns that lasted from December 1862 to December 1864. One can only hope that future research will continue to enhance the reputations of all three campaigns.

Index

Little, Brig. Gen. Henry, 122, 133, 135–36, 138

Lockett, Samuel H., 19–20

Loomis, Col. J. Q., 204

Louisiana Third Infantry, 129, 134–35, 145, 173

Louisville KY, 37–38, 43, 45, 56, 61, 70–72, 77, 80

Lovell, Maj. Gen. Mansfield, 122, 141–42, 145, 147–49, 153–54, 65, 170–71, 174, 185–86

Lumsden, Capt. Charles L., 98–98

Lytle, Col. William H., 89, 98–100

Magee, John Euclid, 105, 113, 118, 217

Magoffin, Gov. Beriah, 25

Maney, Brig. Gen. George E., 92–94, 96–97, 205, 209

Manigault, Col. Arthur M., 205–6, 209

Manson, Brig. Gen. Mahlon D., 37–42

Marshall, Humphrey, 26, 45, 47, 51, 107, 111, 113

Martin, Col. John D., 134–36

Mason, Frank H., 51

Maury, Brig. Gen. Dabney H., 122, 139, 142, 145, 153–54, 159–60, 162, 165, 169, 171, 173–74

McArthur, Brig. Gen. John, 130, 145, 147–48, 167

McClellan, Maj. Gen. George B., 3, 8, 13, 54, 74, 119

McCook, Maj. Gen. Alexander McDowell, 9, 25; in battle of Stones River, 197, 203, 207, 212, 217–18; in Kentucky campaign, 58, 60, 64, 77, 79–80, 82, 85, 87–89, 94, 96, 98, 100–104, 106–7, 111, 120; in Stones River campaign, 178–79, 183–84, 187–88, 190–95

McCook, Col. Daniel, 86–87

McCown, Maj. Gen. John P., 20–21; in battle of Stones River, 197, 199–200, 202–3, 205, 207, 213, 215, 224, 226, 228; in Stones River campaign, 185, 187, 190–91, 193–94

McCray, Col. T. H., 39–41

McKean, Brig. Gen. Thomas, 144–45, 148–49, 151–52, 167, 172

McKinstry, J. A., 161, 163–64

McLain, Col. Robert, 155, 159

McNair, Brig. Gen. Evander, 194, 199, 201–3

McNeill, Henry C., 71

McPherson, Maj. Gen. James B., 166, 168, 171–73

Mendenhall, Capt. John, 223–25

Mersey, Col. August, 157

Michigan troops, First Michigan Engineers and Mechanics, 11

Miller, Col. John, 209–10, 212, 220, 224

Miller, Col. William, 98

Mims, Jemison, 44

Minty, Col. Robert, 184, 88

Mississippi River, 5–6, 14

Mississippi troops: Jefferson Flying Artillery, 201; Seventh Infantry, 65; Ninth Infantry, 65; Tenth Infantry, 63, 65; Fifteenth Infantry, 171; Twenty-second Infantry, 147; Twenty-seventh Infantry, 210; Twenty-ninth Infantry, 65; Thirtieth Infantry, 207; Forty-first Infantry, 21, 98; Forty-third Infantry, 155; Forty-fourth Infantry, 65

Missouri troops: St. Louis Battery (C.S.), 169; Sixth Infantry (C.S.), 151; Eleventh Infantry (U.S.), 161, 163

Mitchell, Brig. Gen. Ormsby McKnight, 6–7, 9–10

Mizner, Col. John K., 144, 152

Moore, Col. James, 65
Moore, Brig. Gen. John C., 148, 160–63, 169
Moore, Col. William H., 155, 160, 164
Morgan, Brig. Gen. George W., 7, 10, 23, 31–32, 34, 37–38, 45, 47–52
Morgan, Col. John Hunt, 12, 24, 45, 47, 50–52, 185, 187
Morton, Capt. James St. Clair, 178, 208, 211, 213, 220
Morton, Gov. Oliver P., 78
Mower, Col. Joseph A., 150, 162
Munfordville, battle of, 63–70
Murfreesboro: battle of (*see* Stones River, battle of); raid on, 12
Murphy, Col. Robert C., 128

Nashville, 32, 61–62, 73, 118, 120
Negley, Brig. Gen. James, 120, 188, 193, 209, 227
Neil, Lieut. Henry M., 135, 139, 140, 159
Nelson, Maj. Gen. William, 9, 37–38, 40–43, 72, 77–78

Oglesby, Brig. Gen. Richard J., 147–52, 157
Ohio troops: Third Infantry, 98; Fifth Cavalry, 158, 171; Seventh Battery, 168; Eleventh Battery, 134–40, 159; Fifteenth infantry, 200; Nineteenth Infantry, 222–23; Twenty-first Infantry, 209–10; Thirty-third Infantry, 97; Forty-second Infantry, 50, 52; Forty-third Infantry, 161, 164; Forty-ninth Infantry, 199; Sixty-third Infantry, 154, 161–63, Eighty-first Infantry, 147, 158; Ninety-fifth Infantry, 40; 105th Infantry, 92–93
Oliver, Col. John M., 144–45, 147–48
Ord, Maj. Gen. Edward O. C., 130–33, 136–37, 139, 143, 168–70

Palmer, Brig. Gen. John M., 188, 210
Palmer, Col. Joseph B., 214–15, 218, 220, 222
Parsons, Capt. Charles, 89, 92–94
Pegram, Col. John, 35, 44
Pemberton, Lieut. Gen. John C., 173, 185–86
Pennsylvania troops: Seventy-seventh Infantry, 201; Seventy-eighth Infantry, 224; Seventy-ninth Infantry, 96
Perryville KY, 84–85, 108, 111; battle of, 84–105, 118, 137, 190, 194, 197, 233, 238–39, 243
Phifer, Brig. Gen. Charles W., 155, 160, 162–63, 165, 169
Pillow, Brig. Gen. Gideon J., 220, 222
Pinson, Col. R. A., 145
Polk, Maj. Gen. Leonidas, 185–87; in battle of Stones River, 213–14, 225–26, 228; in Kentucky campaign, 57–58, 60–62, 67, 81–88, 102, 104, 107, 115; in Stones River campaign, 190–91, 194
Polk, Col. Lucius, 39, 200, 202, 204, 208–9
Pope, Col. Curran, 98–99
Post, Col. Philip S., 197, 200–202
Powell, Col. Samuel, 100–101
Preston, Brig. Gen. William, 214, 217, 220, 222, 224
Price, Col. Samuel, 218–20, 223
Price, Maj. Gen. Sterling, 21–22, 81, 121–22, 124, 126–27, 174–75, 233; in battle of Corinth, 142–53, 155, 164, 166; in battle of Davis's Bridge, 169–71; in battle of Iuka, 128–41
Prime, Capt. Frederick E., 144

railroads, 10–13
Rains, Brig. Gen. James E., 200, 202–3, 208
Reid, Whitelaw, 117

In the Great Campaigns of the Civil War series

Six Armies in Tennessee
The Chickamauga and Chattanooga Campaigns
By Steven E. Woodworth

Fredericksburg and Chancellorsville
The Dare Mark Campaign
By Daniel E. Sutherland

Banners to the Breeze
The Kentucky Campaign, Corinth, and Stones River
By Earl J. Hess

The Chessboard of War
Sherman and Hood in the Autumn Campaigns of 1864
By Anne J. Bailey